St. Victor

P. St. Victor

St. Geneviève

P. St. Marcel

P. St.
Bernard

Les
Bernardins

Coll. de Navarre

L'Ile
Notre
Dame

PL MAUBERT

Notre
Dame

RUE DE LA BÛCHERIE

Petit
Pont

Le Petit Châtelet

P. St. Jacques

Pont Notre
Dame

RUE DE LA VIEILLE JUIVERIE

Les Mathurins

Coll. de Sorbonne

P au Change

Sainte
Chapelle

Pont St.
Michel

Châtelet

Pont aux
Marchans

Le Palais

Les Augustins

Germain
Auxerrois

Louvre

St. Germain
des Prés

RIVER SEINE

TUILERIES

N

Blood
Royal

ALSO BY ERIC JAGER

The Last Duel

The Book of the Heart

The Tempter's Voice

Blood Royal

A True Tale of Crime and Detection in Medieval Paris

ERIC JAGER

LITTLE, BROWN AND COMPANY
New York Boston London

Little, Brown and Company
Hachette Book Group
237 Park Avenue, New York, NY 10017
littlebrown.com

First Edition: February 2014

Little, Brown and Company is a division of Hachette Book Group, Inc. The Little, Brown name and logo are trademarks of Hachette Book Group, Inc.

The publisher is not responsible for websites (or their content) that are not owned by the publisher.

The Hachette Speakers Bureau provides a wide range of authors for speaking events. To find out more, go to hachettespeakersbureau.com or call (866) 376-6591.

Endpaper map: "Plan of fifteenth-century Paris," from *A Parisian Journal, 1405–1449,* translated by Janet Shirley (1968), fig. 4, pp. 386–87. By permission of Oxford University Press.

Library of Congress Cataloging-in-Publication Data
Jager, Eric
    Blood royal : a true tale of crime and detection in medieval Paris / Eric Jager. — First edition.
        pages cm.
    Includes bibliographical references and index.
    ISBN 978-0-316-22451-2 (hc) / 978-0-316-27749-5 (int'l pb)
    1. Orléans, Louis, duc d', 1372–1407 — Assassination.   2. France — History — Charles VI, 1380–1422.   3. Regicide — France — Case studies.   4. Assassination — France — Case studies.   5. Murder investigation — France — Case studies.   6. Crime — France — History — To 1500.   I. Title.
    DC101.7.O7J34 2014
    944.026092 — dc23   2013028257

10 9 8 7 6 5 4 3 2 1

RRD-C

Printed in the United States of America

For Peg,
as always

The detective as knight-errant must nonetheless sally forth, though he knows that his native chivalry ... is as hopeless as it is incongruous.

— David Lehman, *The Perfect Murder*

Contents

Blood
Royal

Introduction

———◆———

IN THE 1660s, an unusual parchment scroll was discovered at an old château in the French Pyrenees. Thirty feet long and filled with small, neat script, the scroll had been lost for more than two and a half centuries. It was the original police report on a high-level assassination whose violent repercussions had nearly destroyed France.[1]

On a chilly November night in 1407, Louis of Orleans, controversial brother of the French king, had been hacked to death in a Paris street by a band of masked assassins. After knocking him from his mount, they split open his head with an ax, splattered his brains on the pavement, and stabbed his body to a bloody pulp before throwing it on a pile of mud and disappearing into the dark.

The crime stunned the nation and paralyzed the government, since Louis had often ruled in place of the periodically insane king, Charles VI. As panic seized Paris, an investigation began. In charge was Guillaume de Tignonville, provost of Paris—the city's chief of police. Knight, diplomat, man of letters, and man of law, he was also very likely one of history's first detectives.

Guillaume soon learned that behind the murder lay an intricate conspiracy. But who had plotted it? A jealous husband avenging one of Louis's flagrant seductions at court? A foreign power eager to sow chaos in France? The mad king, who had once drawn a sword on Louis and tried to kill him?

Over the next several days Guillaume solved the case,

astounding the city all over again as the mystery behind the crime was revealed. Yet his official report—committed to the scroll—eventually disappeared, and with it many details. Now, in the 1660s, more than two hundred and fifty years later, it had come to light again.

The parchment scroll. "In the year of grace one thousand four hundred and seven..."

Like a torch ignited in the dark, the long-lost scroll revealed the gruesome facts of the assassination. It contained firsthand accounts of the grisly autopsy and the ensuing investigation as well as sworn depositions from shopkeepers, housewives, and other eyewitnesses who had seen the actual murder or the killers escaping afterward.

The parchment scroll also captured a great national calamity in the making. For Louis's murder had plunged France into a bloody civil war, leading to a devastating English invasion under Henry V, followed by a brutal foreign occupation that began to lift only with Joan of Arc.

Guillaume's inquiry took place hundreds of years before the

advent of police detectives in the nineteenth century and the creation of the modern detective story by Edgar Allan Poe, Arthur Conan Doyle, and others. But literary murder mysteries are as old as Shakespeare's *Hamlet* and Sophocles's *Oedipus Rex,* whose title characters each pursue a criminal inquiry.[2] And Guillaume de Tignonville's real-life investigation shows that one literary scholar is wrong to claim that "as long as the officially practiced, universally accepted means of crime detection was torture, the detective story was impossible."[3] Indeed, Guillaume led the investigation with what an expert on medieval law describes as "a remarkable legal and scientific rigor."[4]

A brilliant sleuth, Guillaume directed the scores of officers and clerics under his command to examine the crime scene, collect physical evidence, depose witnesses, lock Paris's gates, and ransack the city for clues. The priceless scroll gives us a unique inside look at his investigation, conducted without modern forensic tools and mainly with shoe leather, intelligence, and a courageous pursuit of the truth.

There are some things we will never know about the case. The decadent court of the mad king swirled with scandalous rumors of adultery, poison, witchcraft, and treason. But the tattered scroll provides a rare window onto a turbulent week in Paris that changed the course of history, recording developments almost as they took place and before their huge, enduring consequences for millions became apparent.

The scroll also gives us a glimpse into the lives of ordinary Parisians who were going about their daily routines when they were suddenly caught up in great events. These people played small but crucial roles in the drama, speaking for themselves and in their own voices, as carefully recorded by the provost's scribes. Along with other surviving records spared by the teeth of time, the rediscovered scroll tells a story of conspiracy, crime, and detection that would be hard to believe were it not true.

This is that story.

I

The Provost

———◀◉▶———

ONE DAY NEAR the end of October 1407, when Louis of Orleans had less than a month to live, a cart carrying two condemned men rumbled through the huge fortified gatehouse at the Porte Saint-Denis, across the wooden drawbridge, and into the northern suburbs of Paris.[1] Behind the departing cart and its well-armed escort, above the great encircling wall, rose "the city of a hundred bell-towers," the largest metropolis in Europe, a mile-wide panorama of spires and steeples all reaching toward Heaven amid a smoky haze exhaled by tens of thousands of kitchen fires.[2]

Veering right, away from the freshly harvested vineyards covering the slopes of Montmartre in autumnal red, the execution party headed for another, more infamous hill to the east.[3] The two felons in the cart, their hands bound and hemp nooses already around their necks, could see the grisly public gibbet looming before them as they lurched along an unpaved track toward the hill known as Montfaucon. They may have smelled it too—scores of blackened corpses dangled there, exposed to the wind and the sun, pecked and nibbled by the crows and rats that scavenged among the dead.[4]

Riding on his horse at the head of the somber procession

was the provost of Paris, "superb in his furs and scarlet robes."[5] He was followed by his lieutenant and his bodyguard, a dozen mounted sergeants known as the Twelve.[6] Behind the sergeants rode a gray-cloaked friar who would hear each prisoner's last confession.[7] Then came the burly executioner atop his horse, and behind him the rattling cart containing the two prisoners.[8] After the cart came a troop of sergeants, some mounted, others marching on foot with wooden staff in hand.[9]

Following along behind the sergeants in a less orderly fashion was a crowd of spectators, larger and noisier than usual.[10] Some of them had come because they had nothing better to do, simply for their own amusement, eager to watch the two hanged men struggle and kick their way out of this world and into the next. But others were there in protest, for the case involving the two men had aroused a good deal of controversy. Some, wearing the hooded robes of coarse black or brown woolen cloth that marked them as university men, were even shouting angrily at the provost and his officers, denouncing the imminent hanging. The prisoners, as if still hoping to be rescued during their short, final journey to the gibbet, loudly joined in, crying out, *"Clergie! Clergie!"*—"We're clergy!"[11]

The gradual upward slope of the ground soon turned steeper as the group began to ascend Montfaucon, or Falcon Hill— named for "the ghastly sight of those birds of prey plunging down on to crows and ravens as they flew away with gobbets of flesh from dead bodies."[12] Shouts from the approaching crowd now competed with "the cawing of crows and the cries of birds of prey."

The immense gibbet towered some forty feet in the air above the hilltop, "a hideous monstrosity" visible for miles around and lurid with the whitewash daubed onto it from time to time.[13] Sixteen massive limestone piers stood in a rectangular array on a raised foundation about forty feet long and thirty feet wide. Three separate tiers of heavy wooden beams held the

Montfaucon. The huge public gibbet was the reputed haunt of sorcerers and body snatchers.

weathered ropes and rusty chains that could suspend at least sixty bodies at one time. Even so, the continuous demand for space often kept the gibbet filled to capacity.[14]

The place "was like an outdoor Chamber of Horrors" with its vast "crowd of skeletons swinging aloft, making mournful music with their chains at every blast of wind." In addition, "the remains of criminals previously beheaded, boiled or quartered were brought from all over France to hang in wicker baskets beside the people actually executed in situ." And "delinquents and blasphemers" were chained alive to the pillars, in the company of the dead.[15]

The odors of the grisly place and the cries of these unfortunates kept most people away, except when there was a hanging. And Montfaucon's evil reputation for body-snatching and sorcery ensured that almost everyone avoided it after dark. "Dabblers in black magic were reputed to steal and use not only the bodies of dead criminals, but also pieces of rope, chains, nails, and wood from the gallows."[16] The gibbet, some said, was haunted by the Devil himself.[17]

—◇—

The provost of Paris leading the procession that day amid the crowd's taunts and protests was a knight named Guillaume de Tignonville.[18] Sir Guillaume, who had been appointed provost by the king, was essentially Paris's chief of police, although he also had the powers of a judge, district attorney, and head of the local militia. In matters of law and justice, the provost, "after the king, was the most important person in the city."[19] As the king's top law officer, Guillaume was responsible for maintaining order, investigating crimes, presiding over the city's chief tribunal, and carrying out the sentences handed down there. Shortly after he took office in 1401, his powers had been further enlarged by a royal ordinance authorizing him "to do justice to all malefactors throughout the realm."[20] In a civil emergency, Guillaume could close all the city gates, muster troops and post them in the streets, and call for the townsmen to arm themselves—with staffs, clubs, knives, or "whatever they had handy"—and keep watch in front of their houses, with big fires burning in the streets all night.[21] He could also order great iron chains, specially forged for the purpose, to be stretched across streets throughout the city to prevent the sudden rush of invading enemy troops or mobs.[22] He had wide civic authority as well, since a popular revolt in 1383 involving the provost of the merchants had prompted the king to abolish that office and grant its powers to the provost of Paris.[23] Guillaume thus enforced the trade statutes governing silk makers, armorers, and other artisans' guilds, and he was responsible for garbage disposal and the half dozen or so leper hospitals on the city's outskirts.*[24]

Besides his personal bodyguard, the Twelve, Guillaume commanded several hundred police sergeants as well as scores of clerics who made and kept the official records.[25] There were two kinds of sergeant: the *sergent à verge,* or tipstaff, who "did the local work," patrolling the city on foot; and the *sergent à cheval,* a mounted officer who "went further afield, both as a policeman and as part of the town's militia."[26] All had the power to make arrests, though some were as dishonest as the criminals they pursued, even to the extent of acting as their accomplices. One officer reportedly "sent two or three fiddlers in advance of him, so that their noisy playing would alert wrongdoers to his approach."[27] But Guillaume himself, said a chronicler, was "a very respected knight" with a reputation for personal integrity and aggressively enforcing the king's laws.[28] As provost, "he refused to do many strange things he was asked to do, such as relaxing the demands of justice."[29]

In 1407, Guillaume was probably in his early to middle forties.[30] Descended from an old noble family in the Loire, he had inherited his father's title, estate, and coat of arms — six gold macles on a field, gules.†[31] Wellborn, he also had great ability and drive. In 1388, when he was probably still in his twenties,

---

* Of the various leper hospitals (*léproseries*), the oldest and best known was Saint-Lazare, about half a mile north of the city wall.

† Gules is red, and the macles, diamond-shaped lozenges, were arranged on the shield in a 3, 2, 1 pattern, from top to bottom. Guillaume's personal seal also displayed six macles but with a helmet and crest.

Guillaume had ridden as a knight banneret, leading troops under his own command, in a royal expedition to the duchy of Guelders, in Flanders.*[32] In 1391 he was appointed a *chevalier d'honneur* and a chamberlain, one of the king's personal advisers. In 1398, he became a member of the royal council—the inner circle of royal relatives and close advisers around the king.[33] A highly valued diplomat as well, Guillaume had served on important embassies to various cities in Europe, including Rome, Milan, and the papal court at Avignon.[34] In the mid-1390s, Guillaume saw further military service during a one-month siege at Montignac, in the south of France, where he helped lead an expedition of "two hundred men-at-arms and one hundred and fifty crossbowmen" who had been sent to crush the robbers and brigands terrorizing the region.[35] As a man-at-arms, Guillaume had battlefield courage and impressive skill with a sword as well as the toughness it took to ride all day and bivouac overnight. And as a well-traveled, well-connected royal official with years of experience at court, he was intimately familiar with the workings of the French government and the levers of power in general.

Guillaume served as provost at the king's pleasure and could be sacked at a moment's notice, but in the autumn of 1407, he had held office for over six years, a lengthy tenure suggesting his competence and success.[36] No portrait or physical description of him survives, but his contemporaries praised him for his mind, character, and personal presence.[37] "Of noble lineage," he was also "wise, knowledgeably and well spoken, and greatly valued by the king for his advice," says one source.[38] Another says that he was "renowned for his mind and his knowledge" and that he spoke in "a loud, clear voice."[39] In all, Guillaume seems to have been "a highly intelligent and cultivated man"

---

* Knight banneret: the second grade of knighthood, below baron and above knight bachelor.

with an "independent mind" who was "moderate in his politics" and, "above all, loyal to the king."[40]

Besides being a knight, diplomat, and officer of the law,
Guillaume was also a man of letters.[41] He was wealthy enough
to keep a personal library, then a rarity, with books such as
Aesop's Fables, an encyclopedia known as *On the Properties of
Things,* and other works in Latin and French, all copied out by
hand and bound in leather or heavy cloth.[42] Like many educated noblemen, Guillaume had written some courtly verse.[43]
More unusually, he had also translated an originally Arabic
collection of philosophical wisdom entitled *Moral Sayings of the
Philosophers* from Latin into French, an achievement that had
earned him a modest literary fame. The translation was probably completed around 1402, after he became provost. One of
the stories collected in the book recounts how Alexander the
Great once refused to pardon a man condemned to hang despite
the man's claims of penitence. "Hang him at once," ordered
Alexander, "while he is still sorry for what he did."[44] A more
measured quote found elsewhere in the text—"There is no
shame in doing justice"—was particularly apt to the challenges
faced by the provost.[45]

A man devoted to the law and to letters, Guillaume was evidently fond of courtly and literary society. His friends included
the celebrated poet Eustache Deschamps, who had died just the
year before, in 1406. Guillaume had also befriended Christine
de Pizan, a rare woman in the male-dominated world of letters, supporting her defense of women in a famous literary
quarrel over the *Romance of the Rose* and even helping her with
legal advice.[46]

Guillaume had a wife named Alix and a daughter, and he
lived with them in the city.[47] As provost, he was provided with a
residence at the Petit-Châtelet, a small château facing the river
on the Left Bank, but Guillaume chose instead to live at his
own house in the Rue Béthisy, not far from the Louvre—the

huge square fortress guarding the western edge of Paris. Guillaume's house had once belonged to the lords of Ponthieu, a
county north of Paris in Picardy. An imposing stone mansion,
located in a prestigious quarter, it identified its owner as a
wealthy, distinguished noble.[48] At the end of a long busy day on
the job—studying documents and writing reports, issuing
orders to his officers, questioning prisoners and witnesses before
his tribunal, or supervising a hanging—Guillaume probably
went home with relief to his family and the neighborhood's
quiet and comfort.

◄○►

The two men whom Guillaume was leading to the gibbet that
day were named Olivier François and Jean de Saint-Léger.
Both claimed to be students at the University of Paris, and this
was the reason their case had caused such controversy and
protest.[49]

They had been arrested earlier that month, charged with
"robbery and murder on the high roads." After their imprison-
ment, they had demanded "benefit of clergy," the right to a
trial in a special ecclesiastical court.[50] The university, known as
"the daughter of the Church" because it answered to the pope
rather than the king, enjoyed great independence in matters of
law, as was typical of universities throughout Europe at this
time. From its founding in the twelfth century, the University
of Paris had been an independent corporation with its own
royal charter granting it special rights and protections.[51] For
example, like priests and friars and monks and nuns, students
and professors were considered clergy and thus were under the
jurisdiction of the Church courts, a separate legal system distinct from the secular courts wherein laypeople were tried.
There was a good reason for this: clerics tried in a Church court
under the authority of the local bishop generally got more
lenient treatment; even those convicted of capital crimes, includ-

ing theft, murder, and rape, often got away with very light sentences or nominal fines.[52]

After arresting the two men, Guillaume had conscientiously "gone to the rector and officials of the university and offered them the malefactors charged in the case" for trial in a Church court.[53] But the university, wanting nothing to do with these accused "murderers, thieves and highwaymen," or "infamous evildoers," as another source describes them, had washed its hands of the matter, refusing to acknowledge the two men as its own.[54] Guillaume next went to the Parlement of Paris, the highest secular court in France, and requested that judges be appointed in order to try the case in that venue. The Parlement duly assigned several magistrates to hear the case. The two men were convicted and sentenced to hang.

Word of their condemnation angered their fellow clerics, who began to complain, raising a vociferous protest intended to rouse the university authorities to action. There were threats of a strike, which meant canceled classes and a suspension of preaching—an attempt to enlist popular support for the cause by withholding spiritual benefits from the people. But Guillaume had carefully followed the law in all of his proceedings, and he held firm in the face of the university's noisy opposition. The provost, wrote a monk, wished to demonstrate "that from now on, scholars and priests would be punished just like everyone else."[55] In his account, the monk, perhaps fearing a new precedent, failed to mention that Guillaume had already given the university a chance to try the two clerics in its own court. But ordinary people may have welcomed the idea that no one was above the law or beyond its reach.

———◄○►———

When the execution party finally reached the top of Montfaucon, Guillaume ordered one of his sergeants to unlock the sturdy gate in the wall surrounding the gibbet.[56] The wall helped keep out wolves and dogs as well as the thieves who stole bodies from the gallows for medical or more occult purposes. The wall also discouraged friends or relatives of the condemned from visiting the site at night to cut down the bodies and give them proper Christian burials.

By now the stench of the place would have been overwhelming. Besides the odor from scores of rotting corpses swinging back and forth above whenever jostled by a breeze, a foul smell arose from the charnel pit below, where the remains of the dead were eventually thrown without ceremony to make more room on the gibbet.[57] Some of the attending officers may have worn scent-soaked cloths over their faces to ward off the smell, although the two condemned men had to withstand its full, unmitigated force.

It was customary to allow the condemned to go to confession before they died, and now the friar in gray stepped forward to perform this office. Confession had not always been allowed to criminals prior to execution, a withholding of ultimate pardon that cruelly added spiritual torment to the physical agony, but attitudes had changed over time, and by the early 1400s, even felons convicted of capital crimes were allowed to put themselves right with God before suffering their sentences.[58] Had not Christ himself forgiven the repentant thief on the Cross?

As the friar led the two men through their final confessions, "assistant hangmen tested chains" and "fixed the halters."[59] When all was ready, the executioner prodded the freshly confessed felons toward one of the half a dozen "long wooden ladders" propped against the gibbet. One after the other, nooses looped around their necks, the two men were forced to climb.[60]

Once a condemned man reached the top of the ladder, he had to wait as the hangman tied the loose end of his rope to the beam. There were no blindfolds or hoods. What he saw in that moment—the gaping crowd below, the circle of sky above, the city's silvery spires in the distance—would have been his last living glimpse of this world.

Finally, he stepped off the ladder; if he did not, the hangman simply pushed him. In some cases, the sudden drop may have caused death, but such a mercy was by accident rather than design. Death by hanging, before the advent of more "scientific" methods centuries later, was often a slow strangulation rather than a sharp snapping of the neck.*[61]

——◄○►——

Eventually the wretched strugglings of the two men ceased, their bodies slack and motionless at last. They now had left the realm of the living to join the vast brotherhood of the dead. Their corpses would hang at Montfaucon for weeks or months, their eyes ripening into fruit for birds, their flesh rotting away, their bones bleaching white in the wind and sun— although popular belief held that hanged men could come back to life, as *revenants,* to haunt the living.[62]

Once the spectacle was over, the crowd began to drift away. Guillaume, his unpleasant task complete, ordered his men to lock and secure the gibbet's gate and then mounted his horse and formed up the procession, now smaller by two.

As Guillaume reined his horse around for the return trip, the whole city lay stretched out before him.[63] Despite the macabre surroundings, the view from the top of Montfaucon was superb, revealing Paris in all its splendor: the great river streaming with vessels of all sorts and lined by shrines and palaces gleaming like polished ivory, the profusion of towers and spires soaring above the horizon, the neat circumference of wall around the whole.[64] Huge and multitudinous, with as many as

---

* According to an eyewitness, a man executed at Montfaucon in 1486 "stuck his left foot and leg out from the ladder as if to push himself off," but the hangman "pulled him back a little, then pushed him off, and he was hanged and strangled."

one hundred thousand inhabitants, the bustling metropolis that
Guillaume was sworn to police and protect now beckoned him
away from the smaller, desolate village of the dead.[65]

*Fifteenth-century Paris. The view is from the north, with Notre-Dame on the
left and the Louvre on the right.*

His officers fell in behind him, followed by the friar, the
executioner and his assistants, and, finally, the additional troop
of sergeants. At Guillaume's signal, the group began to move,
heading down the slope.

Guillaume had probably supervised many hangings during
his six years as provost, even if he often left executions to his
deputies. But this case was unusual in its accompanying uproar.
As Guillaume led the procession back to the city, he may have
suspected that he had not yet heard the end of the matter.

But whatever his private thoughts as he rode back to Paris,
Guillaume could not have foreseen that a new and much bigger
case would soon push the two hanged men right out of his
mind. A far more sensational crime, with tremendous consequences for all of France, was about to break upon the astounded
city, seizing the provost's full attention and that of all Parisians
literally overnight.

2

The Châtelet

———◄o►———

GUILLAUME HAD TO be on duty by seven o'clock each morning at his headquarters in the Grand Châtelet, about a third of a mile from his home in the Rue Béthisy.[1] After rising early, perhaps to a servant's call, and dressing, he probably heard a Mass said by his chaplain or a cleric in his employ and then had a small breakfast with his family—"primarily bread, possibly with cheese, and some ale"—before leaving.[2] To get to his destination, he could follow a series of narrow, winding streets to the east—many of them paved with *carreaux,* flat square stones—then turn right into the wider Rue Saint-Denis and jostle his way south, nearly to the river, through an early-morning crowd of carters, vendors, and shoppers.[3] He could also take a less congested route, turning near his house and heading straight for the river, where he could then proceed east along the busy but more spacious quais.[4] Walking beside the Seine, or riding his horse if he was in a hurry, and doubtless escorted by some of the Twelve, Guillaume would have had a splendid view over the water to the Île de la Cité, the city's main island and the oldest part of Paris.[5]

Along the bank of La Cité, as it was called for short, he would have seen the old royal palace, known as the Palais, its four imposing stone towers lined up like sentinels.[6] The Palais housed the Parlement of Paris, to which Guillaume had referred the case of the two men who claimed to be clerics. Behind it rose the graceful spire of La Sainte-Chapelle, the exquisite shrine of gilded limestone and colored glass built by Louis IX—Saint Louis—to house precious relics from the Holy Land, including Christ's Crown of Thorns and a piece of the True Cross. In the distance behind the spire loomed the two great square towers of Notre-Dame, and behind them the cathedral's even taller spire.

Like ancient Gaul, Paris was divided into three parts.[7] And like a living body, it had a head, a heart, and a stomach. La Cité was its heart, surrounded by the great artery of the Seine and symbolizing the monarchy.[8] Although the king no longer lived in the old royal palace, residing instead at the Hôtel Saint-Pol, farther east along the river, he often came there to sit in state, presiding godlike over his Parlement from a plush, cushioned throne bedecked with the royal emblem—the golden lily, or fleur-de-lis—and tented by a *ciel,* or canopy, of bright blue cloth.[9] To the north of La Cité lay the swelling Right Bank, known as La Ville, where Guillaume lived and worked. Home to many artisans and merchants and built around the great central marketplace, Les Halles, it fed the city's huge appetites with goods of all sorts that came rumbling in on carts and wagons through its winding, shop-lined streets.[10] To the south of La Cité, on the Left Bank, lay the smaller, more cerebral Latin Quarter, also known as L'Université, dotted with colleges and religious fraternities, including the already famous Sorbonne.[11] Its streets buzzed with robed scholars and hooded students from all over Europe, proud of their learning and their clerical status.

As Guillaume drew abreast of the old royal palace on the opposite bank, he may have glanced over to check the time on the great clock tower at its northeast corner, a royal gift to the city and the only public clock in Paris. (Perhaps just a dozen of the larger towns in France had one of these geared mechanical devices for ringing bells or showing the hour.)[12] He was now nearing the two bridges that connected La Ville to La Cité.[13] First was the Pont aux Meuniers, a narrow wooden trestle resting on the stone piers of an earlier bridge and named for the thirteen water mills churning beneath it with the steady river current, grinding grain for baking bread. Behind it stood the wider, sturdier Grand Pont, built entirely of stone and supporting a dozen houses and more than a hundred shops along both sides. Besides the merchants and artisans selling their wares along this commercial avenue, money changers busily converted foreign currency into French coinage, giving the bridge its more common name, the Pont aux Changeurs.[14]

Before reaching the first bridge, Guillaume would have turned left, away from the river, into a narrow curving alley that cut north to the Rue Saint-Denis. The Grand Châtelet—or the Châtelet, for short—was now just to his right, standing squarely across the Rue Saint-Denis, as if blocking its way to the river.

The Châtelet was originally a fortress built to guard the bridge crossing the river—a natural moat—to La Cité.[15] Its most striking feature was "an enormous round tower," which dominated a cluster of smaller towers and turrets, all topped by pointed conical roofs as sharp as spears.[16] Parts of the Châtelet dated back to the ninth century, when Vikings rowed their longships up the Seine from the sea to lay siege to Paris. It had been enlarged by Saint Louis in the thirteenth century, and portions had been rebuilt by Charles V, father of the present king. A relic of an older, smaller city, the Châtelet was no longer needed for defense, but the old gray fortress still frowned over the quarter with a military aspect, its morgue and its prisons inspiring fear among the populace. After the Montfaucon gibbet, the Châtelet, with its forbidding towers, thick walls, and high, narrow windows covered by iron bars, was feared as "the most sinister edifice in Paris."[17]

The Châtelet's evil reputation owed something to its neighborhood, an unpleasant one that it shared with the Grande

Boucherie.[18] This huge abattoir and its adjacent market stalls dominated a stinking row of slaughterhouses and tanneries. Here rough, brawny workers butchered cows and sheep, skinned the carcasses, quartered the meat, and hung the freshly scraped hides to dry. Foul odors filled the air, along with the shouts of men and the cries and groans of dying animals. Blood ran down the streets at times, and offal clogged the central gutter.

———◄◦►———

The Châtelet looked north, facing the Grande Boucherie and with its back to the river. Its front had a vaulted stone entrance leading to a passageway about one hundred feet long and running at street level all the way through to the riverbank and the bridge beyond. Through this darkened passage, just wide enough for two carts to squeeze past each other, flowed a constant stream of city traffic heading to or from La Cité.

The Châtelet. Looking south along the Rue Saint-Denis, with the Grande Boucherie in the foreground at left.

To one side of this passage lay the morgue, where the sergeants of the watch collected a grim daily harvest.[19] Each day about a dozen bodies—crime victims or indigents—were found in the streets or pulled from the river. The corpses were stripped, washed, and placed on view in the morgue for identification; after three days, they were salted and packed in straw to mask the smell. If unclaimed, the bodies were buried in the Cemetery of the Holy Innocents, the city's largest graveyard, just up the Rue Saint-Denis and dedicated to the infants slaughtered by King Herod.

To the other side of the busy passageway lay the prisons, four in all and located on different levels of a large square tower, or *donjon,* next to the great round tower. All were built of stone and had iron-braced doors and locks; the "best" prisons were up high, and the worst down below.[20]

The first prison, on the upper floor, consisted of five cells considered the very best in the building and known, respectively, as the Chains, the Good View, the Moat, the Room, and the Little Glory. The cells were shared, but each prisoner had his own bed, though he had to pay for his accommodations: two pennies per day for his place, and four for the bed, if he chose to have one.[*21]

The second prison, one floor down and not quite so good but "still comfortable," had three chambers: the Butchery, the Beaumont, and the Griesche. Each was subdivided further, with most of the cells reserved for female prisoners. Prices were the same as in the first prison.

The third prison, much worse, was on the tower's bottom floor, a single vaulted chamber known as the Beauvais. It was

---

* Twelve pennies (deniers) made up a shilling (sou), twenty of which equaled a pound (livre). The franc, one of several coins in circulation, was worth about four sous, or one-fifth of a livre. A gallon of ale cost about a penny, and a tradesman earned three to five pennies per day, while a man-at-arms with his own horse, armor, and weapons earned about a pound per week.

for poor and indigent prisoners, "who were piled up here pell-mell, sleeping on mats or bales of straw on the floor, in the middle of which sat a great stone water tub named Grand Pierre." For all of this, a prisoner paid just two pennies per day.

Worst of all was the fourth prison, a dank underground labyrinth lit and ventilated only by airholes high up on the wall. Its four "cells"—the Hole, the Well, the Gourdaine, and the Oubliette—were actually funnel-shaped pits without doors or stairs into which prisoners were lowered by rope from a trapdoor above and where it was impossible to sit or lie down. The prisoners incarcerated here still had to pay a penny per day. Into one of these foul pits, "filled with ordure and teeming with vermin," a man named Honoré Poulard was dropped in 1377 after having poisoned his mother and father, his two sisters, and several others. After a month there, he died.[22]

Despite its risks and privations, prison was not generally intended to punish those confined there but to hold them until they could be questioned, tried, sentenced, or released.[23] Guillaume or his deputy was obliged to visit all the prisoners once a month to ensure their welfare and make sure they were being fed.[24] Every year on Palm Sunday a procession of clergy entered the Châtelet and ceremonially freed a number of prisoners, although the most dangerous inmates were excluded from this amnesty.[25]

———◄◦►———

The main business of the Châtelet, to which the prisons were merely an adjunct, centered on the tribunal.[26] This was an imposing ceremonial room with a tiled floor and a dais at one end where Guillaume held court, flanked by his council, the *examinateurs* who conducted inquiries and the *auditeurs* who served as his deputies.[27] Wearing his scarlet robe and a soft black cap, Guillaume questioned witnesses, consulted lawyers, conferred with his council, and handed down sentences on those summoned *sur les carreaux*—"on the tiles."[28] The tribunal typically convened twice a week, but on any given day the auditors might hear cases for the provost as sergeants and attorneys came and went, examiners deposed witnesses, scribes copied documents, and the *greffier,* the chief clerk, kept all the records in order.

Also on hand at the Châtelet was a special corps of lay experts—barbers, surgeons, midwives, and others—who could be consulted to verify key facts, such as whether a man with a tonsure (a partly shaven scalp) was really a cleric and thus entitled to benefit of clergy, or whether a woman claiming to be pregnant was in fact so, as this might bear on her case or even her sentence.*[29]

A person arraigned before Guillaume's tribunal swore to tell the truth about whatever crime he was accused of and either confessed his guilt or maintained his innocence.[30] Any witnesses were then deposed, and they, too, had to swear on a copy of the Gospels to tell the truth; punishments for perjury ranged from the pillory to death.

After the witnesses had been heard, the judges—the assembled *auditeurs* and *examinateurs*—deliberated while Guillaume or his deputy presided. If the accused had not confessed, the judges sometimes contented themselves with *le procès ordinaire,* in which they sought empirical proof of guilt or innocence. In many cases, however, the judges chose *le procès extraordinaire,* ordering that the accused be "put to the question"—that is, examined under torture.

Judicial torture was on the rise in Europe at this time, and it was "commonly used at the Châtelet."[31] Confession was considered "the paramount proof of guilt," and "pain was perceived...as a means of reaching the truth."[32] If the accused had

---

* Surgeons and barbers were at this time much the same thing, since setting bones, letting blood, cutting hair, and shaving were all considered manual arts. If a surgeon began medical studies to become a physician, a learned art, he had to quit performing operations.

admitted to his crime, he was often suspected of concealing further crimes. If he had not, his guilt was often assumed anyway, and torture was used to make him confess. It seems to have been a damned-if-you-do, damned-if-you-don't situation. But the few surviving records may paint an overly harsh picture; a recently discovered document that covers a one-month period in 1412 shows that the Châtelet was hardly a place of endless torture and interrogation.[*33]

When torture was used, it was generally one of two kinds: *le petit tréteau* or *le grand tréteau*—"the little trestle" or "the great trestle."[34] The accused was stripped naked and placed on an inclined plank, his hands tied to a metal ring attached to the wall about two yards off the ground, and his feet secured to a similar ring on the floor. Then a small wooden trestle was inserted between the ropes and the plank to stretch his tendons. Essentially, it was a crude form of the rack. In addition, a funnel was often placed in his mouth and cold water poured in—an early form of waterboarding. If the little trestle did not get results, a larger one causing more tension and pain was employed, and greater amounts of water were used. These methods usually rendered the subject willing to talk. If so, he was immediately brought to a recovery room, known as the Kitchen, where he was dressed in "good clothes," warmed by a fire, given food and drink, and even allowed to rest. Thus refreshed, he was brought back to the tribunal to answer the questions put to him. If he again refused to confess, the torture was repeated.[†]

---

* A ledger for the years 1389 to 1392 lists 127 arrests, many for capital crimes such as murder, theft, and treason, 51 ending in executions. This record can hardly be complete, since the newer 1412 source shows 114 arrests in just a month, most for minor crimes such as debt, disturbing the peace, and prostitution. Of those arrested, 50 were freed pending judgment, 38 acquitted and released, 8 sent back to prison, and 1 banished. The fate of the other 17 is unknown, but in all likelihood some were convicted and executed.

† The law allowed certain exceptions, and it was illegal to torture a pregnant woman or an epileptic.

In rare cases, even after being questioned under torture, the accused refused to confess. In such a situation, "the embarrassed tribunal sought a middle way," sometimes simply banishing the prisoner.[35]

Once a person's culpability had been established by outright confession, proofs, or admission of guilt under torture, the court deliberated over the sentence and determined the verdict by majority vote. Sometimes the vote was divided, as in the case of eighteen-year-old Jean Petit, accused of theft in 1390.[36] After his guilt was established, five of the ten judges voted for hanging, while the other five, in view of his youth, voted for banishment and the cropping of his right ear. The provost at the time — Guillaume's immediate predecessor — deferred the decision to the next session of the court. The judges voted again, and Jean Petit was hanged.

———◄○►———

In addition to the sergeants, examiners, and clerics who staffed the Châtelet as well as the changing cast of prisoners and witnesses passing through, the place was overflowing with documents: scrolls, books, ledgers, writs, depositions, accounts, affidavits, and inventories, some in Latin, some in French, all written on parchment or vellum (dried and cured animal skins) or on a newer and cheaper but less durable substance called *papier*. And half a century before Gutenberg, all of these records had to be time-consumingly copied out by hand, since there were no printers or official forms or even rubber stamps — just wax seals to attest to a document's authenticity.[37]

The overflow was unsurprising; by this time, written records had replaced many ancient oral procedures of the law. Confessions, for example, "were not valid until they had been written down, read aloud in court to the accused, and approved by him."[38] As a result, legal documents lay piled up throughout the old fortress, stacked on wooden tables and writing desks, sorted onto shelves, cubbyholed in armoires, and stuffed into storerooms, along with the various tools used to make them—goose quills whitened and hardened by heat, silver penknives, black-stained inkpots, pumice for smoothing parchment, and polished wooden rulers and shiny metal styli for scoring straight lines across freshly cut sheets of white, virgin calfskin. Whole herds of cows and hillsides full of sheep had been slaughtered and skinned to make these records of human misdeeds, entire flocks of geese had been plucked, and huge numbers of oak galls had been laboriously collected and boiled down to produce barrels of ink.[39]

Many documents at the Châtelet bore the provost's personal seal, which featured the royal fleur-de-lis.[40] Without these voluminous records, and without the scribes and clerks who copied, sorted, and filed them, it would have been impossible for the provost to administer justice. Indeed, once a fortress and still a prison, the Châtelet was now above all a bustling bureaucracy. And Guillaume, the man in charge, had to have not only a deep knowledge of the law, an encyclopedic grasp of Paris, powerful political allies, great personal courage, and skill with the sword, but also a complete mastery of the written word.[41]

———◦———

The teeming capital that Guillaume policed from the Châtelet with his hundreds of officers and clerics had a population larger than nearly every other European city.[42] Paris in turn was a microcosm of France—a place, as one contemporary observer put it, "filled with a most remarkable crowd of people from all walks of life, ranks and vocations, coming from all the different peoples and provinces of France, and embodying the kingdom in miniature."[43] Simply to supply the huge, hungry metropolis with enough meat, grain, wine, produce, and firewood for its daily needs was a colossal undertaking. Each day, an observer wrote, Parisians drank seven hundred barrels of wine. And every week they consumed four thousand sheep, nearly seven hundred and fifty cattle, six hundred pigs, and countless wagon-loads of grain and vegetables.[44] Parisians also received daily deliveries of fresh fish from seaports to the north, rushed to the city by overnight wagons that clattered noisily each morning along the Rue des Poissonniers.[45]

Even at the best of times, when Paris was not under siege from within or without and food and other necessities were available in abundance at reasonable prices, the city was a noisy, crowded, smelly, dangerous place. Its main defense from the outside world was its "enormous girdle of ramparts," some five miles in circumference and constructed—largely by Charles V, the previous king—to keep out robbers and enemy armies.[46] The wall dominating the ramparts was forty feet high in many places and studded with watchtowers and battlements—notches in the masonry for archers to shoot through.[47] Behind it was a raised earthen platform where additional troops could be mustered for defense. A steep slope or escarpment fronting the wall tumbled to a wide, deep moat filled by water diverted from the Seine. Beyond the moat, in yet another concentric circle of defense, lay a great dry ditch to slow down attackers and make them better targets for archers. Hostile forces thus had to cross more than two hundred horizontal feet of ditch, moat, and steep escarpment, all the while exposed to deadly bolts and arrows, before they could even plant a scaling ladder at the sloping base of the high, forbidding wall. Around the wall's perimeter stood a dozen well-guarded *portes,* or gates, each defended by a large fortified gatehouse and a drawbridge. And two great moated forts, one on the east and one on the west, stood guarding the wall where the river pierced it: the Louvre and the Bastille, built or refurbished by Charles V to protect Paris and the royal family in case of attack or siege. In addition to protecting Paris from human foes, the massive ramparts kept out predators such as wolves, though the wily creatures would swim the Seine or boldly trot over the river ice in winter to hunt and scavenge in the city, digging up newly buried corpses and even attacking and "eating women and children."[48]

The great city wall also kept in a disparate mass of humanity, many of them poor, vagrant, or violent, who scraped out a marginal and often criminal existence. Besides the three main social classes, or estates—nobility, clergy, and commoners—the city teemed with an unofficial fourth estate made up of the itinerant poor who barely subsisted there, vagrants drawn to Paris from all over France hoping to live off the wealthy city's leavings, and the dedicated professional criminals who preyed on everyone. By day, thousands of beggars, pimps, prostitutes, petty thieves, and grifters roamed the city looking for clients or victims or lay in wait for them in darkened alleys, cemeteries, and other familiar haunts.[49]

Cutpurses were a particular menace.[50] Clothes equipped with pockets were rare, and both men and women carried coins, the only form of money in circulation, in small bags—purses—hung on their belts. Quick-fingered thieves armed with knives or scissors would cut off the purses and slip away through a crowd or a busy street. Boldly plying their trade in any well-populated place, they were even active among the throngs watching at the gallows as their fellow thieves were being dispatched.

Every night at eight o'clock—seven o'clock in winter—the churches rang the curfew bells, a signal that all law-abiding folk should be in their homes, their doors barred and their windows shuttered, with their lights and fires extinguished.[*][51] Soon after the curfew bells sounded from the churches, the *guet,* or night watch, a local police force, made its rounds in each quarter to ensure compliance.[52] After twilight, and especially after curfew, the city sank into a profound darkness

---

* Parisians of the 1400s worked, prayed, and slept by the bells rung by their parish churches, since private clocks were still rare. Our word *curfew* comes from the French *couvre-feu* ("cover fire").

unknown in even the worst parts of today's modern cities, and the dangers increased manyfold.

People feared the dark for several reasons, including the threat of the supernatural. The air was thought to be filled with angels and demons continually warring over one's eternal soul, tempting or protecting it, leading it astray by a will-o'-the-wisp or guiding it to safety, waiting to seize or save it at the moment of death. Nighttime was the special haunt of demons and evil spirits—elves, goblins, the incubi who preyed on women and the succubi who sought out men.[53] These were the hours when witches held their covens, and magicians and sorcerers stole bodies from the gallows under cover of darkness.

Night also provided cover for criminals, for "night was the time of crime."[54] Anyone who dared to travel the city streets after curfew was at risk, and those who did so usually traveled in company or carried arms.[55] Most noblemen carried swords or daggers as badges of rank and were armed as a matter of course. Many commoners also went about armed or could turn the tools of their trade—cook's knives, carpenter's hammers—into handy weapons. By night, it was simply foolhardy for anyone to travel the streets alone or unarmed.

Theft was a capital offense, often punished as severely as murder, rape, or treason.[56] A fundamental principle of the law was that the punishment should fit the crime. Thus, stealing at night might mean that the perpetrator's eyes were put out. Penalties increased for repeat offenders: "A first theft might entail cutting off an ear or putting out an eye, but at the second a foot or nose would be cut off; there was no excuse for a third theft—the thief was hanged."[57]

Public executions took place at various sites in addition to Montfaucon, including the central market, Les Halles. Executions, intended as moral lessons for the spectators, were often fraught with ceremony and spectacle. A royal official condemned for embezzling in the early 1400s went to the scaffold at Les Halles "wearing his own colors: an outer coat of red and white, hood the same, one stocking red and the other white, and gilt spurs. . . . They cut off his head and afterwards his body was taken to Montfaucon and hung up as high as it would go, in its shirt and hose and gilt spurs."[58]

People expected executions, like other public rituals, to be done the right way. When Capeluche, the city's executioner in the early 1400s, was himself found guilty of several murders and sentenced to death, he gamely "showed the new man how to go about it" as a rapt crowd watched. "They unbound him and he arranged the block for his neck and face, taking off some of the wood with the end of the axe and with his knife, just as if he were going to do the job on someone else—everyone was amazed. Then he asked God's forgiveness and his assistant struck off his head."[59]

—◇—

As the Châtelet was to Paris, so the walled and moated capital city was to France, standing guard over a sprawling realm that was "beyond question the richest and most populous European country."[60] Outside the city's great encircling wall, along the "high ways" running out in all directions, stretched a kingdom of about ten million people extending from Brittany nearly to the Alps, and from Picardy to the borders of Provence.[61] (England, by contrast, had as few as two million.[62]) Some of the people were settled in towns, where they kept shops, trading or producing goods, but the vast majority lived in outlying villages or hamlets, tilling the soil and tending livestock.[63] Whether townsfolk or peasants, they kept regional customs, prayed to local saints, and spoke separate dialects—Norman, Breton, Occitan, and many others.[64] Although nominally the king's subjects, they entrusted their lives to the local lord, as they entrusted their souls to the parish priest.

All over France, as in the rest of Europe, people lived in constant fear—of famine, plague, robbers, and war. Castles large and small still dominated the land, ruled by great lords who were sworn to the king and by local knights sworn to the great lords. Towns and villages cowered in the protective shadow of these castles, each encircled by its own walls and towers to fend off robbers and marauding troops. (Many remote farms also had walls and moats to protect their cattle, grain, and inhabitants.) Fortified places dotted France, as if the whole nation were braced for a sudden attack.[65] However, in the late 1300s, reports of a magically explosive black powder that could knock down towers and blast holes through walls heralded a new and devilish kind of warfare that threatened to bring the age of castles to an end.[66]

Most people knew little of the larger world. Few could read, even fewer could write, and there were no newspapers anyway.[67] Reports from the "outside" traveled mainly by word of mouth and no faster than a horse—about thirty miles a day, except for urgent dispatches carried by mounted relays.[68] Most of the news available was strictly local, though one village might get word of another from wandering beggars, itinerant peddlers, and mendicant friars who made the rounds hearing confessions and receiving alms. Towns were better informed by the soldiers, merchants, and questing pilgrims who crisscrossed France, bringing word of great events from afar—a battle, a siege, a miracle, the birth of a royal heir, the death of a king.

News of such a death had arrived from England at the close of the previous century, in 1399: Richard II had mysteriously died in prison after being deposed by his usurping rival Henry Bolingbroke, now King Henry IV.[69] Richard's underage wife, Isabelle, daughter of the French king, was insultingly sent back to France, just ten years old and still a virgin but already a widow.[70] The mismatched royal union had been arranged three years earlier, in 1396, to end the long, inconclusive war between England and France. With the end of the royal marriage and Henry's accession, France was again in danger.

Since the 1330s, when a dispute over the succession to the French throne arose because of entangled royal genealogies, English armies had repeatedly invaded and devastated parts of France. The seemingly endless conflict—known to history as the Hundred Years' War—also spilled over into Flanders, Italy, Germany, and Spain, foreshadowing the great European wars of later centuries.[71] During the Crécy campaign of 1346, the English had burned and looted parts of Normandy and Picardy. At the battle of Poitiers, in 1356, they inflicted another humiliating defeat on France and even captured its king, carrying him off to London and holding him for ransom. In 1407, half a century and two kings later, the French still owed England part of the huge royal ransom, to be paid in gold, and English troops still occupied parts of France, holding hostage the great fortress on the coast at Calais and much of the wine-rich Gascony. For now, the two uneasy nations watched each other warily across the narrow blue Channel that moated both.

At the end of October 1407—right around the time that Guillaume hanged the two self-professed clerics—the French navy attacked some English ships in the Channel, threatening the fragile truce.[72] Sailing ships and oar-driven galleys carried crews of up to two hundred who attacked mainly by unleashing showers of arrows at enemy vessels, although some ships carried small cannons as well. When word of the incident arrived, the English court must have wondered who had ordered the attack. The French king? Another lord in the royal council? Or a rogue sea captain?

The confusion of the English was unsurprising. It was often unclear to them who exactly was in charge of the huge, populous realm across the Channel, and for a relatively simple reason: the king of France had been intermittently insane for the past fifteen years.

3

The Mad King's Brother

———◆◇◆———

BY THE AUTUMN of 1407, Charles VI had suffered no fewer than thirty-five spells of derangement, many of them lasting for weeks or even months, and some for almost a year.[1] A strong, vigorous man, Charles loved to be outdoors and in the saddle, hunting or jousting.[2] But during his spells he sat inside, keeping perfectly still for hours, claiming that he was made of glass and that any loud noise or sudden movement might shatter him into a thousand pieces.[3] At other times he would shake and scream, shouting at invisible enemies and running so wildly through his palace that the doors had to be walled up to hide his antics from his curious subjects and prevent him from escaping.[4]

In his mad fits, Charles hurled objects, smashed furniture, and struck courtiers and servants.[5] There are reports that he even hit the queen.[6] He also refused to change his clothes or bathe, wearing his royal finery to rags until his body grew so foul and his presence so odious that his servants had to overpower him, cut him out of his filthy, tattered garments, and forcibly wash him.[7]

During the king's "absences," as his spells were politely called at court, his brother, Louis, took charge of the realm, presiding over the royal council, commanding troops, controlling the treasury. Louis, the Duke of Orleans, was three years younger than the king and next in line to the throne after the underage royal heir, the dauphin.[8] A smaller, slighter man than his brother and less inclined to the joust or the hunt, Louis preferred books and society and collecting expensive things, like the statues of the Nine Worthies and their female counterparts that graced a pair of galleries in his magnificent château at Coucy.*[9] Intelligent and learned—the only peer of France who really knew his Latin—Louis spoke in councils with great eloquence.[10] Apart from the king himself, Louis was easily the richest, most powerful lord in France. But as "the principal authority in the realm" during the king's mad spells, he was regularly challenged and opposed by his uncles and his cousins, who all thought they knew better than he how to govern France.[11] Louis was also widely resented by the people, who loathed his frequent tax levies and his spendthrift ways.[12]

Guillaume, the provost, evidently knew Louis quite well, having served the duke as a chamberlain, or adviser, for many years.[13] Guillaume "often visited" the Hôtel des Tournelles, Louis's spacious palace in the Rue Saint-Antoine, which suggested that the two men were close acquaintances, even good friends.[14] The two shared a love of fine books, and Guillaume had sold Louis some prized volumes out of his own collection.[15] Prior to becoming provost, Guillaume had been bailiff of Chartres, the king's chief law officer in that important town, a two- to three-day ride from Paris, and Louis had attended Guillaume's installation in 1400, a sign of his patronage.[16] When the office of provost became vacant in the following year, it may have been Louis, acting for the king, who appointed

---

* The Nine Worthies were representative heroes chosen from among the Jews (Joshua, David, Judas Maccabaeus), the pagans (Hector, Alexander, Julius Caesar), and the Christians (Arthur, Charlemagne, and the famous crusader Godfrey of Bouillon). The female Worthies often included Deborah, Judith, Esther; Penthesilea, Artemisia, Boadicea; and a varying roster of Christian heroines.

Guillaume to this powerful position as the leading man of law in Paris.[17]

Given Guillaume's close ties to Louis, his frequent visits to Louis's palace, and their shared love of learning and books, it's possible that the provost was also familiar with the duke's private retreat: an exclusive picture gallery that Louis was rumored to have — a collection quite different from the gallery of virtuous female worthies at Coucy, for it was hung with revealing "portraits of the most beautiful women he had enjoyed," most likely wearing the low-cut gowns then in fashion that "exposed the neck, shoulders, and sometimes even the breasts."[18] A great collector of noble titles, territories, and castles, as well as sculpture, books, and jewels, Louis above all collected women. And once he had possessed them, he had them painted in all of their seductive beauty so that they would belong to him forever.

Many nobles and courtiers winked at Louis's seduction of their wives, since they often reaped rewards from these affairs in the form of monetary gifts or advancement at court. But every now and then a cuckolded husband took offense at Louis's exercising a sort of droit du seigneur. Among those outraged husbands was a knight from Picardy named Albert de Chauny whom Louis not only cuckolded but also made the butt of an infamous joke.[19]

De Chauny had an extraordinarily beautiful wife named Mariette, and Louis became so enamored of her that she eventually left her husband to become Louis's mistress. One day the knight himself received a summons from the duke. When he arrived at Louis's palace, he was shown into a private chamber, where a beautiful woman lay on a bed, entirely naked except for a veil over her face. Louis was also there, and he ordered de Chauny to judge the woman's beauty — whereupon the embarrassed knight recognized the odalisque before him as his own wife. As a result of this incident, the outraged knight "conceived an implacable hatred against the duke."[20] The episode of the veiled lady, one of Louis's most notorious amours, became so famous that centuries later it inspired a provocative painting by Delacroix.[21]

While most of Louis's affairs were inconsequential, one of his amorous escapades had shaken the throne of France in a way that no one could have foreseen, helping to precipitate the king's madness and setting the stage for Louis's ultimate demise.

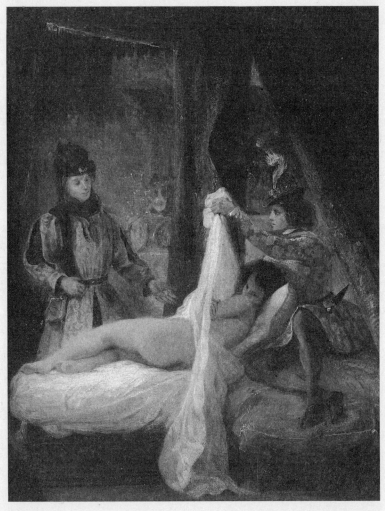

"Louis of Orleans Showing His Mistress." The notorious incident as painted by Eugène Delacroix.

Around the beginning of the year 1392, Louis fell in love with a beautiful young girl and offered her a thousand gold crowns (over \$100,000 today) if she would sleep with him.[22] But before he could consummate the affair, his own wife, Valentina Visconti, daughter of the Duke of Milan, learned of it. She summoned the girl and threatened her so severely that the terrified girl went into hiding. Louis, angered and mystified by her sudden disappearance, blamed a chamberlain he had confided in, Pierre de Craon, and had him banished from court. Craon in turn heard that Olivier de Clisson, the constable of France—the king's chief military officer—had been responsible for his disgrace. On the basis of this hearsay, he secretly returned to Paris, rented a house there, and staffed it with his hired thugs. Late one night, he and his men tried to assassinate Clisson but succeeded only in wounding him. Craon fled to the court of the Duke of Brittany, who refused to give him up to the king. King Charles, outraged at the attack on his constable and at Brittany's protection of the culprit raised an army to bring the rebellious duke to heel and bring Craon to justice.

That is why, on a blazing hot August day later that same year, the young king was riding at the head of a great army—five thousand strong—on a road through a large forest near Le Mans on the border of Brittany.[23] Not far behind him rode his brother, Louis, whose passion for a girl months earlier had been the first link in a long, unfortunate chain of events that would culminate that day in a disaster for all of France. Also riding in the royal army was a newly dubbed *chevalier d'honneur,* Guillaume de Tignonville, who had no idea how the events of that day would alter his own career.[24]

By noon the sun had reached its full height above the leafy forest canopy, and the hot and sweating army trudged on wearily amid the dust, some of the troops half asleep on their feet, marching like somnambulists. Suddenly, a man leaped out from behind some trees and into the king's path. Bareheaded and barefoot, he had a long, scraggly beard and wore a dirty white smock. Some said later that he was a leper or a madman. Seizing the bridle of the king's horse, he shouted: "King, ride no further! Turn back, for you are betrayed!"

As Charles glanced in alarm from this strange figure to the forest around him, the royal procession stopped in its tracks, the line of troops bunching up as the king's entourage blocked the way.

In seconds, the king's infuriated attendants leaped upon the man and began beating and kicking him to make him release the king's horse. Soon he let go. Eluding the king's men, he ran back into the woods, where he continued shouting as before: "King, turn back! You are betrayed!"

Charles nudged his horse forward, and the procession began moving again. The man in the smock kept up, but now at a distance, running through the forest alongside the road and continuing to shout his dire warnings: "Turn back, King! You are betrayed!"

The man kept this up for half an hour, then disappeared back into the forest shadows as mysteriously as he had appeared. All this time, no one interfered with him. The king rode on in silence, apparently brooding over the strange encounter but showing no sign of fright or hesitation about continuing.

In the early afternoon, the army finally emerged from the forest and began crossing a broad, sandy plain under the fierce sun. No longer confined to the narrow forest road, the great lords rode far apart to avoid the dust raised by thousands of marching feet, the king and his brother on one side of the army, their uncle Duke Philip of Burgundy and his son John on the other.[25]

"The sun was dazzlingly bright, blazing down in its full strength. Its beams shone with such force that they penetrated everything....No one was so fit or so hardened to campaigning as not to be affected."[26] The king soon grew very hot in his "black velvet jerkin" and "plain scarlet hat."

Two royal pages rode behind Charles, one carrying his polished steel helmet and the other holding up the king's lance, which had a broad steel head. At some point, the second page dozed off in the saddle and accidentally dropped the lance, which fell and struck the helmet of the page in front of him.

There was a loud clang, and Charles started in his saddle. As though spooked by the strange man in the forest and his warning, he spurred his horse forward, then drew his sword and wheeled around toward the two pages. His face was contorted; he seemed to recognize no one. Raising his sword over his head, he shouted wildly: "Attack! Attack the traitors!"

The young king was an excellent swordsman and in continual practice.[27] The frightened pages reined their horses aside to escape his slashing blade, but a knight riding nearby was not so lucky; the king struck him dead in the saddle.[28]

At this, fear and horror of the king fell over his entourage. "Everyone now fled from him as though from thunder and lightning."[29]

Charles spied his brother nearby and suddenly made for him, brandishing his bloody sword and yelling, "Attack! Attack!"

Louis could hardly believe his eyes, for Charles had always shown him great affection.[30] He spurred his horse and galloped off in a great fright.

Duke Philip and his son John, riding to one side, heard the commotion and looked over to see Charles chasing his brother with a naked sword. "Whoa!" Philip shouted. "Disaster has overtaken us. The king's gone mad! After him, in God's name! Catch him!" And then, as if to urge Louis to safety: "Fly, nephew, fly! The king means to kill you!"[31]

At the duke's cry of alarm, many knights and squires charged off in pursuit of Charles. Soon, a long, ragged line of galloping horsemen, with the king's terrified brother in the lead and the king close behind him, was pounding across the sand, trailing a cloud of dust. Eventually Louis managed to outride Charles, and the men-at-arms caught up with the king. They formed a circle around him as he continued swinging his sword, exposing themselves to great danger as they parried his blows, taking care not to harm him.

Gradually the king's strength waned against the army of friendly foes. Frantic, and still shouting at his imagined enemies, he swung his sword again and again until finally, on one desperate swing, his blade struck another man's weapon and broke in two.*[32]

Charles was now exhausted, he and his horse both drenched in sweat. A knight rode up quietly behind the king and seized him tightly about the waist while others took away his shattered sword. They lifted him from his horse, laid him gently on the ground, and stripped off his velvet jerkin to cool him down. Then they placed him on a litter. "His eyes were rolling strangely in his head, and he did not speak, failing to recognize even his uncle or his brother."[33]

The expedition was called off and the army ordered back to Le Mans.

The king's violent fit threw the court into fear and confusion, for no one knew the cause of his illness. The king's physicians said it was due to an excess of black bile, or *melancholia,* one of the four bodily humors.[34] But others believed that the true cause was poison or sorcery, and rumors began circulating that someone at the court was practicing witchcraft on the king.[35] Guillaume de Tignonville too must have wondered and worried about the king's strange affliction.

For two days, Charles lay in a trancelike state, his limbs motionless and growing colder by the hour. His breath was so

---

* One report says that the king killed four more men before being subdued.

shallow that it would not mist a mirror held to his lips; his heart beat but faintly; and only his chest retained a slight warmth. When his doctors said that the king might die, the court plunged into mourning.

But on the third day of his mysterious illness, to everyone's astonishment, Charles stirred and opened his eyes. Recognizing those around him, he spoke calmly and rationally. Then rising from his bed, he humbly begged pardon from all those he had harmed during his fit. After confessing his sins to a priest, he heard Mass and received the Eucharist.

News of the king's recovery spread through France, and the people celebrated his virtual resurrection from the dead. It was, they said, "a miracle performed by Providence."[36]

———◦———

After a month in seclusion under the care of his doctors at a castle north of Paris, the king regained his strength and eventually returned to the city. By the end of the year, he seemed to have made a full recovery.[37]

In January 1393, prompted by his recent brush with death, Charles issued a decree naming his brother, Louis, as regent in the event that the king died and left an underage heir.[38] (The dauphin was still less than a year old and would not come of age until he was fourteen.) Louis would thus assume great powers if anything happened to the king during the next dozen or so years.

Within days of the king's decree, a tragic event occurred at court that would cast Louis's relation to the crown in a whole new light for years to come.[39] It was announced that one of the queen's ladies-in-waiting was to be married, and, to everyone's delight, the king offered to host the wedding feast and the dancing to follow at the royal palace. A young nobleman, a friend of the king's, proposed privately to Charles an entertainment to add excitement and pleasure to the ball: He and the king, with a few friends, would beforehand and in great secrecy put on linen costumes covered with pitch and stuck full of fine yellow flax that looked like the hair of beasts. Sewn into these close-fitting garments and completely disguised from head to foot as wild men or savages, the king and his friends would burst into the ballroom during the dancing to surprise and amuse the guests. The king thought it a splendid idea, and they set the plan in motion, telling only a few servants whose help they needed. Charles told only the queen.

On the evening of the ball, January 29, all was ready, and after the wedding feast, the six revelers retired to a room in the palace to be sewn into their costumes. One of them, more alert than the others, took the king aside and said: "Sire, command that no one come near us with torches, for if a spark should fall on our coats, the flax will instantly take fire, and we will be burned."[40]

The king saw the wisdom of this and sent a sergeant at arms to the ballroom, where the guests were already dancing, to place all the torches on one side of the room and make sure that no one came near the costumed men when they entered.

Soon afterward, the king's brother, Louis, entered the ballroom with four knights holding torches, evidently ignorant of these precautions.

Moments later, the costumed revelers burst in, Charles leading the other five by a cord that tied the "wild men" or "savages" together like a troop of captives. As knights and courtiers laughed at the comical sight and ladies squealed in mock fright, the five men linked by the cord joined in the dancing, "cavorting among the guests and dashing here and there while making obscene gestures and howling like wolves. Their antics were no more becoming than their cries, and they danced *à la Saracen* in a diabolical frenzy."[41]

The king dropped the cord and went over to show himself to the ladies who were the guests of honor. Passing near the queen, who did not recognize him in his disguise, though he had told her of the plan, Charles went up to his youngest and prettiest aunt, the Duchess of Berry.

Jeanne had married the king's fifty-year-old uncle, Duke John of Berry, three years earlier, when she was only twelve.[42] Now barely fifteen, she excitedly tried to find out who was in the disguise. Flirtatiously taking the king's hand, she said, "I'm not letting you go until you tell me your name."[43]

Across the room, Louis approached the other costumed revelers, evidently "eager to find out who they were."[44] He took a torch from one of his knights and held it close to the face of one. The flame touched the flax, which caught fire, and in moments the man was ablaze.[45] Since the five revelers were tied together, one set light to another, and within seconds all of them had turned into living torches. As the crowd fell back in fear and horror, the screaming and writhing men continued their agonized dance in the middle of the floor. Only one of the five had the presence of mind to snap the cord that linked him to the others and run to an adjacent room where the butlers kept the wine in great vats. By throwing himself into one of the vats, he saved himself, although he was badly burned.

As a cloud of foul smoke rose above the flaming men, many panic-stricken guests, sobbing and groaning, fled the room, the queen among them. The rank smell of burning flesh filled the air, and—in the words of a disapproving monk with an eye for the sordid detail—"as the fire consumed the private parts of the revelers, their genitals fell in pieces to the floor and covered it with blood."[46]

When Charles, still with the Duchess of Berry, saw the men aflame, thrashing and screaming amid the horrified onlookers, he started toward them as if to go to their aid. But the quick-witted duchess threw the long train of her gown around Charles, detaining him.

"Where are you going?" she cried. "Don't you see they're burning? Now, who are you? Tell me at once!"

"I'm the king!" cried Charles.

"Then go, change your clothes, and show yourself to the queen. She's mad with fear that you've burned to death!"

Charles had himself cut out of his costume, dressed, and went to find the queen. When she saw that he was safe, she collapsed with relief and had to be carried to her chamber.

Two of the revelers died on the spot, while two others who were carried alive from the room died of their burns within days. One of the latter was the man who had warned the king about the danger of fire.

The disaster took place around midnight, hours after most Parisians were in bed, but word of it leaked out at once, along with the erroneous news that the king was dead. Before long, an angry mob was at the palace gates, threatening to break them down and avenge the king's death. Charles, still trembling from the ordeal, had to show himself outside to prevent a riot.

The next day, all Paris talked of nothing but the infernal evening at the king's palace, which soon became known as the Bal des Ardents. As the news spread throughout France, people celebrated the king's narrow escape, saying that God had saved him from disaster a second time.

Louis was widely vilified for the fire that killed four men and nearly the king as well. He announced that as penance he would endow a new chapel at the Celestine priory, next to the royal palace.[47] But vicious rumors persisted about his role in the affair. Some said that the king's brother had *thrown* a lit torch at the revelers.[48] Others said he had been privy to the masquerade and was to have joined it but had excused himself at the last minute by saying his costume did not fit. The fatal fire was thus no accident, people said—Louis, recently elevated to regent, had meant to kill the king.

—◦—

The loss of his friends at the ill-fated ball plunged the king into a deep "melancholy," and within a few months he began uttering strange phrases and making obscene gestures "unworthy of a king."[49] This time Charles did not turn violent as before but sank slowly into a state of dementia: "His mind descended into such dense shadows that he completely forgot even the things that otherwise he would have naturally recalled," such as his own name or the fact that he was king. His name was not Charles, he insisted, but Georges; he seemed to be confusing himself with Saint George, the dragon slayer.[50] "By a strange and inexplicable fancy," he even claimed "not to be married and never to have had any children." Whenever he saw the royal fleur-de-lis engraved on an object, he would furiously try to scratch it off.[51]

The king's second spell of insanity lasted much longer than the first, nearly seven months, and he did not recover his wits again until the end of January 1394. In November 1395 he had a third attack, which lasted for two months. In February 1397, he relapsed again, until early July, and shortly afterward he had another weeklong spell. His sixth spell, beginning in March 1398, lasted nearly a year. And so it went, madness alternating with lucidity, dementia followed by an apparent return to reason, in what would amount to more than fifty attacks of insanity over a span of thirty years—a severe, unsolvable crisis of state that plunged the royal family and the government of France into conflict and turmoil for decades.[52]

The fact that the king's derangement seemed to have been grimly presaged by the antics of the "wild men" at the Bal des Ardents only magnified the people's horror and the nation's predicament. For a society bound by rigid hierarchies of birth and class and by strict boundaries between the rulers and the ruled, the mad king—a ruler unable to rule even himself—was an affront, an anomaly, a cipher who did not fit in anywhere and yet whose royal and divinely anointed person had to be faithfully cared for and protected: a *monstre sacré*. Charles, much beloved by his people and known as *le roi bien-aimé* for his likable, approachable manner, had distressingly transformed himself into *le roi fou*, "the mad king."

The king's bizarre symptoms, including his deep fear and suspicion of others, would be seen today as signs of paranoid schizophrenia, a malady that Charles may have inherited from his mother's side of the family.[53] But the several dozen royal physicians knew almost nothing about mental illness and could do little for their patient except bleed him, change his diet, and distract him with amusements.[54] During his spells Charles was confined to his palace, which sank from a proud royal seat where the popular young king had ruled over his realm to a somber royal asylum where he was now quarantined from his people.[55]

Swords, knives, and other sharp objects were carefully kept away from the king, lest he do harm to himself or others.[56] Long after his initial mad fit at Le Mans, during one of his many later spells, Charles was heard to cry out at court: "Save me from the sword-strokes of my brother Orleans! Kill my brother Orleans, for he is killing me!"[57]

With his descent into madness, Charles began to shun his queen, Isabeau, the beautiful Bavarian princess who had so enchanted him when they first met, in their midteens, that he insisted on marrying her after just four days.[58] "Who is this woman whose sight so annoys me?" Charles would now ask when he saw her. "See what she wants, and keep her from always following me around and bothering me with her constant importunities."[59]

At the same time that he repulsed his queen, Charles began showing great affection for his brother's wife, Valentina Visconti. Whenever he saw Valentina at court, he was powerfully drawn to her, calling her *"ma belle soeur"* and preferring her company to that of all other women. Intriguingly, Valentina could calm his fits and soothe his troubled mind when others could not—leading to scandalous talk about the king and his brother's wife, including rumors that she had bewitched him with sorcery.[60]

Such suspicions were not unusual in a world "where poison and sorcery were everyday weapons, and God and demons constantly intervened" in daily life.[61] For example, it was believed that objects consecrated to devils and then rubbed with pulverized bone or pubic hair from a corpse could be used to injure an enemy, and that piercing a small wax image of a person containing his hair or nail clippings with pins could cause that person agonizing pain and even death.[62] The sufferings of the mad— their painful contortions and spellbound trances, like those of the king—were attributed to sorcery or necromancy (that is, conjuring with the dead). Some "magicians," including certain clergy, claimed they could detect and defeat these evil arts, yet as a rule, the Church denounced magic as a fraud when it failed and attributed it to the Devil when it appeared to succeed.

Valentina's origin in Italy, a land associated by the French with "poison and sorcery," encouraged the gossip about her strange power over the king.[63] As the daughter of the Duke of Milan and Isabelle of France, Charles V's sister, she had belonged to the French royal family, the Valois, even before she married Louis, her first cousin. Beautiful, intelligent, and well educated, she was also generous in spirit. When a bastard resulted from Louis's affair with Mariette de Chauny, the veiled odalisque, Valentina charitably took the boy in and raised him as her own.[64] But the royal court and the French people persisted in viewing her with suspicion—as a foreigner, a possible spy, and an ambitious rival to the queen. Valentina, some said, "would gladly have seen her husband made king of France, no matter how."[65] Others alleged that her father, the Duke of Milan, had bewitched the king from afar in order to make his daughter the queen of France. And still others claimed that Louis, coveting the throne for himself, had turned to sorcery after his failed attempt to kill Charles at the Bal des Ardents.

One story in particular aroused a great public outcry. Valentina, it was said, had once tossed a poisoned apple on the floor near where the dauphin was playing with one of her own children, intending for it to kill the royal heir.[66] Instead, her own child seized it, bit into it, and soon died. (The rumor recalled the Arthurian tale in which Guinevere is falsely accused of murdering a knight with a poisoned apple — or an even older tale about a deadly piece of fruit.)[67] It was a baseless charge but still widely believed, in part because Valentina actually did lose a child around this time.*

Isabeau naturally resented her sister-in-law for taking her own place in the king's affections, and popular feeling against Valentina eventually ran so high that she was forced to leave Paris — in effect, banished. In early 1396 she went into exile, moving from one to another château over the next decade but dwelling principally at Blois, on the Loire, several days' ride south of Paris.[68] Her forced departure grieved and angered Louis, and it infuriated her father, the Duke of Milan, who sent ambassadors to France to intercede on his daughter's behalf. As if inspired by stories of Camelot, he even offered to send an armored champion to Paris to prove his daughter's innocence in trial by combat, but this proposal was rebuffed.[69]

After Valentina's exile, evil rumors continued to swirl about Louis, who had "a troubling penchant for magic, sorcery, occult

---

* According to other unfounded rumors, Valentina had a steel mirror from Italy that she used for divination, and she had collaborated with an Italian magician in Paris, via letters sealed with her device, to cast spells on the king.

sciences, astrology and other devilry."[70] Even Richard II of England seems to have believed that Louis was using "diabolical arts" to control Charles VI.[71] Louis's interest in magic may have provided his enemies with a pretext for their accusations, although many princes consulted diviners and astrologers to ascertain their future: dreams, portents and prognostications of all kinds were widely credited and very much in vogue at the French court.[72]

In 1397, the year after Valentina's departure, two Augustinian canons — clerics under vows and living a semimonastic life — arrived in Paris claiming to be magicians and offering to cure the king.[73] Wearing the black robes of their order, they gained the court's trust by pretending to find objects which they had secretly hidden around the royal palace in advance. Lodged in luxury nearby, with all their expenses paid, they prescribed a potion of pulverized pearls for the king and made incisions on his scalp. When Charles failed to improve, they took refuge in the rumors circulating at court and accused Louis of having foiled their efforts with sorcery.

This was a fatal mistake. Louis had them arrested at once, and under torture they confessed to making false charges — perjury — and to being idolaters, apostates, and sorcerers in league with the Devil. They were excommunicated by the bishop of Paris and condemned to death. Wearing white paper miters and parchment vests inscribed with their crimes, they were taken to the city's marketplace, where a large crowd watched the executioner decapitate the two with an ax. Their severed heads were then stuck on spikes, their limbs chopped off and sliced up to be hung up over various city gates, and their dismembered trunks displayed at the Montfaucon gibbet, "feeding the birds and renewed rumors of sorcery."[74]

———◁◦▷———

In 1404, the king's most powerful uncle, Duke Philip of Burgundy, died, removing one of the last checks on Louis's powers during his brother's spells.[75] The two men had long opposed each other, each contending in the royal council for his own policies about taxes, trade, the lengthy quarrel with England, and the Great Schism, a crisis in the Church that had divided Christendom since 1378.[76] While rival popes in Rome and Avignon denounced and excommunicated each other, Louis had repeatedly thwarted Philip's attempts at a reconciliation; Philip, in turn, had probably been behind the scandalous rumors alleging that Louis or Valentina had practiced sorcery on the king.[77] Louis thus may have taken secret joy in his uncle's death, thinking that he could finally rule the king without rival when Charles was sane, and rule in his place when the king was having another of his periodic spells.[78]

Louis also ruled in his own right over a vast domain, which provided him with huge annual revenues through feudal rents and fees — essentially taxes.[79] In addition to the dukedom of Orleans, a large and wealthy territory in central France, he held the counties of Valois, Blois, Beaumont, Soissons, Angoulême, Dreux, Porcien, Périgord, Luxembourg, and Vertus, and he was also lord of Coucy, Montargis, Château-Thierry, Épernay, and Sedan, the last a rich territory in Champagne. In 1394, Louis had allied with his father-in-law, the Duke of Milan, in a rapacious military expedition; they conquered Savona and other territories in Italy, some of which Louis added to his personal domain.

But Louis's colossal personal wealth was never enough to support his voracious appetite. He often dipped into the royal coffers to acquire still more territories or build yet another great castle, like Pierrefonds, a monstrous stone fortress in Picardy with nine great towers and walls nearly one hundred feet high.[80] In order to fund his many costly projects, Louis frequently visited Charles in private, suborning the addled king into signing drafts for huge sums of gold from the royal treasury. The tally of royal gifts and grants to Louis around this time is staggering: In just one year, "from October 1, 1404, through September 30, 1405," Louis received from the royal treasury an annual pension of 12,000 francs, plus 54,000 francs for household expenses; 5,000 francs for his collection of silver plate; 46,000 francs for miscellaneous expenses; 20,000 francs for "the purchase of a single jewel"; 10,000 additional francs as a gift; and 200,000 francs for the Italian territories he had conquered and then ceded to the king. In all, the year's total of royal grants to Louis and his family was over four hundred thousand francs—about fifty million dollars in today's currency.[81]

An aristocrat of the old school, Louis expected the people to pay for his every extravagant fancy no matter the cost. And now that his most powerful uncle was dead, and Louis was virtually king, his greed knew no bounds. In 1405, after he had helped to drain the treasury once again, Louis scandalized the people of France by urging the royal council to levy a new tax—the second new tax that year.[82] Some of Louis's relatives opposed the measure, but in the end the council approved it, on the pretext that England, led by the usurper Henry IV, was planning to invade France and that the funds were needed for national defense.

If the people already resented Louis for his high living at their expense, public outrage boiled over once the Crown demanded payment. Though the official reason for the levy was imminent war with England, it was the French tax collectors who most resembled an army of pillaging soldiers: "The most pitiless men were picked for the job, and they used the most severe methods. All those who resisted or hesitated to pay were thrown into prison. The poorest people were forced to sell all of their furniture, even the straw in their beds, and they still didn't have enough to pay even half the tax. With no other way to avenge themselves, the people vomited out all sorts of curses against the Duke of Orleans, humbly begging God to deliver them from his tyranny."[83]

—<o>—

Remarkably, despite his boundless appetite for women, land, castles, and riches; his spendthrift ways at the people's expense; and his love of "dancers, flatterers, and rioters, as well as great banquets and high living," Louis was also known for his piety.[84] His personal library was filled with edifying works—Bibles, prayer books, and collections of sermons.[85] He wore on his belt two black velvet purses containing saints' relics and a piece of the True Cross.[86] He also gave generously to the poor, albeit with money taxed away from the people. From time to time, he even put on a white Celestine robe himself and retreated for prayers and masses to the priory he had endowed with a new chapel as penance after the Bal des Ardents tragedy.[87]

The priory was located on the Right Bank, directly east of the royal palace and fronting the river. The Celestines, an order of Benedictine monks who first arrived in Paris in the early 1300s, had grown wealthy from royal gifts and pursued their devotions in an elegant cloister and sanctuary built by Charles V.[88] Louis, continuing his father's patronage, was now their principal benefactor. In return for Louis's support, the grateful monks not only said prayers and sang masses for the duke but provided him with overnight lodging in their dormitory whenever he visited. Louis even had his own cell, reserved for him should he arrive without warning, eager to cleanse his soul with holy exercises.[89] Louis was so devoted to the priory that in the will that he drew up in 1402, he made specific bequests to enlarge the dormitory, "which is too small," and to build new latrines, "since the existing ones befoul the dormitory and the surrounding area."[90] (In other words, they stank.) As his custom of wearing a monk's robe suggested, Louis did not visit the priory as a spectator but as a full participant. It was not unusual for him, while he was there, "to attend matins"—midnight prayers—"and to hear as many as five or six masses."[91] In later centuries Louis's humble monastic cell became a kind of tourist attraction for curious visitors, remaining intact right up until the time of the French Revolution.

One night in November of 1407, Louis arrived at the priory and retired to his cell in his usual monastic garb, said his prayers, and went to sleep. But during the night he suddenly awoke in a great fright, shuddering and clutching at the bedcovers. He had had a nightmare—a terrifying vision of his own death.[92]

He had dreamed of a beautiful garden filled with trees bearing wondrous fruit of all kinds. One luxuriant green tree glinted with fruit of gold. But as he went toward it to pick some fruit, his way was suddenly barred by a huge skeleton in a black shroud wielding a great scythe with a long gleaming blade. Death raised a bony finger and spoke, saying, *"Juvenes ac senes rapio"*—"I carry away both the young and the old."[93]

At once the scene changed, and Louis found himself in Heaven among the celestial host, awaiting judgment before the throne of God. Would he be one of the saved and join the company of the blessed saints? Or would he be damned to eternal torment in Hell?

Before he learned his fate, he woke, terrified.

What was this but a divine warning from the other world that he must abandon his sins, especially the delights of the flesh, and repent before it was too late? He was only thirty-six. Must he leave this life so soon?

The frightening dream "so touched his soul" that the next morning Louis went at once to see the prior, a very holy man named Guillaume de Feu. The prior confessed and absolved him, also advising him about his spiritual health. For his part, Louis humbly and contritely "prepared himself for death, as though he were ready to depart from this world."[94]

4

The House in the Rue
Vieille du Temple

———◀◦▶———

FOR ALL HIS piety, Louis did not visit the monks at the Celestine priory nearly as often as he called on the queen at her palace, the Hôtel Barbette. A luxurious stone mansion surrounded by gardens and its own protective wall, the Hôtel Barbette stood in the Marais about a quarter mile from the royal palace and Louis's residence in the Rue Saint-Antoine.[1] Isabeau had purchased this mansion for herself in 1401 to use as an occasional retreat from the stresses of the court. But finding it impossible to live at the royal palace with the insane king, even after ridding Paris of her sister-in-law Valentina, she eventually moved her entire household, including her servants and her children, to the Hôtel Barbette.

Now in her midthirties, Isabeau was no longer the svelte young princess who had married the king twenty years earlier, but she was still beautiful.[2] And she still paid Charles the occasional conjugal visit when he was not ill, continuing to produce royal heirs at regular intervals; she had borne seven children since the start of the king's madness.[3] But she now lived so separately from Charles that, with her approval, he had been provided with a new consort, a pretty demoiselle named Odette de Champdivers. Odette, installed around 1405, had quickly proved her ability to calm and soothe the afflicted king, and she was affectionately known at court as *la petite reine*—"the little queen."[4]

At the Hôtel Barbette, Isabeau ruled over a glittering court of her own, attended by ladies in stylish gowns cut so low that they drew rebukes from friars preaching there. And she hosted lavish balls that kept the windows of her palace lit late at night and scandalized Parisians with reports of lewd dancing until dawn. "The real ruler at her court," complained one indignant priest, "is the goddess Venus."[5]

The king's brother was more than Isabeau's regular guest at these wild, uninhibited affairs. Louis was also rumored to be sharing the queen's bed—an adulterous, even incestuous liaison.[6] And by the autumn of 1407, residents of the Marais had grown well used to seeing the Duke of Orleans and his entourage riding past to visit the Hôtel Barbette.

<hr />

The Hôtel Barbette faced west onto a narrow but heavily used street, the Rue Vieille du Temple, that sliced through the Marais roughly north to south, nearly to the river. Tall wooden houses with tiled roofs lined the street, five or six stories high, each with its own strip of garden in back.[7] Here and there stood more spacious dwellings built around interior courtyards and having their own wells, stables, and latrines.[8] Some houses had shops on the ground floor: a bakery here, a barber there, and now and then a tavern.[9] The street also had a few elegant stone houses belonging to nobles or wealthy merchants, though none so grand as the Hôtel Barbette.

Just south of the Hôtel Barbette, the Rue Vieille du Temple crossed the old city wall of King Philip-Augustus, piercing a former city gate known as the Porte Barbette. The gate, a stone arch more than twenty feet high and flanked by two guard towers, was no longer garrisoned and stood open day and night, since the newer, much bigger wall of Charles V encircled the city a half mile to the north.[10] Continuing south after the Porte Barbette, one soon came to the Rue des Blancs Manteaux ("Street of the White Mantles") on the right, named for the Church of the White Mantles standing near that corner. Next, a block farther down and on the left, was the Rue des Rosiers.

Between these two streets, toward the middle of the block and on the west side of the Rue Vieille du Temple, stood a large, multistory house belonging to Jean de Rieux, marshal of France—a Breton noble celebrated for fighting the English.[11] The marshal, often away from Paris on campaign or at his château in Brittany, rented out rooms to various clerks, squires, and other boarders who were employed by the king, the queen, and Louis of Orleans in their nearby palaces.

Directly across from the Rieux house, on the east side of the street, stood a building known locally as the Maison (or Hôtel) de l'Image de Notre-Dame—the House of the Image of Our Lady. A fairly large wooden structure several stories high that had its own courtyard and stables, it was named for the statue of the Virgin and Child that looked out from a niche over its front gate. The owners were Marie and Robert Fouchier, who lived elsewhere, in the Hôtel du Chantier du Roy, a house at the royal work yard that fronted the river, next to the Hôtel Saint-Pol.[12] Robert was master of the king's works, an architect in charge of important royal construction projects.[13] In 1403, for example, he had overseen repairs to the lofty spire of the Sainte-Chapelle; in 1405, he had supervised work on the city's massive fortifications. Much in demand, Fouchier also took commissions from the king's brother, who had paid him five hundred livres (over three hundred thousand dollars today) for designing Louis's colossal fortress at Pierrefonds. Since the

THE RUE VIEILLE DU TEMPLE

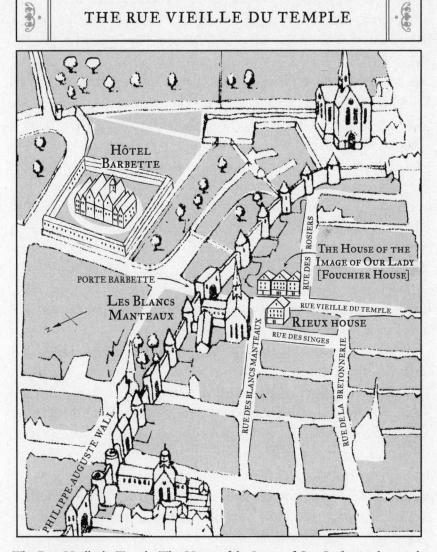

The Rue Vieille du Temple. The House of the Image of Our Lady stands near the old city wall at center.

Fouchiers did not need the house in the Rue Vieille du Temple for themselves, they rented it out, taking in about twenty livres per year.[14] In the autumn of 1407, however, the house had stood empty for nearly six months.

———◄○►———

Right next door to the House of the Image of Our Lady lived Madame Fouchier's daughter Driette Labbé; her husband, Nicolas, who was a carpenter; and their four children.[15]

One day in mid-November—as she would later tell investigators—Driette was at her front door watching the street. It was about ten in the morning, and while she was standing there, a man wearing "a brown robe down to his knee" came up to her and asked if the empty house next door was for rent.

"I don't know," said Driette. But she was related to the people who owned it, and she told him that he could find out by asking Master Robert, who lived at the royal work yard, the Chantier du Roy. The man left.

About two o'clock that afternoon, Driette was at her door again when another man came up to her, wearing "a ratty old coat-of-arms made of white cloth."

The man asked Driette the same question about the house next door.

"I have no idea," she said. And since she did not like the look of him or his clothes, this time she did not supply any more information. The man in the dirty white coat went away.

———◄○►———

The same day—as she, too, would later testify—Driette's mother, Madame Fouchier, received a visitor at her house in the Chantier du Roy.[16] At the time, she was dining with her grandson Perrin Labbé, a young carpenter's apprentice in his early twenties who lived with his grandparents and worked for Monsieur Fouchier.

Madame Fouchier's visitor was an elderly man with a limp whom she had never seen before. He was a broker for rental properties, he said, and he had a client interested in renting the house in the Rue Vieille du Temple.

"You've come to the right place," said Madame Fouchier.[17]

She probably received her visitor in the hall, a large formal room near the front entrance used for entertaining guests.[18] The broker, seemingly lame in one foot, limped over to the door and called to someone outside. In came "a very tall man" dressed as a *cordelier,* a Franciscan friar, in a long brown robe with a red hood.* Madame Fouchier did not recognize him either, nor did he offer his name, though she noticed right away that he was very well spoken. Getting down to business at once, the friar said that he and a friend wanted to rent the house in the Rue Vieille du Temple to store some wine, grain, and other supplies. Madame Fouchier said that she did not want them storing anything there that would overload the granaries and leave the house the worse for wear. The friar assured her that they would be careful and that they would not damage the floors or "do anything they should not do." Then he asked about the price. How much would it cost to have the house until the Feast of Saint John the Baptist—June 24 of the following year?[19]

"Twenty livres," said Madame Fouchier, naming a typical price for a year's rental, although the friar would lease the place for only a little over seven months.

The friar stepped aside to hold a whispered conference with the broker and then approached her again.

"Sixteen livres," he counter-offered, saying he could pay no more.

"Twenty," replied Madame Fouchier, explaining she could not let it go for any less.

The friar insisted that he could not afford any more.

The broker spoke up, probably fearing the loss of a commission. "They are good people," he said, referring to the friar and his friend.

---

* Franciscan friars were known as *cordeliers* because of the simple *corde*, or rope, used to belt their robes, and in Paris many were teachers or scholars affiliated with the university.

"I only do business with good people," replied Madame Fouchier.

Things seemed to be at an impasse. But the house had been empty for months, and apparently Madame Fouchier had no other prospects. After reconsidering, she gave in and agreed to the offered amount.

The friar reached for a purse at his belt, took out a silver coin, and gave it to Madame Fouchier as a deposit to secure the rental. Then he asked about the keys.

"You can get them from my son-in-law, right next door to the house," said Madame Fouchier. And she told him to ask for Nicolas Labbé, who would give him the keys when he showed up for them. After that, the two men left.

The next day, the friar came back, showed Madame Fouchier the keys, and told her that he had brought the rest of the money for the rental.

"But it's not due yet," she said, refusing to take it.

The friar insisted, pressing her several times to take the money. Then he asked her to take at least half of the amount owed, but she still refused. He left but came back a short while later and told her that he really must give her all the money owing, since he would be gone "for three or four weeks." In the meantime, he said, the house would be "very well supplied," apparently referring to delivery of the things he intended to store there.

After the friar's repeated urging, Madame Fouchier finally agreed to take the rest of the money in advance. The friar counted out the sum still owed and handed over the coins. Then he asked for a receipt stating that the full amount had been paid.

"I can't give you a receipt," said Madame Fouchier. "My husband isn't home today." She may have been able to read, but apparently she could not write—a separately learned skill at that time.[20] Business deals often required a receipt written on paper, parchment, or the notched strips of wood known as tally sticks.

The friar said he would come back the next day.

She asked him for his name so it could be put on the receipt. "Jean Cordelant," he replied.

"Are you with the university?" she asked, no doubt surmising this from his robe and hood.

"Yes," he said. But before she could ask any more questions, the friar left.

That evening, Madame Fouchier told her husband, Robert, that she had rented out the house until Saint John's Day for sixteen livres and that the renters were good people, since they had paid the full amount in advance. Then she asked him to write up a receipt indicating that the rent had been paid in full. He said he would have his clerk draw one up.

Robert had his clerk make out the receipt, on paper, then "affixed his own seal" in wax to authenticate it and left the document at his house for the friar to pick up when he returned the next day.[21]

———◦———

One evening later that week, Driette Labbé heard some horses entering the gate of the house next door and then clopping around in the courtyard.[22]

"Listen," she said to her children. "I hear someone next door."

Her children then told her that earlier that day they had seen a load of hay delivered to the house, along with some firewood and oats.

Learning this, Driette said that "some good people" must have moved in, a thought that made her "very happy."

———◦———

Over the next few days, the tall friar in the red hood returned several times to speak with Madame Fouchier about the rental arrangements.

Once he came by with the broker, but Madame Fouchier was not at home. Perrin, her grandson, was there, however, and the two men told him that Madame Fouchier had said they were to have the receipt she would leave for them in the hall, "on a dresser, under a goblet."[23] Perrin left the door, went to the dresser, and found the receipt there under the goblet, just as the two men had said it would be. He took it and went back to the door. He asked the man in the red hood for his name. The friar told him. Looking at the paper, Perrin saw the name written there: *Jean Cordelant*. Perrin gave the receipt to the friar, and the two men left.

◦

For a day or two after she first heard horses next door, Driette Labbé had no idea whether anyone had actually moved in.[24] She did not hear anything from the house, nor did she hear the gate open or anyone coming or going or any horses being led in or out or moving around in the courtyard. But on Friday, November 18, about eight o'clock in the evening, she thought she heard "eight or ten horses" entering the courtyard next door. Soon after this she went to bed. She would not see or hear anything else at the house next door until several days later.

◦

Simon Cagne, a baker in the same street, also noticed some new activity.[25] Simon lived two doors down from the Labbés, on the other side of the Fouchier house, so he was in a good position to observe the goings-on there.

Simon was about fifty years old and married to Jehannette, who was little more than half his age, twenty-seven. Jehannette may have been Simon's second wife, or he may have decided to marry later in life, choosing her because she was young or because she came with a good dowry.

For a full week, beginning in mid-November, Simon and his servants heard "horses coming and going very late at night" and also "very early in the morning" at the house next door. Everyone in the Cagne household was "very surprised," since the Fouchier house had stood empty for months, yet no one ever saw the gate open or anyone going in or coming out. Since the garden behind the house was surrounded by a wall, and there was no back entrance to the property, the horses could have come in only by the front.

Jehannette was just as mystified as her husband about the activities next door. The servants told her that some people were staying there and that they could hear them by day but that no one ever went out of the house "except at night," and they had no idea who the people were.[26]

———<o>———

On Sunday, November 20, at about six in the evening, Jacquette Griffard, a shoemaker's wife who lived with her husband and baby right across the street, on an upper floor of the Rieux house, went out to get a meat pie from a nearby shop.[27]

A man was standing in the street near the door of her house. He wore "a long robe like a priest's and a hat of rabbit's fur."

"Nurse, good lady, sell me a pitcher of water," he said. Seeing her with a baby, he may have assumed that she was a wet nurse.

"I don't have any water to sell," Jacquette replied.

That was the end of their exchange, and she went on her way. When she came back a little later with the pie, the man was gone, and she forgot all about the incident until several days later.

———<o>———

The next day, Monday, at about eight in the evening, Driette Labbé "heard a large number of horses—ten or twelve—going in next door." And then she heard nothing more.[28]

It was all very strange, the mysterious arrivals and departures next door, and she began to worry about what was going on there.

—◦—

On Wednesday, November 23, Girard Lendouil and two fellow water carriers, Jean le Tisserant and a man named Denisot, were approached by a pair of men about delivering water to a house in the Rue Vieille du Temple.[29] One of the strangers wore a robe with a red hood, the other a gray tunic. They did not give their names.

Girard and his comrades belonged to the city's guild of licensed water carriers, many of whom came from the Auvergne, in central France. More than a dozen public fountains built at royal expense were scattered about the Right Bank, all supplied by aqueducts with cool, fresh water from hillside springs north of the city.[30] Fountain water was the purest in Paris, but the supply was limited and it had to be carried a distance. Many people thus used private wells on their own property or drew water directly from the river, although it was often polluted.[31]

One of the royal fountains was situated near where the Rue Vieille du Temple emptied into the Rue de la Tixeranderie.[32] But the two prospective customers approached the water carriers "by the river bank," where Girard and his comrades may have specialized in hauling water in quantity from the Seine.

The two men said they needed a dozen *voies* of water, one *voie* being the contents of two wooden buckets holding about two and a half gallons each, or five gallons in total.[33] (For ease of portage, the pair of buckets were often hung from a yoke balanced on the carrier's neck and shoulders, though larger quantities could be carried a distance by cart.)[34] With buckets attached to ropes and dropped over the quai into the river, Girard and his men began drawing water from the Seine and filling the reservoir on their delivery cart. Once they had drawn a dozen *voies,* about sixty gallons in all, they set off behind the two men toward the Rue Vieille du Temple, pull-ing their cart behind them.[35]

Taking the shortest route from the river, they would have headed north past the Church of Saint-Gervais, then east on the Rue de la Tixeranderie, and then north again on the Rue Vieille du Temple. It was a holiday, the Feast of Saint Clement, and the street would have been crowded with people and some mounted traffic as well, through which the water carriers had to steer their load over the often uneven paving stones. They also had to stay clear of the *ruisseau,* or gutter, a trench running down the middle of the narrow street and often overflowing with mud and debris, including fresh slops from nearby houses.[36]

Since the Rue Vieille du Temple climbed slightly as it went away from the river, and the load of sixty gallons or so weighed about five hundred pounds, plus the weight of the cart, the men may have taken turns pulling the cart as they negotiated the route, nearly a third of a mile long.[37]

Eventually they passed the Rue de la Bretonnerie on their left, and then the Rue des Rosiers on their right, finally stop-ping where the two customers indicated, in front of a house with a statue of the Virgin and Child over the front gate. After the gate was opened, Girard and his comrades followed the two men into the courtyard, pulling their cart behind them.

What happened next may have surprised them a little. The two men from the house "did not allow them to go any further onto the premises," either to the house itself or to the stables where the horses were kept, but told them to pour the water "into a cistern standing near the entrance under a covered way" that sheltered it from sunlight and debris.

After the barrels had been emptied into the cistern, the men paid the water carriers, and Girard and his comrades left. The empty barrels, the downhill grade, and the coins in their purses would have made for a more pleasant return trip to the riverbank.

———◄o►———

Later, at about six in the evening on Saint Clement's Day, Driette Labbé was at home talking with her twelve-year-old daughter, Blanche.[38] By now Blanche seemed to have been aware of her mother's worries about the new people next door and their strange habits.

Blanche told Driette that earlier that day she had seen some men leading eight horses out of the house to water them.

At about seven, after supper, Driette told her daughter that they would go upstairs together and take a peek next door to see what they could find out about the men staying there and make sure that they "were not bad people."

Sunset came early in late November, at around four in the afternoon, and there was no moon that night.[39] A shopkeeper would later describe the night of Saint Clement's as *bien obscur*—"very dark."[40] And a chronicler would say it was *assez brun,* meaning much the same thing but with a literary touch suggesting that this particular night was especially "somber," "unfortunate," even "funereal."[41]

Driette and her daughter climbed up to the attic, where they could look out into a room of the neighboring house. It was now dark, and they saw a candle burning in the room. By its light they saw "eight or nine men, some dressed in white and others in black." Driette did not recognize any of them, but she now "imagined that some bad people were staying in that house," and she became "much more worried than before." Even so, that night she still went to sleep "naked in her bed," as was the usual custom for people, highborn and low alike.[42]

Not long after, Driette suddenly awoke to the sound of people shouting in the street just outside her house.

5

A Cold, Dark Night

———◄○►———

THERE WAS ALMOST no street lighting in Paris after dark
except for the occasional candle or lantern in a shop doorway.[1] And because of the extreme danger to the flammable
wooden houses in the tightly packed streets, all lights and fires
had to be covered or extinguished when the curfew bell rang at
eight, plunging the city into darkness.[2] Afterward, the night
watch made its rounds, putting out any lights still burning and
warning offenders.

The city was not only darker than usual on that moonless
night but also very cold for that time of year. There are reports
that it even began to snow.[3] But no one knew that a great storm
was on the way, the worst in at least a century, a storm that
would plunge France into a long and deadly winter freeze.

———◄○►———

Jean Pagot, a nineteen-year-old clerk who lived in the Rue
Vieille du Temple, returned home that evening around the
time the curfew bell rang.[4] Jean was employed by Pierre Cousinot, a lawyer who represented clients before the Parlement of
Paris.[5] That evening, Jean had been "kept busy in town," perhaps copying some documents for his master.

When he arrived at the Rieux house, where he rented a room,

Jean saw "two big fellows in black" standing in the street near the door. It was very dark by now, even if candles were still burning in some houses. As Jean came up to them, the two men "peered closely at his face." They seemed to be looking for someone.

"What do you want?" he asked.

"Nothing," one of the men replied simply, despite their menacing appearance.

Jean went into the house and closed the door behind him, no doubt relieved to be safely inside and out of their sight.

———◦———

Just up the street and around the corner, in the Rue des Blancs Manteaux, was a tavern called the Shield of France.[6] It was a lively, convivial place that evening. People who had to get up early for work the next day were drinking, eating supper together, playing at dice, and enjoying the last of their holiday. Wine was the most popular drink in the city's several hundred taverns, although beer consumption was on the rise.*[7]

Perrin Fouchier, son of Madame Fouchier and a valet in the king's service, was there having supper with some friends. His table companions included three men—Ermequin, Billecocq, and Le Camus—a woman named Haquenée, and two others.

Haquenée worked for the queen at the nearby Hôtel Barbette, so the news and gossip shared at the table that evening may have included talk of the unfortunate outcome of the queen's childbirth just two weeks earlier.[8] The child, the queen's twelfth and a boy, had died shortly after birth, lasting only long enough to be hastily baptized. The grief-stricken queen, it was said, had spent most of the last two weeks "in tears."

While Perrin and his friends were eating supper together, a

---

* Many Parisians, not just official vintners, were in the wine business, "and one could get a drink as easily at a Carmelite friary as at a lawyer's office or a goldsmith's shop." As for beer, in 1369, Charles V had granted licenses to twenty-one *brasseries,* as breweries and their attached drinking rooms were then called.

man named Maillefer came into the tavern "holding a lighted torch in one hand, and four arrows in the other." Maillefer said he had found the arrows outside in the street. Some men had been running along and dropped them, he said. At this, everyone began "to make fun of him," laughing and saying that he could not possibly be telling the truth.

◄○►

Around eight o'clock, a messenger arrived at the queen's palace, just up the Rue Vieille du Temple. Isabeau was still "confined to childbed," and Louis, continuing to visit the queen, had gone to the Hôtel Barbette that evening "to sup with her" and try to "cheer her up."[9] The child she had recently lost may even have been his.

The messenger, who gave his name as Thomas de Courteheuse, one of the king's valets, said he had an urgent message for the duke: "Sire, the king orders you to come to him at once. He wants to speak with you about a very important matter concerning both you and him."[10]

Soon after this, Louis stepped into the palace courtyard and prepared to depart. Although he commanded a personal retinue of six hundred men-at-arms in Paris, Louis had with him that evening only two squires and four valets, suggesting that he felt perfectly safe traveling about the city at night with only a few lightly armed attendants.[11]

A horse and a mule were brought into the darkened courtyard. Louis, like some great lords, preferred the smaller, more tractable mule to a horse when riding through the narrow, often crowded city streets. While several of the valets "held torches," the duke mounted his mule, and the two squires "mounted the one horse" that they shared.[12]

Two of the valets with torches ran ahead to light the way, and the two squires sharing the horse went next. Then came Louis on his mule, and finally the other two valets on foot.[13]

The short procession clip-clopped "slowly" through the palace gate, turned left into the Rue Vieille du Temple, and headed south through the sleepy city.[14] Despite the unseasonably cold weather, Louis rode "bareheaded," with a woolen muffler wound carelessly around his neck for warmth. Apparently in a good mood after his visit to the queen, he was "humming a tune."[15]

———◦———

All of Paris now lay in deep darkness pierced only by an occasional passing torch. Most shops were closed, and many houses were already barred and shuttered against the freezing night air and its swarms of evil spirits.

As the duke and his men made their way down the dark, narrow street, a few tardy laborers hurried home wraithlike through the night, pressing close to the tall wooden houses to keep clear of the passing hooves. Soon Louis and his retinue came to the old city wall and the Porte Barbette, set into the wall where the street ran through it and arching high over their heads in the chilly gloom.

The procession passed through the old stone gate flanked by its twin guard towers, as before: the two valets with torches, then the horse carrying the two squires, then Louis on his mule, and the remaining valets behind him on foot. One block south of the old gate, they passed the Rue des Blancs Manteaux, where the Shield of France was still open for business, although taverns ordinarily closed at curfew.[16] As Louis and his men passed by, the sounds of people talking and laughing indoors may have carried down the street.

Louis's party neared the Rue des Rosiers. Just ahead, on the right, was the Rieux house and, across from it, the House of the Image of Our Lady.

———◦———

On an upper floor of the Rieux house, at a window "high above the street," Jacquette Griffard, the shoemaker's wife, was watching for her husband to come home and taking in some of her baby's linen, which had been "drying on a pole" stuck out the window.[17] As she looked out, she saw "a great lord" with a number of attendants riding down the street from the direction of the Porte Barbette. "Two or three" of the men carried flaming torches to light the way. The lord was bareheaded and "playing with a glove, or a muffler, as he rode along." And she could hear him singing. After watching for a moment, Jacquette left the window to put her baby to bed.

—◇—

At the Fouchier house, right across the street, a gate suddenly opened below the niche where the Virgin and Child looked out. A band of armed men swarmed into the street in front of Louis, their faces masked with cloth or hidden in their hoods.[18] They brandished swords, axes, crossbows, and wooden maces studded with big iron spikes at the business end.[19] Many held torches, adding their light to the flickering scene.

Louis, finding his path blocked by this heavily armed gang, halted his mule and stared around in alarm at the masked men and their gleaming blades.[20] It was against the law to go about the city embrunché—that is, with a covered face—and at this hour, these masked and well-armed men had to be up to no good.[21]

"I'm the Duke of Orleans!" he shouted. "Stand back!"[22]

But Louis had with him only six lightly armed attendants, and he was not at court, where everyone jumped at his command. His shouted order, rather than warding off danger, sealed his doom.

"It's him," said one of the masked men.[23]

"Kill him! Kill him!" shouted another. And they all closed in.

A tall man in a red hood, evidently their leader, raised an ax and swung it at Louis "as though in a diabolical rage."[24] The stroke severed the hand "which held the saddle-bow." As the clump of bloody fingers flew to the ground, Louis screamed in pain. Then the assailants knocked Louis from his mount, and he "somersaulted" off his mule onto the street, "striking his head on the pavement."[25]

The assassination. A nineteenth-century depiction.

The skittish horse carrying the two squires, frightened by the commotion and "the clatter of weapons," began "to rear up." Suddenly "it bolted down the street," the two squires clinging desperately to its back as it galloped off into the dark.[26] Two of the valets, although seeing their master under attack, apparently fled the scene, dropping their torches in their haste to get away.[27]

A third, more loyal valet, Robinet Huppe, drew his sword and fought with the assailants, despite their overwhelming numbers, only to be frightfully slashed on the face and the arm and forced to retreat in order to stanch his bloody wounds.[28] The fourth valet, a German named Jacob de la Merré, also tried to defend his master, bravely running toward the attackers and shouting, "Spare the duke, the king's own brother!"[29] No such mercy would be shown.

———◇———

Jean Pagot, the young clerk who lived in the Rieux house, had been home for only "a quarter of an hour" when he heard a commotion in the street outside.[30] Someone was raising the hue and cry, shouting, *"Haro! Haro!"*—a traditional call for help indicating a crime in progress. Was the crime being committed by the two big men in black he had seen by his door a little earlier?

Pagot's room had no window onto the street, so he opened the door to see what was the matter. The instant he did so, an arrow shot past the doorway, flying "right alongside the house." He jumped back and slammed the door shut "in a great fright." Listening from behind his closed door, he heard "the sound of blows" and "cries of pain."

———◇———

Several stories up, Jacquette was putting her baby to bed when she heard a noise in the street and then someone shouting, "Kill him! Kill him!"[31]

Had her husband gotten into an altercation on his way home?

She rushed back to the window, still holding her baby, and stared down at the street. But her husband was nowhere in sight.

The great lord was now right below her window. No longer mounted, he was "kneeling in the street," surrounded by "seven or eight men wearing masks and holding swords and axes." Several of the men also held torches. One of the lord's hands was missing, and blood gushed from his severed wrist.[32] Another man, apparently one of the lord's attendants, lay motionless on the pavement nearby.

Jacquette saw the lord glancing around in terror at his assailants. "What is this?" he cried out. "What are you doing?"

They answered with their weapons. As blades flashed in the torchlight, the lord desperately "threw his arms in the air to fend off their blows."[33]

Jacquette watched in horror as a sword struck one of his upraised arms, nearly taking off the lord's remaining hand.

In an instant, they were all "chopping and stabbing" at him. They "hammered" him as he swayed on his knees in their midst, blood flying everywhere.[34]

Despite the onslaught, it took the man a long time to die.

Finally, a great ax blow from above "split open his head down to the teeth," and he fell forward onto the pavement.[35] A piece of his brain, knocked loose from his shattered skull, landed in the mud nearby.

Even after the lord lay "stretched out" in the street, clearly dead, the assassins kept up the attack, chopping and stabbing "as hard as they could" at his lifeless body, "beating" his bloody corpse—Jacquette would later say—"like a mattress."[36]

"Murder!" she screamed. "Murder!"

One of the killers looked up and yelled at her: "Shut up, you damned woman! Shut up!"

———◆———

Drouet Prieur, a young valet who also lived at the Rieux house, several floors below Jacquette, was heading downstairs and out to the stables to check on a horse when he heard some noise outside.[37] The downstairs windows facing the street were high up on the wall, so he could not look through them. But he could see torchlight flickering on the opposite wall, and he could hear the shouts of men and the clatter of weapons.

Prieur hurried back upstairs to see what was going on. By now, everyone was at the windows, staring into the street: his master, Henri du Chastelier, who was one of Duke Louis's squires; du Chastelier's page; another squire named Jean de Rouvray, who lived in the same house; and a barber who also happened to be there.

Joining them, Prieur looked down and saw "a torch lying on the pavement, still burning." By its light he could see "twelve or fourteen" heavily armed men. "Some of them held unsheathed swords, some had axes, and some of them falcon-beaks, and wooden maces with iron spikes."[*38] They were striking and stabbing at someone in their midst, shouting, "Kill him! Kill him!"

To get a better look, Prieur raced back downstairs, opened the *guichet*—the little barred window in the door—and peered out. As soon as he did so, a masked man came over and "brandished an ax right at the window." Prieur, "afraid that he might get hurt," immediately slammed the window shut and hurried back upstairs.

———◁○▷———

Far down the Rue Vieille du Temple, in the direction of the river, the duke's two squires finally managed to halt their run-away horse. They heard approaching hooves, and suddenly their master's riderless mule trotted up. "Thinking the duke had fallen off his mount," they hastened back up the street on their shared horse, towing the mule behind them "by the bridle."[39]

---

* Falcon-beak: a halberd, a versatile combination of ax, pike, and spike or hammer.

When they arrived at the scene, they saw their master lying on the pavement, covered in blood, a gang of masked men chopping away at the body.

As the squires took in this horrible sight, several of the attackers turned to menace them, brandishing their weapons and shouting, *"Allez! Allez!* Get out of here! Or we'll kill you too!" At this, the two frightened men spurred their horse back toward the Hôtel Barbette. All along the dark and shuttered street, they shouted, "Murder! Murder!"

———<o>———

Jacquette was still at her window, holding her baby and staring down.[40] She saw a horse coming up the street carrying two men, a mule trotting along behind. Some of the masked men turned to shout at the riders, and again their horse bolted away into the dark.

As the shoemaker's wife watched, the gate opened again across the street. Out ran a tall man in a friar's robe with a great red hood pulled down over his face. She heard more yelling: "Put out your lights! Let's go! He's dead! Take heart!"

At once the assailants left off their bloody work and made as if to leave. More men came out of the house with torches, some leading horses.

———<o>———

Drouet Prieur, still watching from a lower floor in the same house with his master and the other men, saw "five or six" riders come out of the gate across the street.[41] Nearby stood a man wearing a friar's robe with a great red hood and holding a huge iron-tipped mace.

Prieur could see that the victim lying on the ground wore "a jacket of black damask trimmed with martin fur." The hooded man with the mace began to strike the prone figure, again and again. After a final blow to the head, he dragged the body over to a pile of mud and dropped it there. "With a wisp of lighted straw," he inspected the body, apparently to make sure that his prey was truly dead.[42]

◄○►

From her much higher window, Jacquette saw some of the attackers flee on foot.[43] They ran down the street to the Rue des Blancs Manteaux, pausing there to put out their torches "in the mud." Then they turned the corner and disappeared into the night.

A torch still "burning on the ground" near the lord's body flamed up. Blood was oozing from his butchered trunk, his severed wrist, his shattered head.

Again Jacquette shouted down into the street: "Murder! Murder!"

She heard another woman cry out as well, just around the corner in the Rue des Rosiers.

As Jacquette watched, the second victim—the man who had lain in the street the whole time, as though dead—began to move. "Raising his head" from the ground, he cried weakly, *"Mon maistre!"* or *"Mon seigneur!"* Watching and listening from high above, she could not quite make out his words. Soon the torch lying near the dead man flickered out, and the street was plunged back into darkness.

◄○►

Drouet Prieur and the other men watching from their window also saw the assassins flee, running away on foot or riding off "as fast as they could in the dark without any light."[44] The masked killers headed north, then turned west into the Rue des Blancs Manteaux, the clatter of their retreating horses echoing down the darkened streets.

No one at the window, not even du Chastelier, the duke's own squire, recognized the figure in black damask lying in the street. Someone at the window said it was Monsieur de Boqueaux, a royal chamberlain. But the light was bad, and the man's body was mangled and bloody.

———<o>———

Simon Cagne, the baker who lived next door to the Fouchier house, had been getting ready for bed with his wife, Jehannette, when he'd heard the shouting in the street.[45] Since the queen lived in their quarter, he thought "it must be some of her pages arguing or fighting among themselves," as they often did at night as they passed by. Nevertheless, to see what all the racket was about, he went downstairs, walked through the shuttered bakery, and opened his front door to have a look.

He found a man stretched out on the ground right outside the entranceway. Glancing around, Simon saw no one else.

"Frightened and very upset," the baker quickly shut his door without checking to see if the man was dead or alive or to find out who he was or anything else about him.

———<o>———

Drouet Prieur and the other men still watching from their window saw "a lot of smoke" at the Fouchier house, and they heard shouts: "Fire! Fire!"[46]

They rushed downstairs and into the street to look at the dead man "by the light of one or two burning torches which they carried." The body lay "belly up, all stretched out on the pavement," and was horribly mutilated.

To their shock and dismay—and with cries of *"Hélas!"*— they realized that it was the Duke of Orleans. Du Chastelier, Louis's squire, may have recognized the body first, from the clothing, since the face was all sliced up. The duke had two great wounds in the head, "one across the forehead so that you could see his brain, the other toward the top of his head," and "his left hand and arm" had been cut off.

A few yards away lay another man. Drouet went over to look at him. It was one of the duke's attendants who had valiantly tried to defend his master. He was still alive though badly wounded and "moaning terribly as though he would die." Some of the men began tending to him.

Drouet went back "to look at the body of the Duke of Orleans where it lay headlong on the pavement."

Jean Pagot, the young clerk who was still cowering behind his door on the ground floor of the Rieux house, had heard "a great many people" rushing along the street on horseback and on foot.[47]

Then he saw a gleam of light through a small hole in his door. Peering out through the hole, he saw a man approaching with a lit torch. Stopping near Pagot's door, the man cried out, *"Hélas, monseigneur est mort!"*

After hearing more people arrive on the scene and more cries of lament, Pagot finally dared to open his door again and go outside. He saw two bodies lying in the street not far from his door, both "badly cut up and very bloody."[48] Then he saw something else lying "in the mud." It was a man's hand. It had been "cut clean off."

Someone said that the hand belonged to the Duke of Orleans.

Amelot Lavelle, a florist, about thirty-six, lived in the Rue des Rosiers, right off the Rue Vieille du Temple.[49] She'd been at home working when she heard someone in the street outside shouting, "Murder!"

Amelot opened the door, and a badly bleeding man wearing

"a gray-brown coat" tumbled in. He had "a terrible wound across his forehead" and another wound "on his right arm near his elbow."

"Save me!" he cried weakly.

After quickly shutting the door behind the man, Amelot did the best she could, perhaps trying to stanch the bleeding with some cloth. But seeing how badly injured the man was and fearing that he would die in her house "without making confession," she decided to go out and get a priest before it was too late. This was risky, since the man's attackers might still have been lurking outside.

Leaving the wounded man in her room, she headed to the Church of the White Mantles, about a block away.

As she turned into the Rue Vieille du Temple, Amelot saw torchlight flickering on the buildings and heard shouts and cries. Smoke hung in the air, and people were rushing about with water buckets.[50]

Amelot saw "four or five men dressed as squires" lifting a man from the pavement. The man was "all covered in blood" and seemed to be dead. They carried him across the street into the house of Marshal Rieux.

Another squire came along behind them, carrying "the brain which had come out of the dead man's head." Holding it carefully in his hands, like a relic, he followed the other squires into the Rieux home.

Amelot ran past the commotion to the church just around the corner and pounded on its door and shouted. No one answered. She ran back to the Rue des Rosiers to the house of a priest she knew, Jean Vaillant, roused him, and immediately brought him to her room to confess the wounded man.

Afterward she asked the wounded man who he was and who had attacked him.

He replied that his name was Robinet, adding, "I serve in the Duke of Orleans's storeroom. Just now I was coming from the queen's palace with the duke, and I saw him attacked. I don't know who did it or why, and I shouted, 'Murder!'" The man also told Amelot that the duke had been "injured" in the attack, seemingly unaware that Louis was dead.

———◄◦►———

After Perrin Fouchier had finished supper with his friends at the Shield of France, one of his companions, Le Camus, proposed a game of dice.[51] But just as the game began, they heard shouting in the street.

"Fire! Fire!"

Someone announced that the fire was in Nicolas Labbé's house, in the Rue Vieille du Temple. Hearing this, Perrin had become "very worried," since his sister, Driette, was married to Nicolas.

Perrin rushed outside and sprinted toward the Rue Vieille du Temple. Along the way, he heard people saying that "two dead men were lying in the street."

When he reached the Rue Vieille du Temple, he discovered that the fire was actually in the building owned by his parents, the House of the Image of Our Lady.

Perhaps the gate to the house was locked or perhaps there was too much smoke coming out, because instead of going inside, Perrin ran next door. He entered his brother-in-law's home, stripped down to his shirt, and, with his cousin Beaugrant, who was also there, he ran upstairs to the attic where Driette had spied on the men next door and from there went out onto the roof. The two cousins then climbed over to the roof of the Fouchier house, where they "made a hole," apparently by prying up some roof tiles, "so that they could get in."

Once inside, they made their way down the smoky stairs to the main room on the ground floor, where they found a frozen domestic scene: "the fireplace ablaze, along with two made-up beds," and, in the back room, "a table set for a meal, with bread and one or two shoulders of roast mutton." They doused the fire in the front room and then searched the rest of the house, upstairs and down. They found no one there, and the place looked as though it had been abandoned in great haste.

After leaving the house, Perrin and Beaugrant ran into several people who apparently had managed to open the front gate and were coming in "to put out the fire." They all went out together.

As Perrin secured the gate behind him, one of his neighbors, Simon Cagne, came running up. Leaning close, he whispered: "The Duke of Orleans has had a scare. He's over at Monsieur Rieux's house."

Perhaps the baker was pretending to know less than he actually did to cover for his failure to act earlier. In any case, after Cagne ran off, a stranger came up to Perrin. He wore a sword on his belt, the mark of a nobleman.

"Whose house is this?" he demanded angrily.

"My father's," Perrin replied. "Why?"

Clutching his sword hilt, the man said, "You're lucky I don't kill you!"

A bit shaken, no doubt, Perrin went next door, got dressed, and then returned. On his way back, he heard neighbors in the street saying that the Duke of Orleans had died that night, though he did not realize yet that the duke had been murdered.

———⟨◦⟩———

Gilet, a salt seller in the Rue Saint-Martin, was in his shop that night at about eight thirty with his son Jean, who worked for him.[52] Their shop, located where the Rue Saint-Martin met the Rue aux Oues, was nearly half a mile northwest of where Louis had been struck down.[53] They had already closed up and were about to leave for the night when they heard a number of "very strong horses running at a clip down the street." The horses were going north as if heading for the Porte Saint-Martin, a gate in the old city wall that stood just fifteen or twenty yards up the street from the shop.

Gilet told his son to open the door to see what was going on. Jean did so.

"What do you see?" asked Gilet.

"Men-at-arms. Lots of them."

Gilet hurried to the door to see for himself. Looking out, he saw "twelve or fifteen men-at-arms riding hard" along the street. Their faces were covered.

The riders turned left from the Rue Saint-Martin into the Rue aux Oues, heading west. Gilet leaned out for a better view and watched from behind as they rode down the street.

"Several lights" were still burning nearby, despite the curfew, and Gilet could see that some of the riders "had quivers of arrows, and some had crossbows." Others were carrying "half-lances or larger spears tipped with iron."

Just down the Rue aux Oues was a barbershop belonging to Jean le Roy that was still open. Gilet heard one of the riders shout to the people there: "Put out your lights! Close up!" Then the horsemen rode off "very fast."

Gilet heard some more noise in the Rue Saint-Martin. "Two or three men on foot" were coming along after the riders, comrades, apparently, since they carried "half-lances or other iron weapons."

They also ran past the salt seller's shop and turned the corner into the Rue aux Oues. When they got to Jean le Roy's shop, Gilet saw one of them "raise his weapon and strike the candle in the candleholder hanging in the barber shop," and another shouted: "We're the watch!"[54] Then they sprinted down the street after the horsemen, disappearing into the darkness.

THE RUE ST. MARTIN AND
THE RUE ST. DENIS

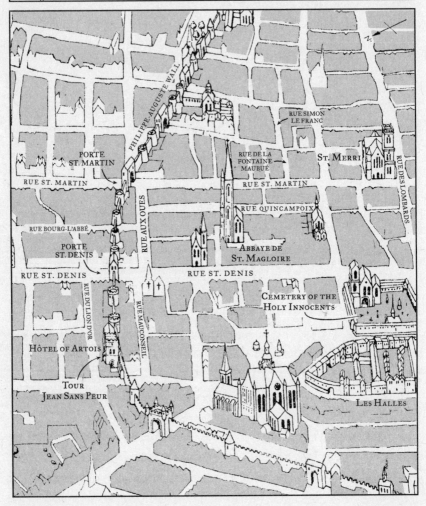

The Rue Saint-Martin and the Rue Saint-Denis. The Rue aux Oues, where the assassins were last seen, is at center left.

Jean Fovel, a barber's apprentice, was in Jean le Roy's shop with three other apprentices. One of them, Jean Porelet, known as Petit-Jean, was shaving a customer's beard—again, well after curfew.[55]

Suddenly they heard horses approaching, making a terrific noise.

As Fovel peered out, he saw "twenty or twenty-four riders" racing by, along with about "a dozen men" on foot. The riders were armed with axes and crossbows. Some of them wore livery and carried half-lances, while others had "naked swords." The mounted men were riding hard, "going as fast as their horses could trot but not at a run," while those on foot were trying to keep up. They all rushed past the barbershop "as if they were making for the Rue Saint-Denis."

Two of the men in livery stopped in front of the shop and came in. As the startled barbers watched, the men raised their lances and "struck the candle-holder that hung there from a chain," putting out the lights. Then they left.

----◦----

Guillemin Moricet, a barber farther down the Rue aux Oues, at the corner of the Rue Quincampoix, was eating supper in his shop when he heard a large number of horses coming along the street.[56] He was sitting "at a table in an alcove, behind a wooden screen" through which he could see the street. His assistant, Jehanin de Bourg, was also in the shop.[57]

Looking up as the horsemen went by, Guillemin saw "twenty or thirty" of them, all riding along at a good clip toward the Rue Saint-Denis. Their faces were "covered," and some of them "were carrying crossbows and quivers full of arrows."

Right behind the horsemen came several figures, also masked, running on foot. One had a lance, and another held an unsheathed sword. They came into the shop, shouting, "Put out your lights! Ruffians! Put them out!"*

The man with the lance struck the candleholder, where a single candle burned, extinguishing it at once.

---

* *"Éteignez! Ribauds! Éteignez!"*

Then they hurried out, running up the street after the others, leaving the two startled barbers in the dark.

Shortly after the men on foot had disappeared down the Rue aux Oues, Gilet the salt seller was out in the street "talking with some of the neighbors about what had happened."[58] No one had heard yet about the events in the Rue Vieille du Temple, and they all stood around wondering why armed men with covered faces had been noisily racing through the darkened city after curfew claiming to be the watch and violently extinguishing any lights they found along their route. What was going on?

A man named Michelet came by and showed them a curious object he had found in the street. It was a caltrop—a fist-size cluster of sharp metal spikes designed to land with one spike upright so as to cripple horses and men on the battlefield.[59] Warlords often ordered them by the thousands for military campaigns. Apparently the masked men had thrown it down behind them in order to delay any pursuers.

Soon after this, some men of the watch—the genuine watch—came by with torches. They stopped at one of the barbershops and told Jean Fovel that they were searching for caltrops and that they had already found "a dozen" of them in the streets.[60]

After they went on, Fovel lit a candle and went out to search the street, soon finding a caltrop himself. Later he gave it to his master, Jean le Roy.

Gilet the salt seller heard that a neighbor, a baker, had found "two or three more caltrops" in the same street.[61]

It was all very strange.

6

Post Mortem

---◄o►---

GUILLAUME DE TIGNONVILLE was at home that evening in the Rue Béthisy. He knew nothing of what had just happened on the other side of Paris, in the Rue Vieille du Temple, the better part of a mile to the east. Saint Clement's was a holiday for many people, and even if Guillaume had spent the day working at the Châtelet, he probably did not expect to have to attend to any business that evening.

Well after curfew, "between eight and nine o'clock at night," there was a sudden noise and commotion at the provost's gate, where several sergeants stood guard, and then some shouting in the courtyard.[1] The servants, accustomed to messages arriving for the provost at odd hours, most likely answered the door. There they found a man named Guillaume de Herville, also known as Tetine—a squire to Charles d'Albret, the constable of France, the king's chief military officer.[2] Tetine, perhaps a bit out of breath, said he had an urgent message for the provost.

As soon as Guillaume appeared, Tetine burst out with the news:

"Monsieur d'Orleans has been killed!"

"What?"

"The Duke of Orleans has been murdered!"

"When? Where?"

"Just now, in the Rue Vieille du Temple. Right in the street, as he made his way along it."

The news must have stunned Guillaume. He had known and served the duke for years. But the news was more than a personal shock: An attack on the king's brother was tantamount to an attack on the king himself. It was high treason, and this was a national emergency.

Guillaume at once sent word to his lieutenant, Robert de Tuillières, summoning him, along with a number of his officers. Robert lived just around the corner in the Rue de l'Arbre-Sec, so it would not have taken him long to arrive.[3]

Guillaume then set out with his men for the scene of the crime. All of them carried arms. It is not known whether they traveled on foot or waited long enough to saddle their horses. Either way, they must have carried torches, for the night remained pitch-dark.

"I hastened to the Rue Vieille du Temple," Guillaume later wrote in his report, "where this crime was said to have been perpetrated, accompanied by master Robert de Tuillières, my lieutenant, and many other officers of the king, our lord, in a large troop, armed and at the ready, to see what had happened and find out the truth of the matter and also what should be done about it."[4]

The trip was about three quarters of a mile by the most direct route — eastward on the Rue Béthisy, then north along the Rue de l'Arbre-Sec, then east again on a series of wider streets leading into the Rue de la Verrerie, and finally, after about another half mile, north along the Rue Vieille du Temple.

Much of the city was now asleep, and the streets were nearly deserted. Traveling up the Rue Vieille du Temple, nearing the Rue des Rosiers, Guillaume and his men would have smelled smoke and glimpsed flickers of torchlight up ahead. After a slight rightward bend in the street, they would have caught sight of the Rieux house and a crowd of people in front of it. By now, the fire set by the assassins had been put out. It seemed that the whole quarter was awake, and the street was full of curious neighbors who had come out to see what had happened.[5]

The constable's soldiers were on the scene, standing guard with half-lances or halberds, controlling the crowd of excited onlookers. There was blood on the pavement in several places in front of the Rieux house, and the mud in the street was heavily trampled, but no bodies were now in sight.

The provost, with his lieutenant and other officers, went up to the door of the Rieux house, also under guard. They were admitted at once.

———◦———

At the Rieux house, Guillaume wrote later, "I found the body of the late Monsieur d'Orleans, all dead and very bloody, stretched out on a table, covered with a cloth of black damask, injured by many wounds."[6]

The body was most likely laid out in the hall, the large room generally located near the front door. Standing by the table, Guillaume stared at Louis's butchered body.

Even by candlelight, the corpse looked horribly mangled, and Guillaume may have hardly recognized the duke at first, the head and face were so badly disfigured. As Guillaume later described what he saw:

Item, two wounds to the head, one running from the left eye to the right ear, and the other running from the left ear almost to the right ear. And the wounds were of such a kind, and so enormous, that the head was all sliced up and the entire brain protruded.

Item, his left hand was severed completely from the arm between the thumb and the wrist.

Item, his right arm was broken so that the master bone protruded below the elbow, and the arm also had a great wound in it.[7]

Louis of Orleans.
The damaged hand
eerily recalls one of
Louis's actual wounds.

Guillaume was well acquainted with death in its many ugly forms from the battlefield, the gibbet, and the morgue, and his report is anatomically precise, even clinical. As a knight, he was familiar with various kinds of weapons and the terrible wounds they could inflict. Had he studied medicine as well?*[8] Or had he simply acquired a coroner's observant eye during his six years as provost? Despite his experience, though, he must have been shocked to see what the assassins had made of the duke with their swords and axes. As Guillaume took in the pitiful sight, his mind must have churned with questions. Who had done this? And why?

Louis was not a popular prince, and he had many enemies. Had one of the jealous husbands he had cuckolded over the years finally taken his revenge? Louis was rumored to be sleeping with the queen, which made the king a cuckold too. Dur-

---

* The city's first recorded medical dissection had taken place that same year.

ing Charles's first fit of madness, he had chased after Louis with a drawn sword, and during a later fit at court, he had shouted something about killing Louis.

Or was the crime part of a foreign conspiracy? France had many enemies, most prominently the English, against whom Louis had often urged war. Had English agents assassinated the king's brother? If so, war was even more likely.

Another question loomed as well: The king was often insane, and now that the king's brother was dead, who would rule the nation during Charles's bouts of madness? The assassins had nearly decapitated not just Louis but all of France.

—◁◦▷—

Before Guillaume could start questioning the "many people present" at the Rieux house, some of the men there showed him another victim of the attack.[9] The second body, too, was bloody and repeatedly slashed.

"Item," Guillaume wrote, "at the same hôtel I found the body of the valet of the said Monsieur d'Orleans, all bloody and completely dead, injured by many wounds in the head and elsewhere—and this valet was known as Jacob de la Merré."[10]

Careful not to jump to conclusions, Guillaume noted that "it appeared" that the wounds he observed on both victims had caused their deaths.

The men at the Rieux house then told him that a third victim, a valet to the duke, had also been very badly wounded and lay in another house nearby. This was no doubt Robinet Huppe, rescued by the florist in the Rue des Rosiers.

"But I did not see the said valet," Guillaume wrote.[11] The wounded man might have provided useful descriptions of the assassins, and Guillaume very likely planned to question him. But for now he focused on the witnesses at the Rieux house, where the two bodies were: "Those present told me that the Duke of Orleans and his people were killed and murdered in the said street in front of the house while passing along the street, and that those who had done this thing had fled, leaving the body all dead in the mud of the street."

As soon as he learned this much, Guillaume sent word to the lords of France, dispatching officers to different parts of the city to report Louis's murder to the four royal dukes in the king's council: Berry, Bourbon, Anjou, and Burgundy.

———◦———

Rumors were already running through the city.[12] When they heard the news of Louis's murder that night, "many nobles armed themselves" and hastened to the palace to help guard the king, "not knowing what was going on or what would happen next."[13]

Soon the queen learned that Louis had been murdered only minutes after leaving her door. "In a state of great fright and horror," Isabeau ordered her servants to begin packing at once for her immediate departure. A litter was prepared, since she was still recovering from childbirth, and soon she was on her way to the Hôtel Saint-Pol to take refuge near the mad king whose presence she had once fled. When she arrived, the terrified queen lodged herself "in the chamber next to the king's for greater security."[14]

———◦———

The messengers Guillaume had dispatched to alert the royal dukes soon returned with more news. The lords of France were calling an emergency meeting of the royal council—minus the king—at the palace of Duke Louis of Anjou.

Interrupting his investigation, Guillaume left the crime scene and hurried back down the Rue Vieille du Temple, then east along the Rue Saint-Antoine toward the Hôtel d'Anjou, which stood near the royal palace. On arriving there, he was admitted at once. Guillaume found all the great lords of France "already assembled": the Dukes of Anjou, Berry, Bourbon, and Burgundy, along with Bourbon's son the Count of Clermont; Burgundy's younger brother the Count of Nevers; the constable of France, Charles d'Albret, who had summoned the provost to the crime scene; Count Waleran of Luxembourg; the Count of Tancarville; "and several other of our lords of France and of our lord the king's great council."[15]

Louis II of Anjou, hosting the emergency session of the council that night, was just thirty years old and the youngest of the four royal dukes.[16] But the quick-thinking Anjou would emerge as a leader in the royal council, as Louis's murder nearly paralyzed the rest of the government. Anjou was also called the king of Sicily because of the House of Anjou's ancestral but disputed claim to that land. He had inherited vast territories in France from his father, Louis I of Anjou, brother of Charles V. Just before his death, in 1380, Charles V had carved out several large dukedoms as bribes to his three jealous, ambitious brothers — Anjou, Berry, and Burgundy — so as to protect the life and royal title of his vulnerable young heir, Charles VI, only eleven years old at the time.[17]

Duke John of Berry, sixty-six, the current king's last surviving paternal uncle, was old enough to remember the battle of Crécy and had fought as a youth at Poitiers a half century before.[18] But Berry's tastes ran less to war and politics than to art.[19] Known as John the Magnificent, he was the greatest connoisseur of the age, a patron of the famous Limbourg brothers, who lavishly illustrated Berry's luxurious life in the *Très Riches Heures* and other sumptuous books that he commissioned.[20] Whenever Berry could escape the cares of state, he devoted himself to aesthetic pursuits, for he was above all a passionate collector — of beautiful white châteaux bristling with towers and turrets, of beautiful illuminated manuscripts, of beautiful Italian sculpture, and of beautiful young men.[21]

Louis of Bourbon, seventy and the king's sole maternal

uncle, was the most kindly of the royal dukes.[22] More attentive to Charles's health than anyone else in the royal family, Bourbon had brought handpicked medical experts to court when the several dozen royal physicians seemed unable to do anything for the afflicted king.[23] One doctor whom he brought to Paris was an expert at "purgation by the head"—that is, trepanation, or the drilling of holes in the skull to relieve the foul humors believed to cause madness.[24] Charles had undergone this operation at least once and reportedly had been none the worse for it.

The fourth royal duke, John of Burgundy, had long lived in the shadow of his illustrious father, Philip the Bold—a young hero at Poitiers who had bravely ridden with sword in hand in front of his own father, the ill-fated King John II, although he had not been able to prevent their capture by the English.[25] At Philip's death, in 1404, John had assumed control of the vast Burgundian domains in France and Flanders.[26] The most warlike of the royal dukes, John had first tasted blood at the disastrous battle of Nicopolis in 1396, where the Saracens had slaughtered the crusaders, and he had barely escaped with his life—he was spared and held for ransom as hundreds of Christian captives were beheaded.[27] Later, in the summer of 1405, John had nearly gone to war against the now-dead Louis over who controlled the dauphin; eventually, the two royal cousins made peace and ordered their armies to stand down.

It was this formidable array of royal dukes and other great lords that Guillaume de Tignonville faced as he entered the council chamber at the Hôtel of Anjou to deliver his preliminary report on Louis's murder.

———◇———

As soon as they saw Guillaume enter, "the lords called him over" and began asking what had happened.[28]

Guillaume reported to the hushed room what he had seen

in the Rue Vieille du Temple at the Rieux house. As he described the terrible wounds on the body of the king's brother, the reality of Louis's gruesome murder sank in.

"Who is responsible for this?" the lords demanded.

Guillaume replied that he had not yet found out.

The lords then declared a state of emergency, ordering Guillaume to shut the city gates at once to prevent anyone from leaving Paris "until the truth of the matter was known."[29] They also ordered him to post guards in the streets throughout the city "to prevent any disturbances" among the populace.[30] And they ordered him to begin an immediate investigation into the murder of the Duke of Orleans. Guillaume was to "diligently investigate and find out what had happened, who had done it, and do so with all dispatch."[31]

———◇———

The gravity of Louis's murder and the powerful shock it sent through the French establishment is recorded by Nicolas de Baye, chief clerk of the Parlement of Paris, who wrote the following journal entry for Wednesday, November 23:

> *This evening, at about eight o'clock, Messire Louis, son of King Charles V and brother of King Charles now ruling, Duke of Orleans, count of Valois, of Blois, of Beaumont . . . was struck down and killed by eight or nine armed men who had been hidden in a neighboring house for a week or two. They cleaved his head in two with a halberd so that he was knocked from his horse and his brains strewn on the pavement.* One of his hands was cut clean off and, with him, they killed one of his valets, who had thrown himself on him to protect him. . . . Thus he,

---

* De Baye refers to Louis's horse (*cheval*), apparently unaware that he actually rode a mule to his death. In the margin, a crude drawing of a sword and a severed head appears.

who was such a great and powerful lord, and to whom naturally, whenever there was no effective ruler, the government of this realm belonged, in so brief a moment ended his days, hideously and shamefully.[32]

The sudden, unexpected downfall of a great lord or prince was often attributed to Fortune — Fortuna, pictured as a blindfolded woman turning a great wheel around whose rim kings and princes sat precariously as they rose or fell in the world. "When they are right on top and think themselves secure," wrote a chronicler of the time, "Fortune flings them back into the mud" — just where Louis ended up.[33]

◇

After receiving his orders from the lords of France, Guillaume immediately had all the city gates closed. He also directed that "a great many guards" be posted in streets throughout Paris to prevent any civil unrest.[34]

Accompanied by his lieutenant and officers, Guillaume then returned to the Rue Vieille du Temple and began gathering information from the residents of the street "as best and as diligently as we could in order to learn the truth of the matter and find out who was responsible."[35]

Guillaume and his men soon learned that the assassins had lodged right across the street from the Rieux home, in the House of the Image of Our Lady; that they had waited there to ambush the Duke of Orleans; that the house belonged to Robert Fouchier, master of the king's works; that after committing the crime, the perpetrators had set fire to the building; that they had thrown caltrops behind them in the street while fleeing the scene; that they had numbered at least eighteen or twenty; and that some of them had escaped on horseback while others had left on foot.[36]

But this was all they knew at that point. "We could not find out," said Guillaume, "who the culprits were or where they had gone or anything else about the business."[37]

One of the provost's top priorities was to gather any available physical evidence from the crime scene and its vicinity before it got damaged or disappeared. To speed up the investigation, Guillaume divided his men, delegating various tasks to them, each going "as duty required."[38] He ordered his lieutenant, Robert de Tuillières, to go to the house where the assassins had lodged "to see the state and disposition of the place and to gather information as best he could and in all possible ways about the event and the circumstances and to report back to me."

Guillaume commanded Jacques Cardon, one of his officers from the Châtelet, to draw up an inventory of everything found at the house where the perpetrators had lain in wait.[39] Cardon was an *examinateur,* an officer who specialized in the *enquête,* the official inquiry into a crime or a pending legal case.[40] It was possible that during their hasty departure, the assassins had left behind some of their clothing or belongings, and these could be used to trace their identities or whereabouts.

Finally, Guillaume ordered some of his officers to begin collecting information from people in the neighborhood who might have witnessed the crime, who happened to observe the assassins in the vicinity prior to the murder, or who saw them fleeing the scene afterward. Anyone who had seen or heard anything noteworthy, who knew anything at all about the perpetrators, or who had had any sort of contact with them was to be brought to the Châtelet to make an official sworn statement so as to help Guillaume "find out who was responsible for the said crime, where they had gone, and how they had proceeded."[41] It was critical that all of the relevant witnesses be located, questioned, and deposed as quickly as possible, while the events were still fresh in their minds and before they started talking among themselves and mixing up their stories. The case was of the highest urgency, and the likelihood of tracking down and identifying the culprits would slip away with each passing hour.

In addition, criers were sent "to all the cross-streets in Paris ordering every innkeeper to bring a written list of the names and surnames of all his guests to the provost or his lieutenant."[42] Guillaume wanted information about all visitors to the city who were lodging in public houses, for it was possible that the names of some of the conspirators would turn up there.

As the city gates were closed by guards, and as soldiers were posted at street corners everywhere, sleepy Parisians began waking to the astounding news that the king's brother had been murdered the previous night by assassins unknown, news that "sowed terror throughout the city."[43] The king himself might be in danger, along with the capital, and perhaps all of France as well.

7

A Mass for the Dead

───◄◦►───

THE SAME NIGHT Louis was killed, the lords of France ordered that Louis's corpse be removed from the Rieux house and carried up the street and around the corner to the nearest church, the Church of the White Mantles.[1] The church, originally founded by the Augustinians, was now inhabited by the Guillemites, the followers of Saint Guillaume.[2] The sanctuary, sacristy, cloister, and refectory together filled a rectangular block between the old city wall of Philip-Augustus to the north and the Rue des Blancs Manteaux to the south. Although built of cut and finished stone, the church was simple and small, only forty feet wide and one hundred and fifty feet long; it had no transept, and a plain wooden rood screen divided the nave from the choir. It was a modest venue, but "it was the church nearest to the place where Louis had been killed" and thus convenient for the vigil that would begin that night and the Funeral Mass to follow on the next day.[3] After these ceremonies, the body would be borne to the much grander precincts of the Celestine priory, Louis's favorite church, for a Requiem Mass and then burial amid the splendor of other princely tombs and richly decorated chapels.[4]

Before the body was moved from the Rieux house, it was blessed and then prepared for the funeral. Killed without warning after a morally questionable visit to the queen, Louis had died in a state of sin, without the confession and absolution and other last rites that even one of his badly injured valets had received.[5] Louis's soul was thus at risk of Hell. At the very least, it was destined for Purgatory, where it would have to endure the purifying flames until it was fit for Heaven, a process that could last for decades or even centuries.

After opening a book of hours, a priest began chanting the Office of the Dead, a series of prayers intended to hasten the soul's release from Purgatory and speed its flight to Heaven.[6] Since the dead could not pray for themselves, clergy, relatives, and other mourners had to pray on their behalf, enlisting the prayers of the heavenly saints as well to reduce the suffering of the deceased.

As the office was chanted, the body was washed and prepared. When burial was delayed by the need to transport the body over a distance, the internal organs were removed and the body cavity filled with aromatic spices—thyme, aloes, myrrh, lavender, saffron, and the like—to ward off decay.*[7] Louis's will, however, specified that his body be buried intact, *"tout entier"*—a last wish nearly spoiled by the assassins' hideous mutilations.[8] But Louis's severed hand, found in the muddy street near the murder site, "was placed in the coffin with his body," along with additional pieces of his scattered brains that had also been collected from the street by the duke's attendants.[9]

After the body had been reassembled and washed, it was sewn into "a white shroud," a snug cloth sack encasing the entire body and typically stitched down the front with coarse black thread. "A black veil" went over the shroud, and the body was placed in a wooden coffin.[10] In its shroud and coffin, Louis's body was then borne up the street "with great ceremony" to the Church of the White Mantles.[11]

---

* When nobles died on long journeys or on distant battlefields, their bodies were sometimes boiled down to bones so the remains could be shipped back without concerns over putrefaction.

At the church, the wooden coffin was enclosed in a larger, heavier "coffin of lead" and placed on a bier before the altar.[12] Then it was covered by a pall, a heavy black cloth decorated with golden fleurs-de-lis.[13] Beginning a vigil that would last through the night, black-robed clergy gathered around the bier to serve as mourners and continue to repeat the Office of the Dead.[14]

Close to midnight, Louis's relatives began arriving, "along with many other princes, knights, and squires." The great lords who had gathered earlier that evening to hear the provost's preliminary report on the case now came to the church, "all in great sorrow."[15] The Duke of Anjou came, and Berry, and Bourbon, as well as Burgundy, along with Bourbon's son Clermont, Burgundy's younger brother the Count of Nevers, and Count Waleran of Luxembourg. John of Burgundy, clothed in black and seated among the principal mourners, wept copious tears and was overheard to say, "Never was there a more treacherous murder!"[16]

As the family remained in audience, "the clergy of that church kept vigil all night, saying prayers and singing psalms."[17] The tapers near the altar grew shorter, and the crowd grew steadily larger as more mourners continued to arrive, including additional relatives and friends, members of the royal court, and people from the neighborhood and throughout the city.

———◦———

By morning, the little church was packed with "a great multitude of the people of Paris."[18] Although Louis had been widely hated for his heavy taxes and high living, Parisians were stunned by his murder, and many who had privately vilified him when he was alive publicly mourned him in death.

When all was ready, the officiating priest announced the beginning of the Requiem Mass, also known as the Mass of the Dead, by intoning the Miserere from Psalm 50: "Have mercy on me, O Lord."

Louis's body remained on its bier under the pall and before the altar. But now a catafalque had been placed around it, a wooden framework filled with lit tapers. The candles illuminating the bier at the front of the church symbolized the *lux perpetua,* "perpetual light," petitioned for the Christian dead.[19] Smoke wafted up from smudge pots, earthenware jugs filled with burning charcoal and placed on the floor near the bier "to purify the air and protect against contagion."[20] As the clergy's prayers and psalms filled the chilly sanctuary, sobs and laments arose from the congregation, many of whom were swathed in mourning clothes.

The climax of the Funeral Mass was the Elevation of the Host.[21] The priest faced the altar with his back to the congregation, flanked by the black-robed mourners on one side and the choir on the other, as several clerics held tall, flickering candles to illuminate the Host—the consecrated wafer miraculously transubstantiated into the body of Christ and now to be shared in remembrance of his Passion. With joined hands, the priest raised the Host high over his head so that all could see it. Bells were now rung, and the priest similarly raised the chalice filled with the consecrated wine. In the days to come, Louis's followers would not hesitate to liken his bloody, wounded body to that of the suffering Savior and Louis's murderers to the arch-traitor Judas.[22]

Notably absent from the ceremonies were Louis's brother, the king, and Louis's purported lover, the queen, both of whom remained in seclusion at the royal palace. Also conspicuously absent was Louis's wife, Valentina, still living in exile from the royal court because of her rumored sorcery against the king. Nor were her now fatherless children—three sons and a daughter—present. In fact, Valentina probably had not yet heard the terrible news of his assassination, since she lived a good day's ride from the capital by the fastest horse.[23]

———◇———

After the Funeral Mass, Louis's body was carried from the Church of the White Mantles and borne through the streets in a grand procession. Before the bier went a clutch of black-clad bell ringers, followed by "a great number of knights and squires in black, each carrying a lighted torch before the body."[24] Next came the bishop of Paris wearing a white miter trimmed with gold, holding his crosier and flanked by his clerical entourage.[25] The bier followed, accompanied by the four royal dukes serving as pallbearers—Anjou, Berry, Bourbon, and Burgundy. Each duke held one corner of the heavy black cloth covering the bier as he walked alongside it, "weeping and mourning loudly."[26] After the bier and the royal dukes came a long line of the mourners, "each according to his rank—princes, clergy, and barons, all commending Louis's soul to God his Creator."[27]

After turning into the Rue Vieille du Temple, the procession headed south toward the river, retracing Louis's last journey and crossing right over the spot, in front of the House of the Image of Our Lady, where he had been murdered the night before.[28]

A funeral procession. As blood from Louis's coffin stained the pavement, "a great murmuring" arose from the crowd.

All along the cortège's route, Parisians came out of their homes or gathered at the windows of their tall wooden houses to watch the company pass.

When it reached the Rue Saint-Antoine, the procession turned left and headed eastward, past the royal palace, where the king and queen remained sequestered and under heavy guard. Finally it turned onto the grounds of the Celestine priory, next to the palace and fronting the river.[29] There the heavy lead coffin was solemnly borne past the cloister and into the sanctuary, where the clergy would celebrate another Requiem Mass.

During the journey to the priory, something strange happened: Louis's body slowly "leaked blood into the coffin," and the blood dripped out along the procession route, leaving red stains on the pavement as the cortège passed. At this sight, "a great murmuring" arose from the people.[30] A newly bleeding corpse was a sure sign, according to popular superstition, that the murderer was present and that the body was calling out for vengeance.

———◅◦▻———

Later that same day, "after a very solemn service"—a separate and lengthy Burial Mass—Louis was interred at the Celestine priory with full honors, laid to rest in the same chapel he had endowed almost fifteen years earlier as penance for his role in the fatal fire at the Bal des Ardents.[31] "A large and very beautiful chapel built of cut stone," it stood not far from the monastic dormitory that contained the humble cell where the duke had recently dreamed of his own death.[32]

Louis was buried near the altar in a tomb of "black marble and white alabaster" raised just "three inches from the floor" and inscribed in "letters of gold" with his name, arms, titles, and the date of his death.[33] A silver oil lamp burned continuously in his memory, and masses were to be chanted in perpetuity over his tomb and at thirteen other chapels all around France.[34] The loyal valet who had died trying to defend Louis was buried in the same chapel, at his feet.[35] Yet although Louis was buried with all the pomp befitting a great lord, his funeral also had a humble touch. Before interment, his body was further clothed in the simple white robe and cowl of a Celestine monk that he had worn during his visits to the priory for prayers and penance.[36] It was not unusual for great lords to be buried in clerical garb, a last pious gesture after a life of worldly pursuits. Louis had asked to be buried directly in the ground "on the clay," without a coffin, a common practice for the lowborn but unusual for people of high rank.[37] And he had directed that the effigy on his tomb likewise depict him in a Celestine cowl and robe, its head and feet resting on a simple rough-cut stone just a few inches off the floor.

By the time of Louis's burial, late in the afternoon on the day after the crime, the news of his murder was spreading far beyond Paris. Despite the state of emergency, the city still needed to be provisioned with meat, grain, firewood, and other necessities. One report says that two city gates were still open, though "well guarded" and closely watched.[38] So word of the sensational murder probably traveled beyond the city walls on the lips of carters, tradesmen, boatmen, and others who supplied the daily needs of the huge, hungry capital.[39]

In all likelihood, the news was also carried out of the city in the saddlebags of couriers sent galloping to all parts of France, from Picardy to the Pyrenees. Garrisons at far-flung castles and guard posts had to be alerted, lest the enemies of France — especially the English — take advantage of the national crisis to mount a surprise attack.[40]

At the same time, other couriers traveled to courts and capitals beyond the borders of France. Paris was a great crossroads of Europe, and French affairs were closely entangled with those

of England, Italy, Germany, Flanders, and the various kingdoms in Spain on account of war, trade, royal intermarriages,
and the Great Schism. Given that the king had been periodically insane for over a decade, the murder of the king's brother
immediately raised the question of who would now govern
France—a question of pressing importance to not only the
stricken nation but also its wary neighbors.

One of the couriers departing from Paris with news of the
murder galloped south toward Orleans and Tours, eventually
made his way to the southwest corner of France, and then
crossed over the Pyrenees into Spain. His destination was Pam-
plona, the capital of Navarre, a tiny but influential kingdom
just beyond the mountains.[41]

Navarre had once been ruled by a very dangerous enemy of
the French: Charles II, known as Charles the Bad.[42] As both
king of Navarre and Count of Évreux, Charles was related to
the French royal family and had claimed the French throne for
himself. For nearly four decades, until his death in 1387, he
fought and intrigued against the French kings, operating from
a chain of fortresses infesting Normandy. Once he even sent an
assassin to Paris to poison the young Charles VI; the assassin,
discovered at court with the poison sewn into his clothing, was
caught before he could harm the king.[43]

Charles the Bad's eldest son, Charles III, had succeeded him
to the throne of Navarre. Unlike his father, Charles III enjoyed
a good reputation, becoming known as Charles the Noble. For
twenty years, since his accession in 1387, he had pursued a policy of peace with France, posting his brother, Pierre, the Count
of Mortain, to Paris, not only to keep Charles III informed but
also to serve as his ambassador and help maintain good relations. Pierre regularly appeared at court with Charles VI and
served on the royal council, and he had even jousted with the
king in earlier days, before Charles's catastrophic madness.[44]

Pierre was in Paris at the time of Louis's murder and may

have been present to hear the provost's initial report on the crime.[45] Ideally positioned to know all the latest news, Pierre kept his brother, the king of Navarre, well supplied with information and up to date. Indeed, it was he who dispatched the courier to Navarre.[46]

After Charles III received the dispatch, he sent it on to Castile, an allied kingdom. In Castile, the letter became part of an official Spanish record, a digest, in effect, of the latest international news.[47] The report of Louis's murder garbles a few facts, but on the whole, it is quite accurate:

> Vos çertifico que . . . *I can tell you for sure that on the twenty-third of this month of November, the Duke of Orleans was killed while going from the queen's residence to the house of the count of Tancarville. And it is certain that the first blow cut off his arm, which fell to the ground, and that the second blow split open his head, and that the third blow sliced open his body through the back, and that he fell dead from his mule to the ground. And one of his squires threw himself upon the duke as soon as he saw what was happening, and he was killed at once as he lay over his master's body. And they also killed a valet who was carrying a torch to light the way, because he refused to flee the scene.*

The letter goes on to provide some other details, including how the assassins made their escape by throwing caltrops in their wake. It closes by mentioning that Pierre of Navarre had sent the news to not only his brother, Charles III, but "numerous other lords as well." Those lords, alert to any signs of change in France, were undoubtedly alarmed. Louis's assassination was the worst crisis to strike the French government since the onset of the king's madness. Now the main buttress against the king's insanity was gone. What sort of wider madness might follow?

8

The Inquiry

———◄◦►———

GUILLAUME DE TIGNONVILLE had no time to attend Louis's funeral. Instead, he showed his continued loyalty to the slain duke by devoting himself fully, with all the resources at his command, to tracking down Louis's killers.

Following his orders from the lords of France, Guillaume had posted soldiers throughout Paris and closed all the city gates except for two "well guarded" points of access.[1] The assassins were thus trapped in the city, unless they had managed to climb over the city wall during the night and cross the deep, water-filled moat or drift down the river in boats small enough to slip under the great iron chain stretched across the Seine at its western portal.[2]

Guillaume had also mobilized his army of officers and the sergeants of the watch to begin collecting evidence, including any belongings left behind by the assassins at the house where they had lodged and the caltrops they had thrown down behind them as they fled, showing which way they had gone—and possibly pointing to where they were now hiding.

But as dawn broke on the morning after the murder, Guillaume's most urgent task was to collect crucial information from anyone who had happened to witness the murder or observe the assassins' activities before or after the crime. And he had to collect this information quickly, while it was still fresh, so as not to miss "any useful clue, however slight."[3]

◄◦►

On Thursday morning the great city woke and began to stir, accompanied by the usual cacophony: vendors crying their wares, shopkeepers opening up for business, drovers cursing their stubborn teams, boatmen shouting alongside the busy quais, and university students joking and laughing after a night's carousing.[4] But now residents also heard bells tolling throughout Paris for the dead duke, and criers shouting in every quarter for innkeepers to bring lists of their guests to the Châtelet.[5]

Astonished Parisians who woke to the news of Louis's death likely paused in their morning routines to gossip with neighbors about the murder, perhaps in whispers, since soldiers stood guard on street corners throughout the city. Especially in the Rue Vieille du Temple and nearby streets, people who had seen or heard the commotion the night before traded stories, while neighbors who had known nothing stood listening with mouths agape. Along the Rue Saint-Martin and its side streets, where the assassins had made their escape, people also exchanged news of the sensational events.

For some Parisians, the news soon turned more serious when sergeants from the Châtelet suddenly swarmed into their streets, pointing with their staffs and stopping people to question them, pounding on doors and gates, bursting into shops, demanding names, and summoning "for interrogation" anyone who might know anything about the murder or whoever had perpetrated it.[6]

The sweep turned up several people who had witnessed the crime, including Jacquette, the shoemaker's wife, who had watched the whole thing from her window, and the young valet Drouet Prieur, who had even gone down to see the duke's fresh corpse in the street. The sergeants also tracked down Madame Fouchier, wife of the master of the king's works, who owned the House of the Image of Our Lady. And they summoned many others—clerks, barbers, shopkeepers—who had seen the murderers making their escape and might be able to provide descriptions or information about where they had gone.

Soon the Châtelet was bustling with sergeants, examiners, and anxious witnesses brought there for questioning, in some cases under arrest to be held in prison for safekeeping. As quickly as possible, they all had to be sworn in and deposed and their statements studied and compared for clues about the crime.

Depositions were normally taken by two-man teams, one examiner questioning the witness while the other took down the testimony in writing.[7] Special characters were used to catch the fleeting human voice, a kind of shorthand consisting of scribal abbreviations used for centuries—such as a *p* with a line through the stem to represent the first syllable of a word beginning with *per-* or *pro-*, which saved the scribe precious time and enabled him to keep up with the speaker.[8] Once the scribes wrote down what the witnesses said, the ephemeral events of the night before—these traces of memory and emotion, fact and supposition—would be fixed into a permanent record that might help fill in the picture of what had happened and why.

At the center of all this activity was the provost: directing lines of inquiry and delegating tasks; sorting the essential from the incidental; scanning fresh depositions brought to him with the ink still damp, setting some aside for later study and poring over others at once in search of vital clues; and now and then even summoning and questioning a key witness himself.

———◇———

One of the first witnesses brought to the Châtelet for questioning on Thursday was Marie Fouchier, who had unwittingly rented out her house in the Rue Vieille du Temple to the assassins.[9]

Madame Fouchier was no doubt stunned and alarmed to find herself at the Châtelet for questioning. She thought she had rented her house to some "good people." How they had deceived and lied to her! Not that she herself was suspected of any role in the crime; she was the wife of an important, respected man, a loyal servant of the king. But still, it all must have been very frightening and upsetting.

Madame Fouchier was probably questioned in one of the six rooms at the Châtelet used for deposing witnesses.[10] An examiner named Nicolas Lanchelet asked her questions as a fellow examiner, an unnamed scribe, wrote down her testimony.

She was first told to state her name, age, and place of residence for the record. (Like many witnesses, she could give only an approximate age—in her case, "sixty-two years or thereabouts"—since people often did not know their exact year of birth.) After her personal information was recorded, she was "deposed under oath," swearing beforehand on a copy of the Gospels that her testimony would be true and complete.[11] Madame Fouchier described how one day in the previous week, "either Tuesday or Wednesday," she thought, a certain broker or rental agent had come to her. She had never seen him before, although her grandson Perrin said that he had. The broker, lame in one foot, had asked if she had a certain house for rent in the Rue Vieille du Temple. When she said she did, he replied that he had a man interested in renting it, to which she replied that he had come to the right place.

Marie then told how the agent had brought in a very tall man "dressed as a cleric" in a long brown robe with a red hood. She had never seen him before either.

Dressing as a cleric (*en estat de clerc*) was not quite the same as *being* one, and considering this in retrospect, Madame Fouchier may have been voicing some doubts about her tenant's true identity. Clothing was a mark of class and vocation, and there were even sumptuary laws against dressing contrary to one's actual rank or occupation, but perhaps she now suspected that the clerical robe was, in all likelihood, a disguise.[12]

Marie then related that she and the cleric discussed the terms of the rental—how long, how much, and so forth. They finally agreed on a price that was somewhat lower than what she wanted and made arrangements about the keys. After the cleric gave her a deposit, she said, the two men left.

The next day the cleric returned, showed her the keys, paid the rest of the money, and asked for a receipt, giving his name as Jean Cordelant. Madame Fouchier then told the examiner she had asked Cordelant if he was with the university. He said he was, and she believed him because he was so well spoken.

In all, Madame Fouchier appears to have been a very cooperative witness who gave all of this information quite readily. There are no follow-up questions in the record, suggesting that her story seemed complete and credible.

But the examiner—and later the provost—must have noticed that the name given by the tall cleric in the brown robe was very generic. Jean was the most common name in France, and Cordelant was very similar to *cordelier,* a common name for Franciscans.[13] It was almost as if the cleric had given his name as John Smith—or John Clark.

There was also the question of why he had dickered over the cost of the rental, working Madame Fouchier down from twenty livres, her asking price, to just sixteen. Twenty livres was a bit high, but were the assassins really so hard up for cash?

One explanation may be that buyers or renters were usually expected to bargain. Agreeing at once to the asking price might arouse suspicion. Indeed, it would have seemed especially odd if a man dressed as a "poor scholar" and claiming an affiliation with the university had *not* tried to bargain down the price.

After Nicolas Lanchelet had deposed Madame Fouchier, he showed her out and called in her grandson Perrin Labbé, who had also seen and spoken with the two men involved in renting the house.[14]

Perrin stated his personal information, including his age, "twenty-two years old or thereabouts," and was sworn in. Then he said that he had been at his grandmother's house when the broker arrived with his client. Confirming that the broker walked with a limp, Perrin also mentioned that the man was a foreigner—a Lombard—new information that might prove useful to the investigators.[*][15] As for the broker's client, he "wore a long robe like a scholar's."

Perrin described the ensuing conversation about the house and the terms of the rental agreement. He also reported that, on the following day, he had given the receipt to the man in the friar's robe when he had called for it, finding the paper under a goblet on a dresser. Perrin could no longer remember the client's name, though he had seen it written on the receipt and had checked with the man at the time to make sure the name was right.[†]

After Perrin's statement, the examiner was eager for more information about the mysterious scholar.

"This scholar, do you know who he is?"

"I don't know his name, but I think I saw him once before, prior to this rental business, coming and going around Paris. But I don't know whether I saw him dressed as a scholar."

"Would you recognize him if you saw him again?"

"Yes, if I saw him wearing the habit he wore to the house. Then I would know him at first sight, I'm sure."

"Is there anything else?"

---

[*] *Lombard* was a term used for Italians in general.

[†] Perrin's inability to recall the client's name confirms that he was deposed separately from his grandmother and had not talked to her beforehand, at least not about this detail.

"I think I heard my lady"—Madame Fouchier—"say that when she asked the man who looked like a scholar whether he was with the university, he said yes. I would say from the clothes I saw him wearing that he was a scholar. That's all I can say."

Once Perrin was deposed, the examiners probably released him and Marie Fouchier, likely advising them that they might be summoned again to identify one or the other of the two men if the broker or his client could be found.

While Nicolas Lanchelet was busy deposing Marie and Perrin, another examiner, Guillaume Marescot, was questioning Jacquette Griffard, the shoemaker's wife who had watched the whole murder from her window above the street.[16]

After swearing her oath, Jacquette told Marescot that she had been holding her baby at the window, waiting for her husband to come home, when she saw a great lord riding down the street with his attendants; a short while later, as she was putting her baby to bed, she had heard someone in the street shouting, "Kill him! Kill him!"—at which she had rushed back to the window.

Jacquette went on to describe the murder in great detail and reported that the assassins had fled the scene afterward. "A tall man in a red hood," she said, seemed to have directed the whole business.

Marescot then asked her a long series of probing questions.

"Where did the assassins go?"

"After they ran into the Rue des Blancs Manteaux? I have no idea."

"Would you know any of them if you saw them again?"

"I don't think so."

"What about their clothing? Was it long or short?"

"I couldn't really see. It was too dark."

"Any other details that you recall?"

"I was so upset, I didn't really—Well, the man in the red hood who was in charge, he was definitely the tallest of them."

"Did you hear any of them say why they were doing this, or who they were?"

"No."

"The tall man, what was his nationality?"

"I really couldn't say, except that he spoke good French."

If the man spoke a foreign tongue, this might point to a conspiracy from abroad. Or if he spoke a regional dialect of French, his accent might help to place his origin. Paris itself was regionalized, with people from different provinces settling with their own kind in different neighborhoods.[17] Thus a distinct accent might help to track the ringleader to a certain part of the city or even a particular street. His speech might also be a clue to his true social class or vocation, assuming that his clerical garb was a disguise.

Jacquette's reply, that the tall man spoke good French, suggested an educated man from the court, the university, or even the Church.

"How long did the House of the Image of Our Lady sit empty?"

"Ever since the Feast of Saint John the Baptist."

"Who owns it?"

"I don't know."

"Who was staying there? Did anyone visit the place?"

"No one that I knew of, not since the Feast of Saint John."

"No one?"

"Well, a few times I saw the neighbors drying laundry on the wall."

Then Jacquette seems to have recalled the incident the previous Sunday when she had gone out with her baby to get a meat pie and found by her door a tall man in a cleric's robe with a hat of rabbit's fur who had asked her to sell him a pitcher of water.

She told the examiner about it.

"Do you know where the man came from?"

"No."

"Where did he go afterwards?"

"I have no idea."

"Would you know him if you saw him again?"

"I don't think so."

———◦———

Around the time that Jacquette was being deposed, another examiner, Guillaume Paris, was in a different room with his scribe questioning Drouet Prieur. This was the young valet who also saw the murder from the Rieux house and afterward went down with his master, Henri du Chastelier, and several other men to see the duke's body in the street.[18]

When asked to tell what he had seen the night before, Prieur gave the following statement: "Yesterday evening about eight o'clock, I came down from my master's room to go and look at a horse he had given me and which was stabled behind the house. One of the rooms has several windows that were open and that look out into the Rue Vieille du Temple. It's right across from the House of the Image of Our Lady, which belongs to Master Robert Fouchier. As I passed one of the windows, I heard a great noise in the street like that made by swords and other weapons. And I saw by the light of those openings that the people making this noise were holding torches and shouting: 'Kill him! Kill him!'"

Prieur went on to describe how he raced back upstairs to watch from a window with his master and the others. They could see a gang of armed men attacking someone in the street. Prieur then reported that he had gone downstairs and opened the little window in the door for a better view, at which point a masked man brandished a great ax at him, and the startled valet had slammed the window shut and fled back upstairs. He said he had seen a tall man in a red-hooded friar's robe carrying a great mace. And he recounted how the assassins made their escape, after which he and the others went out into the street. Only then, after a close look at the victim's body, did they realize that it was the Duke of Orleans.

After Prieur finished, the examiner asked him some questions. One question was about the people who had lodged at the House of the Image of Our Lady. Prieur had no idea who they were. But his answer to another question would have a powerful effect on the course of the investigation.

"Do you know who killed Monsieur d'Orleans?"

"No. But it's common knowledge that Monsieur Albert de Chauny, captain of the guard at Ghent, did it or had it done."

De Chauny was the knight whose beautiful wife had been taken by Louis as his mistress and then reportedly shown to her husband naked except for a veil over her face. Prieur doubtless had heard rumors of the infamous episode, and as a valet to one of Louis's squires, he may have known further details of the duke's private life. Even before Drouet Prieur named the knight as a likely suspect, the provost may have suspected de Chauny because of the rumors and the gossip or due to his own personal knowledge of Louis's affairs. De Chauny, said a chronicler, was an obvious choice, "the first person to be suspected of the crime, because of the great hatred he had for the duke, who had seduced his wife and taken her to live with him."[19] And when the valet drew a direct line from Louis's murder to the knight's guilt, and the examiner brought this fresh information to his superior, it moved de Chauny right to the top of the list.

With a named suspect and a clear motive for the murder, Guillaume and his officers began an urgent search for information about the knight's whereabouts and activities.

—◦—

By now the officer responsible for searching the assassins' hideout and drawing up an inventory of its contents had completed his task and filed his report. Attesting to the truth and accuracy of his findings, Jacques Cardon, examiner, wrote, "I went to the house in the Rue Vieille du Temple near the Porte Barbette and belonging to Master Robert Fouchier," where "I found the following things":[20]

> *First, one empty barrel.*
> *Item, one table and two wooden benches.*
> *Item, one old chair.*
> *Item, one old tablecloth and a towel.*
> *Item, four small beds in poor shape.*
> *Item, four pairs of old torn drapes.*
> *Item, one wicker basket.*
> *Item, about twelve pounds of hay.*
> *Item, about fifty fire logs.*[21]

This list of mundane items did not look very helpful at first. Judging by their condition, most of the household furnishings were quite old and may have been at the house long before the assassins arrived. But after completing his inventory, Cardon selected one of the items, the basket, and had it "brought to the

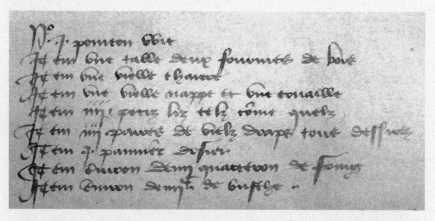

Jacques Cardon's inventory. The list begins with Primo, ·i· poinçon vuit *("First, one empty barrel").* Primo *is abbreviated as a crossed* P *followed by a superscript* o.

Châtelet." As one of the smaller, more portable things found, the wicker basket was likely to have been brought to the house by the assassins and thus might be traceable to a shop whose owner might recall who purchased it.

——◄◊►——

As some officers deposed witnesses at the Châtelet, others collected physical evidence around the crime scene, and still others tried to track down Albert de Chauny, information was pouring in from the city's inns and taverns in response to the orders of the criers whom the provost had sent throughout Paris.

One of the many innkeepers who delivered lists of guests' names was Isabeau la Guionne.[22] Isabeau, about forty years old, according to her deposition, managed a lodging house called the Angel in the Rue Saint-Martin. She had a connection with the Châtelet and may have known the provost or his lieutenant personally, since she was "the widow of Guillaume la Guion, horse-sergeant at the Châtelet"—that is, her husband had been one of the mounted officers in the provost's corps who patrolled the Paris suburbs.

Isabeau's list, delivered "in writing" to the provost's lieutenant, noted five people staying at the Angel: two from Rouen (a knight named Hector de Ste. More and a lawyer named Regnier Cousin), and three from Gisors (Guillaume de Sens, Pierre la Macé, and Maciot Baquet). The knight and the lawyer had lodged with her for the past month, but the three men from Gisors had been there only since Tuesday of that week, the day before the murder.

The arrival of the three men at her inn on the eve of the murder may have led to Isabeau being singled out for special questioning, although a large and bustling city like Paris saw a constant "stream of travelers"—hundreds if not thousands of people came and went each day.[23] Isabeau, one of only two innkeepers to be deposed, may have attracted attention also because the Angel was located in the Rue Saint-Martin, one of the streets along which the assassins had made their escape the night before.

But Isabeau affirmed under oath that "yesterday around nine o'clock at night, when she heard that Monsieur d'Orleans had been killed, all of her guests were in bed at her inn, except the said Pierre la Macé, who was tending his horse in the stables out back." There were no further questions, and nothing suggests that any of her guests were summoned to the Châtelet to be questioned themselves.

———◁◦▷———

The second innkeeper was not so lucky.

It turned out that Albert de Chauny had repeatedly lodged at a tavern called the Sheep in the Rue Saint-Denis—the same street toward which the assassins had fled the night before. Jean de la Bué, the proprietor of the Sheep, was arrested, along with his wife, Etiennette, and their chambermaid, Margot, and all of them "were led as prisoners" to the Châtelet.[24] The arresting officer was Jean Larchier, examiner. The stated reason for the arrests was that "it is said that they had received in their house Messire Albert de Chauny, knight, by whom the late Monsieur d'Orleans is said to have been killed, on account of the hatred he bore against him."

The ages of the three prisoners are not recorded, almost as if these details were omitted in the haste to depose them. Margot, the chambermaid, may still have been in her teens, and all three were probably frightened out of their wits to be seized and brought as prisoners to the Châtelet—to be led down the Rue Saint-Denis as their neighbors stared and then taken all the way to the gloomy old fortress, through the dark passageway below, past the morgue and the prisons, and upstairs to face questions from the suspicious authorities about the murder of the king's brother.[25]

De la Bué was not just summoned and deposed, like most of

the other witnesses, but "arraigned for judgment before the provost and in the presence of master Robert de Tuillières, his lieutenant." Arraignment meant that de la Bué—the two women, it seems, were not so treated—was suspected of possible involvement in the crime. And the fact that Guillaume and his lieutenant heard the depositions in person, most likely in the tiled tribunal chamber, meant that they were keenly interested in these particular witnesses, who had some direct knowledge of the leading suspect.

No initial statement from de la Bué is recorded. After the taverner was sworn in, the interrogation immediately got under way with a series of very direct questions. The principal examiner, Larchier, probably asked the questions while the provost listened from the dais, and the second examiner, his quill scratching on parchment, recorded the results:

"Did you know the said Messire Albert de Chauny, knight?"

"Yes."

"How?"

"Several times he stayed at my house with Monsieur d'Aufemont."

"And when did Messire de Chauny last stay with you?"

"At least a year ago."

This answer may have disappointed Guillaume. If de Chauny had not stayed at the Sheep for over a year, it was unlikely that he had been involved in the crime.[26] Then again, if he was in fact behind the murder, would he have been so foolish as to lodge openly at a public house while lying in wait for his victim? Perhaps, like Pierre de Craon, who had tried to assassinate the constable of France in 1392, de Chauny had secretly rented a house in Paris and hired some thugs—in this case, the assassins who had stayed at the House of the Image of Our Lady—to do the deed for him.[27]

"Were any of his people staying with you on the day that Monsieur d'Orleans was killed?"

"No."

Another disappointing answer. Neither de Chauny nor any of his associates had been recent guests.

Then, perhaps desperate to produce some information that would appease the provost without incriminating himself, de la Bué added something further:

"But last Saint Martin's Eve a fellow named Watier, who was Messire de Chauny's cook but now serves Monsieur d'Aufemont, came to my house and stayed there a day or two and then left at night with Monsieur d'Aufemont. But after Watier, no one else attached to Messire Albert has visited."

Watier was merely a former servant of de Chauny's, but even so, he had stayed at the Sheep — in a street now under a cloud of suspicion — on Saint Martin's Eve, November 10, less than two weeks before the murder.

The examiner, Larchier, or perhaps Guillaume himself, sprang the next question on the nervous taverner, as if to catch him by surprise and judge his reaction:

"Do you have any idea who killed Monsieur d'Orleans?"

"No!"

The record states that de la Bué "confessed" to nothing further, another clue that he was treated more like a suspect than a witness.

After they had finished with the innkeeper, the officials turned to his wife and the chambermaid. The two women were also sworn in and then deposed, "one after the other." But they could not, or did not, tell the authorities "anything more."

In all likelihood, Guillaume did not release the three witnesses but instead ordered them to be confined in one of the Châtelet's prisons while he and his officers sought more information about de Chauny and looked into de la Bué's claim that he had not hosted the knight for the past year or more.

As the initially promising lead had begun to look like a dead end, or at least a cold trail, Guillaume started pursuing several new lines of inquiry. After reviewing "the investigation as already recorded"—that is, once he finished sorting through and studying the depositions collected so far—he focused on another person of interest: the tall friar with the red hood who appeared to have led the assassins.[28] Even if the friar, or the man dressed as a friar, had been hired by someone else to kill Louis, solving the crime probably depended on finding him. Under interrogation, or even under torture, he might reveal who or what lay behind the whole business.

The shoemaker's wife and the young valet who witnessed the crime had both seen the tall friar shouting orders and directing the mayhem at the murder site. And the friar, judging by his distinctive clothing and his unusual height, was almost certainly the same man who had rented the Fouchier house. Both Madame Fouchier and her grandson Perrin had seen the friar with the broker who had arranged the rental. Perhaps the broker knew something of the friar's whereabouts and could lead them to him.

"To learn the truth of the matter," Guillaume now directed his officers to find and arrest the broker. "I commanded that the broker who had rented the house where the culprits had lodged and lain in wait, as mentioned in the depositions of various witnesses, be found wherever he was, arrested, and imprisoned at the Châtelet, in order to be examined in connection with the case."[29] The provost delegated this task to two sergeants, Adam Boucart and Jean Le Gendre, who set off at once to track down the broker and bring him in.

Guillaume started another line of inquiry as well, one involving the household items found at the assassins' hideout and inventoried by the examiner Jacques Cardon. It was possible that people who had sold these things to the assassins might recognize the items and recall something useful about the buyers. Guillaume ordered "that all the goods found at the house be shown to the shopkeepers and merchants who stock such things, in order to find out who had sold them, and who had bought or taken them, so as to identify the criminals who had lodged at the house."[30] This time-consuming task was made slightly easier by the fact that merchants and artisans selling goods of a certain kind—wicker baskets, say—often congregated in a particular street or frequented the central market, Les Halles. Still, in an age without modern forensic tools—materials science, product tracking, and computerized records—to speed the investigation, shoe leather and determination would have to do.

9

A Break in the Case

―◄○►―

SOMETIME ON THURSDAY, probably after the noon bell had rung and perhaps even late in the day, Guillaume got some good news. The two sergeants he had dispatched to find and arrest the broker returned to the Châtelet with a prisoner in custody.

The prisoner, "an old, lame man" who worked as a "rental agent," closely fit the description of the broker given earlier by Marie Fouchier and Perrin Labbé.[1] His name was François d'Asignac, and he lived in the Rue Saint-Martin. He was a foreigner, a Lombard, like the man Perrin had described.

Guillaume had d'Asignac brought before him, probably in the tribunal room, along with Marie and Perrin, whom he summoned back to the Châtelet and "into his presence." There were no protocols, such as a lineup, and no attempt to shield the witnesses from the prisoner's eyes.

Face to face with the old man, Madame Fouchier and Perrin studied him closely. The prisoner may have been told to say a few words, since both witnesses had spoken with the rental agent the week before and might have recognized his voice.

"After they had seen and looked over the said François," they both agreed: "Together they affirmed under oath" and were deposed to the effect that "the said François was the broker who had arranged the rental of the house in question."

A scribe recorded the old man's testimony, and the broker, no doubt terrified to be hauled in for questioning in connection with the murder of the king's brother, told quite a story.

He had first been approached by his client months earlier, he said, "around the feast of Saint John the Baptist," in late June. It all began one day when he was attending Mass at Saint-Merri, his parish church, and "a young man dressed as a scholar"—the friar, presumably—came to see him. D'Asignac did not know his name or who he was, though he "would recognize him if he saw him again."

The scholar asked d'Asignac if he knew of any houses for rent "in the Saint-Pol area," near the king's palace, particularly "in the Rue Saint-Antoine"—the street where Louis of Orleans lived.

The broker said he didn't know of anything currently available there but that he would make some inquiries and begin looking. The scholar thanked him and left.

Sometime later—d'Asignac could not recall exactly how much later, whether days or weeks—the scholar came back to see if the broker had found anything. D'Asignac had not, and the scholar left again.

A third time he came back, but once again d'Asignac had not been able to find anything in the Rue Saint-Antoine or nearby. Then the scholar asked the broker if there was anything available "in the Rue Vieille du Temple, near the queen's palace."

Guillaume concluded that the assassins had been spying on Louis and had learned that he regularly passed through the Marais—in particular, along the Rue Vieille du Temple, riding back and forth to visit the queen.

The scholar, apparently eager to find something soon, told d'Asignac that if the broker found a suitable house in the new location, he would "pay him with some good wine."

"So I began to look around in the new quarter," recalled

the broker. Clearly worried now about being thought a co-conspirator, d'Asignac added, "I didn't think there was any harm in it."

Shortly after he started searching in the Rue Vieille du Temple, he learned about the Fouchier house.

"About two weeks ago," d'Asignac said, the scholar came by to see him again, once more at Saint-Merri.

"Have you found anything?" he asked.

"Yes," said d'Asignac, and he took his client to the Rue Vieille du Temple, where he showed him the Fouchier house.

"C'est bon," said the scholar, clearly pleased. He said he wanted to talk to the owner right away about renting it.² D'Asignac took him to the Chantier du Roy.

There, after bargaining a bit with Madame Fouchier, the scholar rented the house, paying her sixteen livres and then paying d'Asignac his commission. After that, the scholar left, and d'Asignac claimed that he never saw or spoke to him again.

But there was more. On close questioning, d'Asignac revealed that after he had heard about Louis's murder, he had gone back to the Rue Vieille du Temple and asked the neighbors there what had happened. This must have been just hours before he was arrested and brought to the Châtelet. The neighbors told him that the assassins had attacked the duke "from the very house he had rented to the scholar."

"When did you first learn about this business?" asked Guillaume, referring to the plot against Louis's life.

"I didn't know anything about it until afterwards, and then only by hearsay," said the broker.

Obviously eager to prove his innocence, he added, "When I got involved in renting the house, I had no idea about the scholar's *mauvais propos*"—his evil plans.

Apparently the provost believed him. The old, lame man didn't seem to know any more about the conspiracy than

Madame Fouchier. All he had done was unwittingly help the assassins find and rent their hideout.*

The record states that d'Asignac "confessed nothing further." His testimony finished, at least for now, he was "led back to prison" for safekeeping, to make sure he was on hand to identify the elusive scholar if the latter should turn up.

◄◦►

The broker's testimony gave Guillaume his first real glimpse into the conspiracy behind the assassination. Originally the assassins had tried to find a house for their ambush right in the victim's own street, the Rue Saint-Antoine. Failing to do so, they apparently spied on Louis's activities and hit on the stratagem of attacking him on his way to or from the queen's palace in the Rue Vieille du Temple.

D'Asignac's testimony seemed to confirm that the man dressed as the scholar, or friar, was the ringleader, since he had initiated the attempt to rent a suitable house for the ambush. And it revealed that this ringleader had been planning Louis's murder for some time. The fact that he had begun looking for a house all the way back in June and persisted in his search for nearly five months surely meant that he—or whoever was behind the murder—had a powerful motive to kill Louis, although what that motive was remained unknown.

But who was this mysterious scholar who had orchestrated things from the start, renting the house in question from Madame Fouchier, presumably under a false name and wearing a disguise? His repeated visits to Saint-Merri, where he had found the broker, suggested that he lived in that quarter, in or near the Rue Saint-Martin. And while his offer of a reward in the

---

* Madame Fouchier's husband, Robert, was not deposed, but it must have struck him as sadly ironic that the assassins had used his own house to attack Louis, since he had designed one of Louis's greatest fortresses, Pierrefonds.

form of "some good wine" was an intriguing detail, it was too general to be of any help. Wine arrived in the city every day by wagon and barge from all over France—Burgundy, the Loire, the Rhône, and a host of other regions.[3] And no particular vintage had been mentioned.

On the positive side, the broker thought he would recognize the scholar if he saw him again. But first the hooded man had to be found and arrested.

By all accounts, Guillaume was a fair and high-minded man. But it was the provost's duty to find those responsible for killing the king's brother. The law allowed torture as a means of determining the truth in criminal matters—it even prescribed it—and Guillaume would use every means at his disposal if it came to that.

———<o>———

As the day wore on, the provost's sergeants continued to sweep the city and bring in more witnesses.[4] Jacques Cardon, who had inventoried the contents of the assassins' hideout, deposed one of the next-door neighbors, Driette Labbé, daughter of Madame Fouchier.[5] Driette, he learned, had also seen and briefly spoken with "a man wearing a long brown robe down to the knee" when he came by to ask her about the house next door. Once the house was rented, Driette testified, she had grown suspicious of the men next door and their furtive comings and goings. She described how, the previous night, she had gone up to the attic with her daughter, Blanche, and looked into a window next door, where she saw "eight or nine men" by candlelight; this led to her conclusion that "some bad people" were lodging there. She and her daughter had probably seen the assassins making their final preparations for the attack, although at the time they had no idea what they were witnessing.

Also summoned to the Châtelet were the neighbors on the other side of the Fouchier house, the baker Simon Cagne and his wife; they were separately deposed by an examiner named Pierre de Campagnolles.[6]

Simon described how, the previous night, he had heard some noise in the street, gone down to have a look, and found a man lying on the pavement right outside his door.[7] Alarmed, he shut and locked his door at once without trying to learn who the man was or whether he was alive or dead. When he opened his door again a few minutes later to help put out the fire next door, he said, the man was gone.* Then he overheard some people in the street saying "that the Duke of Orleans, God save him, had been killed"—although another witness, Perrin Fouchier, testified that during all the commotion, Cagne had dashed over to say that the Duke of Orleans had merely "had a scare."[8] Saying he knew nothing more about the business, the baker concluded his statement by telling de Campagnolles that for the past week, he and his wife, as well as their servants, had heard noises coming from the house next door at odd times, including the sound of horses.

After Simon's lengthy but not very informative account—the major revelation of which was that Simon was probably the first person to see the freshly murdered duke and had done nothing about it—de Campagnolles began to grill him.

"These people with the horses lodging next door, who were they?"

"I never asked about that."

"When did they go in and out?"

"I never actually saw anyone going in or out. The door was always shut."

"Was the lock broken, or had the door been forced?"

"I don't know."

"Who lived there last, as far as you know?"

---

* Simon's actual phrase was *environ demi quart de heure après* ("about half a quarter-hour later"), perhaps his attempt to minimize the interval.

"A surgeon, Nicolas du Car. He moved out at the end of June." The baker, without being asked, eagerly supplied the surgeon's new address.[9]

"Who has the keys to the house now? Did the surgeon return them to the owner, Robert Fouchier?"

"I don't know."

Clearly hoping to divert attention from himself, Cagne now dragged a poor chambermaid into the business.

"But it's very notable, I think, that one day, sometime after the Feast of Saint John the Baptist, last"—June 24—"I can't be sure exactly when, I saw Robert Fouchier's chambermaid going into the house."

"Her name?"

"Jeanette."

"Surname?"

"I don't know. But it's well known that she works for Monsieur Fouchier where he lives, at the Chantier du Roy."

"What else do you know about her?"

"Well, I don't really know who she is, or where she's from. But I've often heard people say she's from the Vexin, in Normandy. But I don't know her native village, or anything else. I never asked."

The examiner brought the evasive baker back to the main business.

"The house itself, does it have a back entrance?"

This may seem an odd question, since the provost's men had searched the premises and presumably knew the layout. Perhaps de Campagnolles, already knowing the answer, was testing the baker's truthfulness. Then again, he may not have known the full extent of the information gathered so far, since the investigation was proceeding so quickly and along so many different lines of inquiry. Only some of the provost's men had been to the crime scene. The examiner's job was to depose the witness thoroughly, without assuming anything; the provost, the mastermind of the investigation, would then sort out and compare the details.

"There's no back entrance," said Simon. "But the back gardens are quite big. Perhaps they used ladders to climb over the walls and get into the property, then opened the front gate."

Simon apparently had an active imagination. Maybe the assassins had taken over the house by scaling the garden walls—an escalade!—before sallying forth against the duke. "But if they climbed over the walls into the garden," he acknowledged, "then they would have had to get into somebody else's garden first."

"Who set the fire in the house?" asked the impatient examiner, abruptly changing topics.

"I have no idea."

"None at all?"

"Well, I guess it must have been those men with the horses."

"And who were they?"

"I don't know."

"Why were they staying there?"

"I don't know."

"Why did they set the fire?"

"Again, I don't know."

"When did they bring the horses to the house?"

"Once again, I don't know."

De Campagnolles, clearly frustrated by his witness and apparently realizing that he would get nothing more out of him, finally ended the session. He concluded his report by saying that he examined the baker "diligently" but that he questioned him no further after the last fruitless exchange, or *débat*. If Simon managed to escape an overnight stay in one of the Châtelet's prisons, he was lucky.

———◇———

After Cagne was shown out, de Campagnolles called in his next witness, the baker's wife. Jehannette, twenty-seven, was a better subject than her husband, more direct and more forth-coming.[10] Although she did not know much, she did not claim to know more (or pretend to know less) than she actually knew, and she did not try to implicate others.

She told the examiners that around eight o'clock the night before, she and her husband had heard people shouting in the street that their house was on fire, and Simon had sent the servants rushing out to fill their water buckets. The fire turned out to be at the house next door, and after it was put out—Simon claimed to have helped, but Jehannette said nothing about this—the servants told her that the duke had been killed and that his body had been carried into the Rieux house across the street. But they had no idea who had done it, and they hadn't seen or heard anything else.

Questioned about the house next door, Jehannette said that it had been empty since late June but that her servants had told her that for the past week some people had been staying there; they could be heard by day, although they went out only after dark.

"Do you know who these people were?"

"No, I don't."

"What about your servants?"

"I never heard them say who it was."

The household had ten servants in all, some of them presumably employed in the bakery.[11] Perhaps they had seen or heard something useful that they had not shared with Simon or Jehannette. De Campagnolles concluded the deposition by telling Jehannette that she was to order her servants to appear at the Châtelet for questioning.

At a stroke, that made ten more witnesses, ten more oaths, ten more statements, and ten more examinations. It was going to be a very long day, and the depositions might continue well into the night.

Another resident of the Rue Vieille du Temple to be deposed that day was Jean Pagot, the young clerk who had returned home the previous night to find two big fellows in black lurking outside his door.[12] Pagot, giving his age as "nineteen or thereabouts," the youngest of all the witnesses to be deposed, was sworn in and questioned by an examiner named Jean Briand.

Like the baker, Pagot had slammed his door shut in alarm and fright after an initial peek into the street — in his case because, just as he peered out, an arrow flew past the house. Cowering behind his closed door, listening, he heard what must have been Louis screaming in pain as the gang of assassins cut him to pieces outside. Pagot had not dared to open his door again until after he heard the assailants flee, and everything was quiet once more. When he finally looked out, he said, he saw two bodies lying in the street, which some men soon carried away, and also a severed hand lying in the mud. He testified that he overheard the neighbors saying that one of the dead men was the Duke of Orleans and that the men lodging in the house across the street had killed him. But that was all he knew.

"Do you have any idea who did this thing?"

"No."

"Who was staying in the house across the street?"

"I really have no idea."

"How long had they lodged there?"

"Again, I don't know."

Pagot had never actually laid eyes on the assassins and so could not help the investigators identify or find them.

———— ‹◦› ————

More helpful were the barbers and shopkeepers in and around the Rue Saint-Martin, some of whom had gotten a good look at the assassins as they made their escape.

The caltrops collected by the officers of the watch and by

some residents marked the assassins' escape route as clearly as a trail of blood.

After fleeing the murder scene in the Rue Vieille du Temple, according to witnesses in that street, most of the assassins had disappeared down the Rue des Blancs Manteaux, rushing past the little church where Louis's body would soon be borne for the vigil. Since the masked men were next seen in the Rue Saint-Martin, they had probably gone directly west from the Rue des Blancs Manteaux into the Rue Simon Le Franc, then continued straight on into the Rue de la Fontaine Maubué until they came to the Rue Saint-Martin.[13] There they must have turned right and gone north, for witnesses saw them turning from the Rue Saint-Martin into the Rue aux Oues and then heading west once again.

One of the first people from that neighborhood to be summoned and deposed was the salt seller Gilet, whose shop was in the Rue Saint-Martin, right across from the Rue aux Oues.[14] Once again, Jacques Cardon was the examiner. After he had sworn in the witness, who gave his age as "fifty or thereabouts," he took a statement. Gilet related that on the previous night, as he and his son were closing up their shop, they heard a troop of "very strong horses" riding up the Rue Saint-Martin. Watching from his doorway, Gilet saw "twelve or fifteen" horsemen round the corner "very fast" and continue down the Rue aux Oues. Gilet recalled some of the weapons they carried, including crossbows and quivers of arrows as well as half-lances and "other long staves tipped with iron"—spears or maces of some sort.

As the riders headed down the Rue aux Oues, passing the barbershop across from his own shop, Gilet said, one of them shouted, "Put out your lights! Close up!" Then "two or three men on foot," also carrying half-lances and other arms, came running around the corner—comrades, he assumed, of the men on horseback. As they passed the barbershop, Gilet told Cardon, one of them struck the candleholder there with his lance, putting out the lights as he shouted, "We're the watch!" When the examiner probed further as to where the riders and the other men had gone, Gilet said that he "saw and heard them going all the way down the Rue aux Oues to the Rue Saint-Denis."

"And after that?"

"I have no idea."

"How were they dressed? How many of them were there?"

"It was very dark, and I only saw them from behind. Besides, they were riding very fast and all close together. So I really can't say."

Another dead end.

Guillemin Moricet, the barber at the corner of the Rue Quincampoix, farther down the Rue aux Oues, had also seen the horsemen pass.[15] Deposed by Jean Briand, he said there were "twenty or thirty of them," all wearing masks and carrying weapons and heading toward the Rue Saint-Denis. Close behind the men on horseback came two men on foot, said Moricet, one with a lance and the other with an unsheathed sword. The man with the lance stepped into the shop and struck the candleholder, shouting at Moricet and his assistant, "Put out your lights! Ruffians! Put them out!"

Asked who the men were, Moricet said he had no idea, since both had been masked.

"Where did they go?"

"I can't say, since I don't know which way they turned when they reached the end of the street."

"What did you think of all this?"

"At the time, I really didn't think anything of it. And I hadn't heard anything about what had happened."

"When did you hear that the Duke of Orleans was dead?"

"Not until this morning. That's when I also heard that the men seen going down our street last night had killed him."

Questioned further, Moricet could only add that a sergeant

of the watch, Jean le Meignen, later told him that the suspects had thrown some caltrops behind them as they fled.

———◦———

The investigators had been getting nowhere until they reached Jean Fovel, the barber's apprentice who worked for Jean le Roy.[16] Fovel was also unsure where the suspects had gone, but he had gotten a better look at them than the others had and was able to provide some details of their clothing.

Deposed by an examiner named Aubert de la Porte, Fovel gave his age as "twenty-two or thereabouts." In his statement, Fovel said that he and several other apprentices were in the shop the night before, "between eight and nine o'clock," when they heard a commotion in the street.

"I saw lots of men on horseback rush past the shop, as many as twenty or twenty-four of them, along with a crowd of men on foot, a dozen or so of them. Some of the men on foot carried half-lances or unsheathed swords, some had axes or crossbows. They were riding along as fast as they could go, the men on foot hurrying along close behind. They all turned into the Rue aux Oues and headed down the street as if they were making for the Rue Saint-Denis."

Asked to describe the men he saw, Fovel replied: "The men on foot—two or three of them were wearing white fustian jackets, each with two large colored bands around them and crossing over the chest. The overlapping band was blue, and the one under it was green. And both bands were as wide as your palm."

One of the men in livery and two of his comrades, said Fovel, then entered the shop. "With their sticks, they struck the candle-holder hanging there from a chain and put out all the candles."

"These men, who were they?"

"I don't know."

"And the other men you saw on horseback and foot?"

"I have no idea who they were."

"Where did they come from?"

"They came up the Rue Saint-Martin, but where they were before that, I don't know."

"Is there anything else?"

"Right after that, the watch came by, looking for caltrops as they went along the street. They said they had already found a dozen of them. So I went out, with a candle, and found one myself. I gave it to my master last night. Today he gave it to a sergeant of the watch who came here asking for it."

"What else happened last night?"

"Well, after the watch went by, I heard some men out in the street—three fellows, valets, I think, and a brewer—saying that Monsieur d'Orleans was dead, and that they had found some caltrops."

"Who were they, these three fellows and the brewer?"

"I don't know."

—◇—

Jean Porelet, known as Petit-Jean, had also been in Jean le Roy's shop, shaving a customer's beard, when the riders passed.[17] The same age as Fovel, "twenty-two or thereabouts," he agreed in the main with his fellow apprentice but recalled only "twelve or fourteen" men on horseback and thought they passed by somewhat earlier, "around eight o'clock at night and after the curfew bell had rung," for which reason, apparently, he thought "that they were the watch."

After Petit-Jean gave his statement, the examiner, Aubert de la Porte, pressed him for more details about the suspects and where they had gone, clearly hoping to add to the information he had collected from Fovel.

"Would you recognize any of the men, the riders or the men on foot, if you saw them again?"

"No."

"How were they dressed?"

"I really couldn't say."

"How were they armed?"

Petit-Jean could not recall anything about their weapons either, perhaps because he had been focused on his customer and had not seen as much as Fovel had. Indeed, he'd gotten a good look at only one of the men.

"The fellow who came into the shop and put out the lights, he was carrying a half-lance, I think."

"The riders and the men on foot, where did they go?"

"I don't know."

"What street did they turn into?"

"All I can say is that they passed my master's shop and went down the Rue aux Oues. They seemed to be heading for the Rue Saint-Denis. But I have no idea which way they turned there, or even if they went that far, or if they went into the Rue Bourg-l'Abbé, or somewhere else." The Rue Bourg-l'Abbé was a side street running north from the Rue aux Oues, just east of the Rue Saint-Denis and parallel with it.

"When did you hear about the death of Monsieur d'Orleans?"

"About a half an hour later, some fellows passed the shop— I have no idea who they were—saying they had heard that Monsieur d'Orleans was dead. But they didn't say where, or how, or who had killed him."

Though he was clearly a cooperative witness, Petit-Jean said he knew nothing else.

———◦———

The provost's men most likely continued deposing people late into Thursday evening, since new witnesses were still being brought to the Châtelet to be questioned and examined on Friday. By then, Guillaume had widened his net to include the water carriers of Paris.

Although neighbors in the Rue Vieille du Temple had seen or heard the suspects leading horses out to be watered after dark, the assassins may also have had water delivered, since horses consumed great quantities of it. And any water carriers who had supplied the house or who had seen or spoken with the assassins might be able to provide descriptions or other useful information.

Nearly two dozen water carriers were summoned or brought to the Châtelet to be deposed, "one after the other," beginning with Perrin Bouier, a carrier living in the Rue Guillaume-Porée; he was followed by Thomas Guillemen, from the Rue des Lavandières, and then Girard de Fismes, from the same street, and so on.[18] Most of them knew nothing, swearing under oath that they had "never carried any water" to the house in question.

But then, after almost twenty of them had been deposed without any useful results, the examiners found Girard Lendouil, the water carrier who had made a delivery to the Fouchier house on the day of the murder and who had seen and spoken with the apparent ringleader.[19] Girard, who lived in the Rue du Franc-Meunier, testified under oath that on Wednesday, he and two fellow water carriers—Jean le Tisserant and a man named Denisot—had been approached "at the riverbank" by two men asking about a delivery.

Girard, evidently an alert observer with a good memory, recalled that one of them was dressed "in a long brown scholar's robe with a red hood," and the other "in gray."[20] He did not know their names. He went on to say that they had ordered twelve *voies* of water to be delivered to the house in question and that the two men had warily supervised the delivery, preventing the carriers from taking the water around to the stables and insisting that they pour it into "a cistern near the gate, under a covered walkway."

But that was all he knew, and he had not seen either man again after he and his comrades left the premises.

———◇———

Guillaume gave orders on Friday that, in addition to the water carriers, "all those who sell wooden bowls or basins, cutting-boards, and baskets" should be "summoned and examined." If the investigators could speak to the merchants who had sold the housewares found in the Fouchier house, they might be able to discover who had bought them.[21]

A number of vendors and shopkeepers were brought in and deposed, including Richarde Lemperière, a woman who sold kitchenware at the city's busy central market, Les Halles.[22] Questioned about her recent sales, she mentioned several customers and what they bought, but when shown the wicker basket taken from the Fouchier house, she was of no help.

"Did you sell this basket?"

"No. I don't sell baskets like that one."

"Where might someone buy such a basket?"

"I couldn't even tell you that."

Another vendor, Jeanne de la Planchette, who likewise sold goods at Les Halles, recalled under questioning a number of recent sales: a dozen cutting boards to a housewife; five bowls to "a country fellow"; three or four wooden platters, a soup-spoon, and two smaller spoons to some others.[23] But when she was shown the wicker basket, she said she had not sold it and that she did not know who might sell such things.

Eventually a useful witness turned up, a shopkeeper who recognized the basket and remembered the man who had bought it from him. Jean de Pardieu, "sixty-six or thereabouts," had a shop in the Rue au Feurre, near Les Halles, where he sold baskets, platters, and other housewares, and he provided a detailed description of the customer.[24]

About a week ago, he said, a rather odd fellow had come to his shop—"a small man, about fifty or so, with just one eye, dressed in a black coat down to about the middle of his thigh." Revealingly, the man had a silver cook's knife stuck in his belt—an almost sure sign that he was a cook by trade.

Jean had noticed the one-eyed man "passing his shop two or three times" before stopping there. He did not know his name, but he definitely "recognized him on sight," since he had seen the man several times before, he said, working here or there as a cook—one for hire, apparently, or perhaps one who moved frequently from job to job. Jean even knew, by hearsay, that the one-eyed cook had once worked for a man named Guillaume des Bordes.*[25]

When the cook finally stopped by, Jean had asked him if he wanted any of his wares. His shop, like many others, had a front window facing the street. When the shop was closed, the window was covered by a pair of heavy wooden shutters that hinged above and below and locked together in the middle. When it was open, the lower shutter could be used as a display table, the upper one as an awning.[26] Customers could thus shop from the street.

"Do you have any oyster baskets?" the cook had asked, looking over Jean's wares. He said that he wanted a white one.

"Yes," Jean answered, pointing to one.

"How much?"

"Two sous."

"That's too much. All I want is one white basket, at a good price, big enough to hold ten or twelve pieces of meat. I don't need it for long," the one-eyed man added.

Jean then pointed to another basket, a cheaper but less attractive one made of wicker that had hung in his shop for the past three or four years.[27]

The cook had taken it, said Jean, paid just twelve pennies, and then left.

The examiner showed Jean the basket found in the Fouchier house. De Pardieu looked it over carefully.

"This is the one," he said. "I know it for sure."

"Did you sell anything else to this cook?"

"No."

---

* Cooks ranged from the "simple cook" of a burgess or townsman to the "knight's cook" to the "great chef of France" (*grand queux de France*) employed in a ducal or royal household. Wealthier households often hired additional cooks for weddings, funerals, and other occasions.

"Did you see him again?"

"No, I did not."

As soon as the new information gleaned from the alert shop-keeper was brought to the provost, the one-eyed cook became another highly sought-after witness.

Guillaume summoned two sergeants, Thibault Le Natis and Macé Durand, and ordered them "to seek out and find the said cook," arrest him, and "lead him as a prisoner to the Châtelet."[28]

———◦———

By the time that he issued orders for the cook's arrest, Guillaume may have already reached a tentative—but very troubling—conclusion.[29] The case had nothing to do with his initial suspect, Albert de Chauny, who by that point had been dropped from the list, or with the innkeeper in the Rue Saint-Denis who had hosted de Chauny. Nor did the findings so far implicate any of the other people now being held at the Châtelet.

Most of the witnesses in the Rue aux Oues seemed to think that the masked men had gone all the way down to the Rue Saint-Denis. But which way had they gone after that? No one could say. Had they headed south, toward the provost's head-quarters at the Châtelet? This did not seem very likely. Had they turned north, toward the Porte Saint-Denis? No one had reported a troop of armed and masked men riding noisily through that vicinity the night before, and such a cavalcade through the city gate at that hour would have been prevented, or at least reported, by the guards on duty there after curfew.

There was one other possibility: Had the assassins gone straight on, continuing west and crossing the Rue Saint-Denis into the adjoining street, the Rue Mauconseil?[30]

The livery worn by some of the assassins suggested an answer. The sharp-eyed barber's apprentice had recalled that several of the masked men wore white fustian jackets with banding of blue and green.[31] Blue was the king's color, and everyone at court wore it. It probably meant nothing. But green was not so common—it was principally Burgundian.[32]

Supposing the assassins had not turned either way at the Rue Saint-Denis but had simply gone straight on into the Rue Mauconseil—the Street of Bad Counsel? Along this street lay the walled and well-guarded grounds of the Hôtel of Artois— the imposing Parisian residence of Louis's cousin Duke John of Burgundy.[33]

Was this their actual destination? Is this where they were now hiding? And did Duke John himself have something to do with Louis's murder?

Impossible! Why, just this past Sunday, the two cousins, John and Louis, had attended Mass together, and afterward they had dined together in a great display of mutual friendship.[34] After a royal council meeting on Tuesday, John had agreed to dine with Louis again on the following Sunday. And after the murder, he had conspicuously attended Louis's vigil and had served as a pallbearer at his funeral, dressed in black.

Was all of this just an elaborate ruse? A mere pretense of friendship calculated to allay Louis's suspicions followed by a great public show of sorrow to fool everyone else? Had John in fact secretly ordered his cousin's death? Or had the killers worn green so that suspicion would fall on John? Guillaume knew that the attack on Louis was premeditated, a conviction strengthened when the broker's testimony revealed a conspiracy of some kind. But now, as the provost's suspicions shifted to the royal family, his investigation took a momentous turn. And he must have recognized that his search for the truth might put him at great personal risk.

10

Rival Dukes

———◅◦▻———

L OUIS'S CONQUESTS WERE legendary, whereas John lacked his
cousin's good looks and refinement, although he still had
numerous liaisons and managed to sire dozens of bastards.[1]
Rumor had it that Louis had once even pursued John's wife,
Marguerite of Bavaria, "said to be one of the most beautiful
women of that time."[2] The royal palace was often the scene of
late-night masques and balls, and at one such affair, Louis
reportedly followed the duchess into a secluded part of the palace and tried to seduce her. "When she vigorously resisted his
evil designs, he attempted to take her by force," and only by
the greatest struggle did Marguerite manage to escape. When
she told John about it afterward, he "solemnly swore to his wife
that he would avenge the crime with the culprit's blood."[3]

Another version had Louis boasting to John at a banquet
about his private collection of portraits depicting all of the
beautiful women he had enjoyed. One day, while John was visiting Louis's palace, he tried an unlocked door and soon found
himself in Louis's private gallery. "The first painting to meet
his eyes," the story goes, was a portrait of his own wife — proof,
it seemed, that Louis had in fact made a conquest of Marguerite.[4] From that day on, it was said, John secretly began to plot
Louis's death.

Less than a year apart in age, the two cousins could not have been more unalike. Louis was slender and fair, with a round, pleasant face, while John was short and ugly, with a great square head, heavy brows, and a beaklike nose.[5] Louis was outgoing and gregarious, never appearing in public in anything but the finest clothes, while John was wary and suspicious of others and seemed to care little about his appearance. "In everything— cast of mind, disposition, and physique—the two cousins were complete opposites."[6]

John of Burgundy. Portrait by an anonymous Flemish master, circa 1450.

Even in their choice of personal emblems, they clashed. Louis chose as his device a knotty cudgel or club, which he had emblazoned in silver or gold on his shield, his armor, and his rich fur-trimmed robes. John chose as his personal device the carpenter's plane with wood shavings, an emblem he wore with equal ostentation, thus hinting that he could trim Louis's cudgel down to size.[7] The club and the plane were humble everyday devices compared to the noble lion, the royal fleur-de-lis, and other aristocratic symbols, but there was no mistaking the violence threatened by each. Louis's personal motto, *Je l'envie,* "I challenge him," was also a taunt, as was John's own motto in Flemish, *Ich houd,* which translates as "I hold."[8]

Like many great lords, John and Louis enjoyed the hunt. But whereas Louis pursued traditional aristocratic game, such as the fox, the wild boar, and especially the stag, John had a special passion for hunting the wolf—a stealthy, elusive creature with which he had a good deal in common.[9]

For many years John and Louis's rivalry simmered behind the scenes, secondary to Louis's power struggle with John's father, Duke Philip.[10] Uncle and nephew argued in the royal council over everything—taxes, trade, the quarrel with England, the Schism in the Church—and their disputes often turned into shouting matches, until the room seemed too small to contain them both. During one especially heated exchange, it is said, as the younger prince vied with the elder to have his way, Philip angrily burst out: "Look here! If you want to rule the king, you first must learn to govern yourself!" Philip's sharp reproof drove Louis into a blind fury, and he struck his astonished uncle in the face.[11]

Philip eventually repaid his nephew's insult by spreading propaganda about Louis's wife that ultimately drove Valentina from the court amid suspicions that she had used witchcraft or poison to harm the king.[12] But it seems that Philip in turn paid a heavy price for his intrigues against Valentina Visconti. Rumor had it that her furious father, the Duke of Milan, found a way to strike back at Philip where it hurt most, punishing him through his son John.

In the same year that scandalous talk of Valentina's poisoned apple sent shudders through the French court, Europe stirred with alarm at news of the Ottoman Turks, who had overrun the Balkans and crossed the Danube to invade Hungary. In the spring of 1396, the kings and princes of Europe joined forces and raised a crusade to rescue their fellow Christians and fend off the Muslim threat. Nobles everywhere joined the glorious campaign. Duke Philip, a chief contributor, poured in money and troops.[13]

Philip also put his personal stamp on the expedition by sending his eldest son, John, to help lead it. Louis, as the ailing king's brother and regent, could not be risked on such a dangerous foreign adventure. John had jousted in his first tournament at sixteen, and at seventeen he had joined his father for the first time on campaign.[14] Now, at twenty-four, he would help lead a great crusade.

In April 1396, John and the men under his command gathered at Dijon and marched east through the Swiss Alps to Strasbourg and Vienna.[15] At Budapest they joined up with other crusaders and then followed the Danube into the Balkans. Eventually they came to Wallachia, which bordered Transylvania — dark and dangerous lands in the minds of the French, even half a century before the notorious Vlad Dracul, the Impaler, began his reign of terror.[16]

The Christians besieged and captured Vidin, an Ottoman stronghold on the Danube, and put its entire garrison to the sword.[17] Continuing east along the river, they recklessly attacked and plundered several more places. In September they arrived at Nicopolis, a well-fortified city on a high bluff overlooking the river and strongly defended by the Ottomans. An initial attack with mines and scaling ladders failed for want of siege engines.*[18]

---

* If ground conditions permitted, attackers would dig tunnels beneath (undermine) a wall and prop it up from below with timbers, then set fire to the timbers to collapse the wall into the pit. If the defenders detected mining, sometimes by vibrations in a bowl of water placed on the ground, they would dig countermines to intercept the attackers.

Sultan Bayezid, the Ottoman leader, was besieging Constantinople, three hundred miles away.[19] Learning of the attack on Nicopolis, he promptly ordered a rapid march north. His army joined with his Serbian allies at Kazanlak in late September and, ten thousand strong, proceeded toward Nicopolis, arriving on September 24.[20]

The next morning, the crusaders rode out to meet the enemy.[21] Several hundred French knights took the lead, with the Hungarian and German troops drawn up in ranks behind them. John—then known as the Count of Nevers—was in the vanguard along with two famous French crusaders: Philip of Artois, the Count of Eu, and Jean de Boucicaut, marshal of France. The French knights in their emblazoned surcoats formed "a very beautiful array" on their warhorses, as their blue and gold and green banners fluttered above them from a forest of lances.[22]

To cries of "Saint George!" and "Saint Denis!" the French knights lowered their lances and charged the waiting Turks.[23] The crusaders smashed through the enemy line, but their advance then slowed against a storm of arrows falling "thicker than hail or raindrops ever fell from the sky."[24] The French cavalry regrouped and charged again, but now they ran into a field of sharp stakes planted in their way that "pierced their horses' entrails, killing and wounding many men as well who fell off their horses there, while others, though hobbled, managed to get through."[25]

More died in the man-to-man fighting behind the stakes. John, for his part, fought courageously, "acquitting himself so well that he was an example to all of how to fight."[26] But displays of valor on the field were not enough to win the battle. Many Hungarian troops in the rear now fled the field, retreating to Nicopolis and even scrambling across the Danube to safety, while the French and the Burgundians, hemmed in by the enemy and the terrain, fought where they stood, the bodies piling up around them.

Faced with overwhelming odds, the remaining crusaders finally surrendered, including Boucicaut, the Count of Eu—and John. With the bloody defeat and humiliating capture, however, the horrors had only begun.

The next day the sultan ordered his men to begin executing the captives.[27] John and the other high-ranking prisoners were set aside for ransom, seated on the ground, and forced to watch. The Christian captives, stripped to their breeches and with their hands tied before them, were driven forward one by one. Turkish troops, standing at the ready with great scimitars and swords, expertly cut each man to pieces with their whirling blades, "striking horrible blows upon the head and chest and shoulders." One after another, the victims fell, until bloody heads and severed limbs lay piled everywhere. "The Sultan looked on as his dogs pitilessly slaughtered our loyal Christians with their great scimitars, in the presence of the Count of Nevers and right before his eyes."[28]

In the middle of this carnage, John saw his friend Boucicaut hobbling forward, hands tied, toward the waiting swords.[29] John turned to the sultan and signaled that he and Boucicaut were as brothers. The sultan relented and spared him, after being promised another huge ransom.

The killing resumed, and more bodies piled up until, finally, the sultan called a halt to the slaughter, having apparently slaked his thirst for vengeance. One report says that three thousand crusaders perished in this massacre.[30]

For John's ransom alone, the sultan demanded more than two hundred thousand francs. But with interest on loans and other expenses, the total cost of John's return would come to nearly five hundred thousand francs—a colossal sum that forced his father into debt.[31]

In June 1397, after nine months in captivity, John, Boucicaut, and the other ransomed nobles took ship from Gallipoli and sailed south around Greece and then north via the Adriatic

Sea to Venice. From there they traveled overland by horse, taking the Brenner Pass through the snow-filled Alps and finally arriving at Dijon in February 1398.[32]

John had been away from home for nearly two years. No longer an untested youth, he was a battle-seasoned veteran who had endured the horrors of war and captivity, which left him "a bitter and humiliated man."[33] The harrowing ordeal doubtless sharpened John's hatred for Louis, who had stayed home the whole time, far from danger, indulging his many luxuries and vices while vying with his uncle Philip for the reins of power.[34]

Worse yet, it was rumored that Louis's father-in-law, the Duke of Milan, to avenge himself on Philip for Valentina's exile, had kept the sultan informed about "all that was passing in Christendom," including news of the French court and even crucial military intelligence about the crusade. (The duke's own informant at the French court was mostly likely Louis.) The duke sent the sultan a gift of twelve of the finest hawks and falcons, it was said, along with a confidential letter listing the names of the wealthiest crusaders, the ones most likely to provide the largest ransoms if captured. Chief among the targeted nobles was John.[35]

If John learned of these rumors upon his return to France—and Burgundian spies were everywhere—it would have only whetted his appetite for revenge against Louis.[36]

———◇———

Just days after Duke Philip died, in April 1404, John called a council meeting in Flanders.[37] There he announced to his assembled advisers that his top priority as the new Duke of Burgundy was to get rid of his cousin and nemesis once and for all. What, he asked, was the best way to kill Louis that posed the least risk to himself?[38]

Philip had not yet been buried; his body still lay in state at Douai, the black-draped town where John may have called the meeting. Finally in power after years of standing in the wings, John apparently could not wait a moment longer for his cousin Louis to be dead and buried as well.

On hearing that John's first order of business was to kill Louis, his advisers "were stunned," and they desperately tried to persuade their impulsive new lord against such "an atrocious and dangerous policy." At this, John flew into a rage, shouting, "I'm not asking your opinion! I'm ordering you to find a way to do the thing!" After threatening his council "on pain of death," he angrily dismissed them, giving them just three days to come up with a plan.

By the second meeting, John had calmed down enough to take advice. His nervous advisers hesitantly outlined their plan: a massive propaganda campaign that would make the people of France accept and even welcome Louis's death. Louis would be painted as a tyrannical usurper, an enemy of the people who had to be removed for the safety of the king and the good of the realm, while John would be portrayed as the people's sympathetic tribune, their champion against Louis's oppression.

John liked the plan and approved it. He even agreed to a delay of "two or three years" in executing Louis's death warrant. At once, his agents began spreading stories vilifying Louis as a tax-crazy tyrant while promoting John as the people's last hope for justice. John, the story went, "had great compassion for the king's subjects, burdened as they were by so many taxes and duties of all kinds, and he wanted to restore their ancient liberties and free them from these unjust impositions." Such propaganda was put out by letter and writ as well as in tales carried far and wide by friars and beggars, paid agents who knew how to inflame the gullible and unlettered people.[39] The campaign included "all the important towns in the realm," but John directed his main efforts at Paris, whose populace he had to win over in order for the plan to succeed.[40]

All the lords of France used courtiers, clerics, and other

agents to polish their own images, but John specialized in this sort of subterfuge. A Machiavellian prince a century before the type was defined — and like that type, more feared than loved — he rivaled the Borgias with his schemes and lack of scruples. John was not only "willful, brutal, cruel, and without pity," but, in the words of a contemporary, "a subtle, wary, suspicious man who trusted no one."[41] There was "something insidious or stealthy" about him, "an element of cunning," as reflected in "his use of spies, his passion for secrecy, the various conspiracies he organized, and in his devious diplomacy."[42] Even the mad king's beautiful young concubine Odette was one of John's protégées — and most likely one of his spies as well.[43]

John had become Duke of Burgundy at thirty-three, nearly middle-aged for the time, after spending years in his father's shadow, watching and waiting, learning the art of rule from a master, studying the strengths and weaknesses of other men. Once he finally came to power, he was a man in a hurry — "a masterful opportunist who acted impulsively, with speed and decision, on the spur of the moment." But he was entirely lacking in prudence and seemed unable "to weigh the consequences of his actions."[44]

Despite John's shortcomings as a leader, one thing that he really understood was money — how it oiled the gears of government, how it extended a ruler's grasp, how it shaped political reality.[45] He recognized, for example, how deeply the people resented the new tax levies, and, unlike Louis, he did not foolishly ignore the public outcry that greeted them. Not quite a point of principle on his part, neither was this mere opportunism: like the early oil painters of the north whom he patronized, John was a Flemish realist who saw the material world with a clear-eyed precision that his more romantic cousin Louis did not.[46]

In the following year, 1405, Louis proposed his crushing new tax, and John, following the script of his own propaganda campaign, vigorously opposed it in the French royal council, saying, "As I see it, it is tyranny to tax the poor people for a second time in the same year. Especially since the money we've already collected is sufficient to do what we have decided on."[47] John was financially pinched at the time—the Crown had been holding back his rightful payments since his father's death the previous year—but to prove his bona fides, he said that if the council approved the new tax, he would not levy it on his own territories but would make up the difference from his own treasury.

John's speech did not sway the council, who went ahead with the tax on the grounds that England was planning to attack France again and that the funds were needed for defense.[48] But John's vocal opposition burnished his rising reputation as a friend of the people and as the only lord in France who dared challenge the reckless and tyrannical Duke of Orleans.

◄○►

That summer came the crisis that pushed the nation to the brink of civil war.[49] It began with a dispute over the custody of the eight-year-old dauphin, heir to the throne.[50] The king's intermittent madness made his underage son an especially vulnerable pawn in the royal family's constant power struggles, and a key player in this drama was Queen Isabeau, the dauphin's official guardian.[51] Isabeau was now taking an increasingly active role in court politics, allied with Louis of Orleans and possibly his lover by now as well. But the dauphin was also John of Burgundy's son-in-law, married to the duke's eleven-year-old daughter, Marguerite, although (not surprisingly, given their ages) the union had not been consummated.[52] And Burgundy was vying to have himself appointed as the dauphin's new guardian.[53] Trapped in this web of royal intrigue was a sickly young prince prone to nosebleeds and sudden frights.[54]

In June 1405, Charles had another spell of madness; it lasted until mid-July.[55] After recovering, he called together his council, saying he would reform the government. Answering the summons, John set off for Paris in August with seventeen hundred troops, while his brother Anthony marched to the capital with an additional one thousand men-at-arms.[56] Louis, alarmed by news of these approaching armies and perhaps fearing that John was about to mount a coup d'état, decided to flee Paris with the queen and the dauphin.[57]

To cast a cloak of nonchalance over their departure, Louis and Isabeau pretended to go hunting. On August 17, they rode slowly out of the city, attired for the chase. But soon they were galloping toward Melun—about thirty miles southeast of Paris—to take refuge in a castle there.[58] Since the dauphin was in bed with a nosebleed, they left him behind for now, instructing the queen's brother, Louis of Bavaria, and several confederates to bring the dauphin and the other royal children as soon as they could and in great secrecy.

The next day was a stormy one, but Louis of Bavaria and his confederates took the dauphin from his bed and placed him in a boat on the Seine during a driving rain, against his doctor's orders and without telling his uncles, the Dukes of Berry and Bourbon. With the dauphin were his nine-year-old sister, Michelle, and John's daughter Marguerite.[59] The crew had to row upstream in bad weather, and the boat had gone only a few miles past the city walls when the party stopped for the night.

Duke John, encamped with his troops about twenty miles north of Paris, got word overnight of the dauphin's departure. After rising at dawn "to a trumpet blast," he called for his horse and set off for Paris in haste with a small but well-armed troop of soldiers.[60]

He and his men galloped right through the city, "to the great surprise of the inhabitants," and continued south along the Seine.[61] After about twelve miles of hard riding, they caught up with the dauphin and his party, now in a carriage, near

Juvisy. John, "all covered with dust," pulled his horse up alongside them and called out to his eight-year-old son-in-law. One report says he drew his sword and cut the traces connecting the horses to the carriage to stop it in its tracks.[62]

The three children peered out at the troop of armed men on dusty horses.

"Sire," said John to the dauphin, "may I ask where you are going? And whether indeed you wish to go there?"[63]

As the queen's brother watched sullenly from his mount, everyone quieted so they could hear the little boy's response.

"Father," answered the dauphin, "I should like to go back to Paris."

John could hardly conceal his delight. He turned to the coachman: "Driver, take this carriage back to Paris. We will escort you."[64]

The queen's brother protested angrily: "When Isabeau hears of this—"[65]

John cut him off: "We're taking him back. And in front of anyone who cares to watch."[66]

Isabeau's brother, his few men outnumbered by John's heavily armed troops, fell silent.

Soon the coachman had turned around his team of horses, and the carriage containing the dauphin and the two princesses set off for Paris, John and his troops riding alongside. The queen's brother and his men followed glumly behind.

Isabeau and Louis were dining farther down the road at Pouilly when they heard the news that John had caught up with the dauphin.[67] Fearing that Burgundy was now coming for them, they dropped their food on their plates and fled in disarray to the castle at Melun.

As the dauphin's carriage and his Burgundian escort approached Paris, John's cousin Louis of Anjou and two of his uncles, Bourbon and Berry, rode out to meet the party in their armor and accompanied by troops.[68] Together with John's troops, they conducted the dauphin back into Paris, across the city, and to the Louvre, where they posted a heavy guard at every gate.

John had outmaneuvered Louis.

But that was not the end of it. Louis, now in self-imposed exile from Paris, began gathering troops, saying that "he would rather die than allow John's insult to himself and the queen to go unavenged."[69] In response, John mustered his own army and prepared for war. In Paris, he ordered thick wooden barricades placed across all the streets near his residence, the Hôtel of Artois, each fitted with a heavy gate that was guarded day and night.[70]

Parisians, fearing that Louis would attack the city and seize the dauphin and that they would be hostages in their own homes, appealed to the king's eldest uncle and the senior member of the royal council, the Duke of Berry.[71] The council, John of Burgundy included, appointed Berry as guardian of the dauphin and captain of the city, in charge of its defense. Berry—acting through the provost, Guillaume de Tignonville—had most of the city gates bricked up and the rest placed under heavy guard. Parisians stockpiled weapons for their own defense, and hundreds of chains were installed across streets throughout the city.[72]

Meanwhile, the Duke of Bourbon was sent to Louis to ask him to disband his army and allow the queen to return to Paris. Louis angrily refused. Bourbon went to Melun a second time, but his nephew rejected his overtures again. Deputies from the University of Paris made up a third embassy, but Louis only mocked them: "Would you send a troop of knights to settle a question of faith? Of course not. So why send a claque of scholars to decide a question of war? Go back to your schools and your lectures."[73] Finally the Duke of Berry himself went to Melun to beg Louis not to plunge the nation into war, telling him that he and the other princes agreed that John of Burgundy had acted rightly with respect to the dauphin. Louis scornfully rebuffed him too.

All this time, wild rumors flew about. For example, it was alleged that Louis had bribed the guards at the Porte Saint-Martin to allow him and thirty men to enter the city secretly under cover of darkness and carry off from his palace gold and jewels worth more than two hundred thousand livres.[74] Not all such stories were mere rumors, however. One night an armed troop actually sailed down the Seine and attacked the Duke of Berry's palace, which fronted the river.[75] Burgundy led five hundred soldiers to the scene at a gallop, putting Louis's men to flight, and the next day he ordered an enormously heavy chain to be forged and then stretched across the Seine in order to prevent such attacks in the future.

On September 12, John of Bavaria marched up to Paris with an army to reinforce Burgundy, his brother-in-law. Guillaume de Tignonville, acting in his capacity as provost, met Bavaria at the Porte Saint-Denis and had him swear an oath before entering the city that he would keep the peace and "that neither he nor his men would do anything against the town."[76] Burgundy, well aware of Guillaume's close ties to Louis, whose army now threatened Paris, may have watched this ceremony with annoyance and suspicion, viewing Guillaume as little more than Louis's confederate inside the capital.

Despite these reinforcements, fear of further attacks by Louis's troops caused "a commotion in Paris," wrote an eyewitness. "Parisians were in such a panic you would think the whole world had been after them, bent upon their destruction."[77] The two armies, each several thousand strong, were foraging outside the capital, seizing cattle and crops, and soon the whole area "was greatly burdened and oppressed by the troops of both factions."[78] Amid the alarms and maneuvers, civil war seemed imminent.

But with thousands of active troops in his pay and without

Louis's immense cash reserves, John was running out of money.[79] And he saw his popular support erode, as Parisians began to fear Louis's reprisals if they backed John militarily and he lost.[80] In late September, John prepared to disband his army and opened negotiations with Louis at the Château de Vincennes, the towering white fortress set in the royal hunting park several miles east of Paris. After three weeks of talks, the cousins agreed to dismiss their armies, swore to live in peace, and even promised not to speak ill of each other.[81] The immediate crisis was over.

—◇—

Over the next year or so, relations between John and Louis seemed to improve amid various displays of goodwill. In January 1406, John invited Louis to dine with him at his palace, and they dined together again in April.[82] Around the same time, John was named captain-general of Picardy and West Flanders, an important military office he had sought on his own behalf; Louis made no objection.[83] On May 1, the two princes dined together, and then again during the following week. They also exchanged gifts, John giving Louis a replica of his own emblem, a carpenter's plane, decorated with a great pearl, an emerald, and several diamonds.

A double wedding that June prompted further friendly gestures.[84] The king's younger son, second in line to the throne, married Burgundy's niece, and the king's daughter Isabelle, Richard II's sixteen-year-old widow, married Louis's eldest son, five years her junior.[85] At the festivities, John and Louis competed to outdo each other in courtesies, exchanging lavish gifts and swearing oaths of mutual "love and friendship for life."[86] At one of several tournaments held as part of the festivities, John "did honor to Louis by wearing a black surcoat embroidered with Orleanist cudgels," while Louis replied in kind, conspicuously wearing John's emblem, the carpenter's plane.[87]

That summer the two cousins united in another joint venture: Eager to show their loyalty to France after having recently mobilized armies against each other, they went on parallel campaigns against the English.[88] John led his army north to attack the enemy's great stronghold at Calais, a sore spot ever since its capture in 1347, and Louis headed south into Bordeaux, the last piece of the storied Aquitaine still held by the English. But during the fall and winter, both campaigns came to naught. At the end of October, Louis besieged the castle of Bourg-sur-Gironde. But in one prodigal spree, he squandered his army's pay by losing it all at dice.[89] Cold and rain further hampered the siege, as did repeated attacks by the English navy. In January, Louis called off the expedition, having accomplished nothing. Then the king impulsively canceled John's campaign too. John was "infuriated" and seems to have blamed Louis for this embarrassing public setback.[90]

———◦———

John was in Paris by January.[91] By now, his revenues from France had been held back for nearly three years, and the Crown's outstanding debt to him totaled several hundred thousand francs.[92] Again he pressed the government to pay him, and in April the king finally issued letters ordering that John be granted nearly three hundred and fifty thousand francs.[93] A month later, however, John still had not received the promised funds, and again he may have blamed Louis for blocking his rightful payments.

At the end of April, while John was away in Flanders, Louis took advantage of his cousin's absence to reorganize the royal council, purging it of dozens of men, including nearly all of Burgundy's partisans.[94] At a stroke, Louis virtually eliminated John's role in the government, aggressively refusing to share power with him. The period of goodwill was over.

Louis had choked off John's revenues and mounted a virtual

coup d'état behind his back. He had also spent the past three years exploiting the king's illness and using his own powers as regent to raise new taxes, loot the royal treasury, block government reforms, prolong the Schism, and entangle France in a host of ill-conceived alliances throughout Europe—all this on top of his rumored affair with the queen, his having almost killed the king at the Bal des Ardents, and his near assault upon John's wife.

Louis's insult to Marguerite, his purge of the royal council, and his continuing attempts to bankrupt John may have seemed to Burgundy a three-pronged attack—on the vulnerable fronts of sex, money, and power—that no prince could tolerate. John may also have believed the rumors reported by some of his advisers that Louis was plotting to do away with *him*.[95] These were tangible threats, but John felt that Louis's enmity had also cost him "honor and reputation" in the public eye. As a result of all this, his accumulated resentment "knew no bounds."[96]

In June 1407, the friar in the long brown robe with the red hood began looking for a house to rent near Louis's palace.[97]

In October, Louis again started meddling in Flanders, where John was especially vulnerable. Earlier that year, Louis had threatened to seize several castles held by John's younger brother, Anthony.[98] And he had long supported Liège, a Flemish province in open revolt against Burgundy's brother-in-law, John of Bavaria.[99] Now another of Louis's allies in the region, Guelders, signed a treaty with Liège. This alliance ramped up the military threat against John and his brother-in-law.

At the end of October, as if deliberately trying to provoke his cousin even further, Louis recklessly ordered the French navy to attack some English ships in the Channel.[100] Besides risking war with England, the attack imperiled the Flemish wool trade, crucial to John's finances. If Burgundy, having already begun secret preparations for Louis's murder, was still hesitating to kill his cousin, the naval attack was probably the last straw.

Around the time that John gave the final order for Louis's death, he sent a trusted friend named Dino Rapondi to Bruges, one of John's strongholds in Flanders. Rapondi, an Italian financier and also a fixer for the Burgundy family, had helped raise money for John's ransom after the disaster at Nicopolis.[101] In Bruges, Rapondi was "to recruit a troop of Flemish soldiers" who could rush to John's aid in Paris should he suddenly need them.[102]

On November 18, a few days after the friar rented the house in the Rue Vieille du Temple, a courier galloped from Bruges to Paris with secret orders from Rapondi "to inquire about the stabbing of the Duke of Orleans"—a sure sign that Burgundy's paid assassins were about to strike.[103]

———◆◇◆———

The elderly Duke of Berry was as ignorant of the conspiracy as its intended victim was, but fearing that the renewed hostility between his two nephews might lead to civil war, he attempted to broker a truce.[104] He made overtures to John and Louis and got them to agree to bury their animosity for the good of the nation and make a public pledge of peace before God.

On Sunday, November 20—the same day that Jacquette, the shoemaker's wife, found a stranger in a clerical robe outside her door asking to buy some water—the Duke of Berry escorted his two nephews to Mass.[105] The joint communion took place at the Church of the Grands-Augustins, the principal monastic establishment in Paris, right next to Berry's palace on the Left Bank.[106] The church had a cavernous nave nearly eighty yards long, and a great square bell tower ninety feet high.

In the candlelit gloom of the immense sanctuary, before the high altar, John and Louis "together received the body of Our Lord" and "swore a solemn oath" of brotherhood, after which they exchanged the kiss of peace.[107] As the priest blessed the two cousins and intoned the Paternoster, the long quarrel between them seemed to dissolve in the air amid the wafting clouds of incense that drifted toward the ceiling.

Afterward, John and Louis sealed their new accord by dining together with their uncle at his nearby palace, the Hôtel of Nesle. At the banquet, Louis conferred on his cousin the Order of the Porcupine, which Louis had founded in 1393. Louis "personally placed the insignia" around John's neck: a chain with an enameled gold medallion featuring the animal reputed to throw its quills at its enemies.[108] The two reconciled cousins then "kissed one another," and the Duke of Berry embraced both of his nephews "amid tears of joy."

That Tuesday, November 22, John and Louis "sat together" at a royal council meeting called by the king and "drank together" afterward from the customary wine and spices. Louis invited John to dine with him the following Sunday, and John cordially accepted.[109]

To those looking on, including the king and the contented Duke of Berry, all seemed well again between the two most powerful lords in France.

The next day, Louis was assassinated.

II

A Confession

————◄○►————

O NCE GUILLAUME SUSPECTED that John had ordered Louis's
death and that the assassins were most likely Burgundy's
paid henchmen, he had to figure out what to do next. How
could he test his suspicions, or prove them with any degree of
certainty? Guillaume could not just issue orders for Burgundy's
arrest or summon him to the Châtelet to be deposed, let alone
use judicial torture to force the truth from him. As a member
of the royal family, a prince of the blood, a Valois, Burgundy
was not subject to the normal procedures of the law. He enjoyed
an almost royal immunity from investigation and prosecution.[1]
Guillaume could not even pay a visit to Burgundy at his residence, the Hôtel of Artois, to ask him a few circumspect questions. Indeed, his doing so would be presumptuous to the point
of treason. Besides, if the duke had even the slightest hint that
the provost suspected him, Guillaume would suddenly be in
grave danger. The provost's wife, Alix, and his daughter might
be at risk too. And neither his personal bodyguard, the Twelve,
nor his several hundred sergeants would be able to shield him
from Burgundy, who was now the most powerful lord in
France and who commanded thousands.

Of the dozens of witnesses deposed over the past two days
by Guillaume's officers, none had said anything directly con-

necting John with the crime. The incriminating details collected so far—the escape route dotted by caltrops leading toward John's residence, the green livery worn by some of the assassins—were merely circumstantial. Guillaume, having studied the gathered testimony and compared the various reports, may have been the only one to suspect Burgundy so far. "No one knew who had killed the duke," wrote a chronicler, "and no one suspected John, because of the oaths he had sworn with his cousin, and the promises of friendship, and the sacred Host they had shared."[2] As Friday dawned, Guillaume faced a new and troubling dilemma: How should he handle the terrible secret?

The idea that the conspiracy to kill Louis had originated within the royal family and that Burgundy had ordered his own cousin's death was staggering, as explosive and potentially destructive as the new "cannon powder" that was changing the face of warfare all over Europe.[3] If the theory proved true, it could plunge France into civil war, with Louis's outraged relatives and friends seeking revenge against Burgundy. If rumor of the duke's involvement got out prematurely—if Guillaume's unproven suspicions breached the walls of the Châtelet before he obtained proof of Burgundy's guilt—Guillaume's situation would become very dangerous. Attempts on the lives of law officers were not unknown, which is why the provost had the Twelve. In 1368, a royal sergeant had been assassinated while investigating a criminal case.[4] Whatever Guillaume did next, he had to do with extreme care—as cunningly and stealthily as John seemed to have carried out the murder plot.

The lords of France had called another meeting for that morning, this time at the royal palace, the Hôtel Saint-Pol. A key item on the agenda was an update from Guillaume on the progress of his investigation, and the gathered lords doubtless expected the provost to have much more to tell them now than he had reported at their first emergency meeting on Wednesday night, shortly after the crime. And among those great lords would be John of Burgundy.

On Friday morning, as his officers were still deposing the water carriers and vendors, Guillaume had very little time to decide what to do. How should he conduct himself in the presence of the man he suspected of ordering the crime while that man's unwitting relatives looked on? If he openly accused the duke, the whole royal family might turn on him as a traitor. If he asked impertinent questions, he might be hustled out of the room and sent off to his own prisons, or worse. But he could hardly say he had discovered nothing about the crime, that the investigation ordered by the lords two days earlier had not yet produced any useful results. So much depended on his next steps: the outcome of the investigation, his tenure as provost, his own personal safety and perhaps that of his family, the well-being of the agitated city he was sworn to protect, and, very likely, the peace and security of all France.

———◄◦►———

"On Friday," says a chronicle, "the royal council assembled again at the Hôtel St. Pol."[5] Shortly after the council convened, Guillaume was summoned to give his report. When he entered the room, the lords turned to him, and Berry spoke for them all.

"What have you discovered, Provost, about the late duke's death?"

Guillaume replied that he had been investigating the matter "with the greatest possible diligence" but that so far he had been unable to learn the truth.[6]

This was not what the lords—all but one, that is—wanted to hear. They wanted results. They wanted to know who had killed Louis, and they wanted to know now.

But Guillaume was not finished.

"However, if my lords would allow me to enter the houses of the king's servants, including my lords' own residences, perhaps I may discover the truth about the perpetrators, or at least their accomplices."[7]

There was silence in the room as these words sank in.

Had the provost really mentioned "my lords" in the same breath as "the perpetrators" and "their accomplices"? And was he really proposing to search their own sacrosanct and inviolable homes? To ransack their bedchambers and their storerooms, their cellars and their stables, as though the royal dukes were ordinary suspects in an everyday criminal case? This was unprecedented—under the law, no one could search a prince's house or seize property or persons there "without the permission of the lord."[8]

Just a month earlier, de Tignonville had hanged the two self-professed clerics amid protests from the university, a dispute that still lingered in the air. What else would the impertinent provost now do? Attempt to arraign the lords of France before his tribunal? Question and depose them like ordinary citizens? Interrogate them under torture?

The lords pondered the matter, and Guillaume waited for an answer, knowing that he had taken a terrific gamble. All the lords had to do was refuse, and that would be the end of it— his investigation would be over; he might even be summarily sacked, and the crime would remain officially unsolved.

Then again, with a bit of luck, his stratagem might work. Three of the four royal dukes were almost certainly innocent of the crime and knew nothing about the conspiracy, so what had they to fear from a search? And if those three consented, how could the fourth fail to follow suit without betraying his guilt—especially if the masked men who had been seen fleeing toward the Hôtel of Artois were still hiding there or had left traces of their presence?

Finally, one of the lords spoke up; this time it was Anjou who took the lead.

"You have my permission," he said.

"And mine," said Berry, quickly following.

"And mine too," added Bourbon.

Just like that, three of the lords had consented, giving the provost "leave and permission to enter wherever he thought necessary."[9]

Only one, Burgundy, remained conspicuously silent.

But he was now trapped.

When he heard his relatives agree to a search of their houses, Burgundy suddenly "became anxious and fearful."[10] He "changed color" and "turned pale."[11]

"Good cousin," said Anjou, "do you know something about this business? If so, you must tell us."[12]

Still saying nothing, his face still agitated, Burgundy impulsively took Anjou and Berry aside and led them out of the main council chamber into an adjoining room.[13]

———◄◦►———

Only after John had sequestered himself with Anjou and Berry, and the three of them were out of the council's earshot, did John speak.

"I did it!" he burst out. "By the tempting of the Devil, I ordered the thing done!"

The others stared at him in amazement.

He had ordered Louis's assassination?

They could not believe it.

"The two lords, hearing this confession, were so astounded and sad at heart that they could hardly reply."

But once they absorbed what John had just told them, Anjou and Berry "began to berate him for what he had done and how he had gone about it — the cruel murder he had perpetrated on his own cousin."[14]

All this time, while celebrating Mass with Louis, swearing oaths of eternal friendship, and supping with him, he had been evilly plotting his murder! Even now, John was clothed in black, as was his entire household, the better to disguise his guilt.[15]

Berry, who thought that he had successfully reconciled the two dukes a few days earlier, saw his hopes for the nation's peace dashed. As surely as the assassins had split Louis's head, John had sundered the royal family, dooming France to untold violence and grief. The old duke burst into tears, exclaiming, "Now I have lost two nephews!"[16]

There were more tears and recriminations, but Anjou and Berry eventually recovered their composure. Anjou returned to the council chamber but "said nothing" of what had just passed in the other room.[17] He kept Burgundy's confession of guilt a secret — even from the Duke of Bourbon — and abruptly adjourned the meeting.

Guillaume left the palace. Like the others who had stayed in the council chamber, he was not privy to what Burgundy had said to the two lords. But he was in a better position than them to guess the truth: Louis's murderer had finally been unmasked.

Guillaume had no idea what would happen next, and he was hardly out of danger, for whatever had passed in the privacy of the other room, Burgundy must now fiercely hate him for having forced his hand.

As for searching Burgundy's palace, Guillaume had probably never expected to do so. His request for a search had been a ruse, a threat to drive his quarry into view. But even if the quarry had been flushed from hiding, he still remained at large.

And as long as Burgundy was at large, Guillaume had to look to his own safety, and that of his family.

———◇———

At ten o'clock the next morning, Saturday, the lords of France assembled again, this time at the Hôtel of Nesle, the Duke of Berry's residence.[18] The duke's palace fronted the Seine on the

Left Bank, across from the Louvre and near one of the towers anchoring the great iron chain that spanned the river at the city's western portal.[19]

Berry was there, of course, along with Anjou, and they had asked Bourbon to join them, as well as a few other great lords. But many nobles and officials, including the provost, were not invited this time.

John of Burgundy was not invited either. Berry and Anjou apparently wanted to discuss the situation in his absence and just among themselves, the remaining peers of France. A case of murder within the royal family would have national and even international repercussions.

But John defiantly showed up anyway. He came with some bodyguards, left his horse in the courtyard below, and climbed the stairs with his cousin Count Waleran of Luxembourg, who had arrived at the same time.[20]

As the two men were about to enter the council chamber, however, Berry came to the door and stopped John.

The day before, Berry had broken down on hearing John's astounding confession of guilt. But today, the elderly duke was composed and adamant:

"Good nephew, do not come in this time. No one here wants to see you."[21]

Berry went back inside, and, "as the council had ordered beforehand," he had all the doors locked against Burgundy.

At this, Burgundy was "very troubled and confused." He looked at Waleran and asked his cousin to leave with him. Waleran apologized but said he was going in, as he had been summoned to attend the meeting. John abruptly turned around and started back down the stairs "without a word."[22]

On his way, he nearly bumped into his uncle Louis of Bourbon, who had arrived late for the meeting and was puffing up the stairs.

"Where are you going?" Bourbon asked, surprised at his

nephew's hasty departure, still ignorant of John's confession the day before.

"I'm going out to piss," shouted John over his shoulder as he descended.[*23]

John exited Berry's palace, collected his retinue, mounted his horse, and set off for his own palace, "angrily vowing that he would return in force and keep his power despite the opposition of the princes."[24]

———◁▷———

When Bourbon joined his relatives in the council chamber, Anjou and Berry told him about John's confession the day before.

"Why did you let him escape?" asked the astonished Bourbon. "This thing must be handled in the right way. Now we must tell the king."[25] The three royal dukes went down, ordered their horses saddled, and set off for the royal palace.

The queen already knew about Louis's death and had fled her palace in fright after receiving the news on the night of the murder. But it is uncertain whether the king had yet been told the full truth. Since his most recent spell of madness, a year before, his sanity had often fluctuated, and he had "his highs and lows."[26] But if Charles did already know about his brother's murder, then he was about to receive another nasty shock — the news that Louis had been assassinated on the orders of their cousin.

———◁▷———

As his relatives went to see the king, Burgundy stopped at his palace only long enough to collect a couple of extra men — an adviser named Raoul Lemaire and another, Regnier Pot, who had been a comrade in arms at Nicopolis. Then John "jumped

---

★ The source says *"dit qu'il allait pisser."*

on a horse being held at the ready for him" and set off with these two men and four others, all armed and mounted on fast horses.[27]

On the night of the murder, John had made advance plans for an escape, dispatching several trusted men overnight to Lille, one of his Flemish towns, to assure him of a safe route and a ready reception should he need to flee at once.[28] But the next day, his tremendous secret still safe, John had instead remained in the city, boldly attending his cousin's funeral and dressed in mourning.

Now, spurred into action by his frosty reception at the council, he took the planned escape route. He and his men turned from the palace grounds into the Rue Saint-Denis and galloped toward the Porte Saint-Denis, about a third of a mile to the north.[29] The huge gatehouse, through which kings and queens entered the city and condemned criminals left it, was one of only two portals still open to traffic.[30] And it was closely guarded.

Just how John and his men got out of the gate is not known. Perhaps the duke blustered his way through, shouting that he was on the king's urgent business, and the guards, ignorant of his guilt, believed him. Or perhaps he and his party simply galloped through, forcing the soldiers to jump aside to avoid being trampled.

At any rate, soon they were through the gatehouse and thundering over the drawbridge. Once they were beyond the water-filled moat, the great outer ditch around the city wall came into view, and the countryside to the north opened up before them. John and his men spurred their horses past the houses lining the Rue Saint-Denis just outside the ramparts.[31] Any shouts at the gatehouse behind them were soon lost amid the rush of air and the pounding of hooves.

They were headed for Saint-Denis, about five miles distant, where they would skirt the last great loop of the Seine as it wound its way west to the sea. After Saint-Denis, they would take the high road north through Picardy to the county of Artois — Burgundian territory, John's own, where they would be safe.

As they galloped north, passing Montmartre to the west, the suburbs thinned out around them, soon turning to open country sectioned into farms and vineyards and dotted by villages and hamlets.

The weather had turned colder that week, with an early snowfall announcing the approach of winter.[32] But the road beneath the horses was still firm, and John's party could travel fast for the next several hours, while the sun lasted.

———◁◦▷———

The news of Burgundy's sudden flight quickly spread through Paris, and one of Louis's most loyal knights, Sir Clignet de Breban, decided to give chase. After assembling an armed and mounted troop of one hundred and twenty men, he led them out at a gallop through the same gate, the Porte Saint-Denis, vowing to avenge Louis's murder by "putting the Duke of Burgundy to death if they could catch him."[33]

Word soon reached the lords of France that one of Louis's knights had set off in pursuit of John with an armed and mounted troop. At once, the Duke of Anjou sent couriers galloping after Clignet de Breban and his soldiers with orders directing them to turn back and forbidding them to harm the duke.[34]

———◁◦▷———

On the same day, a tall man who had been hiding since Wednesday night at the Hôtel of Artois also slipped out of the city with several accomplices. "Having changed their clothes and disguised themselves," they traveled separately from Paris "by different routes." They were bound for a château in Artois that belonged to Burgundy, where safety and payment in gold awaited them.[35]

———◦———

John and his men raced northward through Picardy, not even stopping to change horses, according to reports, and halting only once while still in French territory.[36]

This was at Pont-Sainte-Maxence, on the river Oise, about forty miles north of Paris. After crossing the wooden bridge there, they stopped, dismounted, and attacked the bridge timbers with axes, breaking them down in order to delay any pursuers.[37] Back in the saddle, they rode on, galloping north past the towns of Roye and Nesle.

John's pursuers eventually reached the shattered bridge, and it stopped them in their tracks. Clignet de Breban reluctantly called off the chase and turned back.[38] There had been little chance of catching John anyway, since he and his men had gotten a good head start, and a small party could travel much faster than a large one.[39] But Clignet's foiled attempt to avenge Louis's death heralded the great conflict and division in France that was to come.

———◦———

By nightfall, John and his men were approaching the river Somme, beyond which lay the county of Artois. They had already covered nearly eighty miles, which was rare speed, as a typical day's journey on horseback was about a third of that.[40]

Sometime after sunset, John and his men crossed the Somme at Éclusier, where they stopped for supper, fresh horses, and a short rest, having long since outridden any pursuers. Still, John "slept scarcely at all" and soon was back in the saddle.[41] Now that it was dark and he was safely in Artois, John slowed his pace a bit. He also sent a courier riding ahead to Bapaume, a town about fifteen miles to the north, with orders to have a hot meal ready for him when he arrived, as well as a priest to celebrate Mass.[42]

At one o'clock in the morning, John and his men finally trotted into Bapaume.[43] It was Sunday, November 27 — the day that John was to have dined again with his cousin Louis. Legend has it that John ordered the church bells to be rung to commemorate his narrow escape from danger, and that "this midnight peal of bells" was repeated every year thereafter on the same date, a ritual that became known as the Angelus of Duke John.[44]

After hearing Mass and eating a very late meal, John finally fell into an exhausted sleep.

◦

By Saturday night, everyone in Paris knew that John had fled the capital — a coup de théâtre that astounded the whole city all over again.[45] Word of John's confession may also have leaked out, but to the popular mind, John's abrupt departure was the obvious proof of his guilt.[46]

If most Parisians recognized John's guilt, however, not all condemned Burgundy for ordering the assassination: "The people of Paris did not like the Duke of Orleans very much or hold him in good grace, on account of the taxes and other duties he had imposed on them. And they began to whisper to one another, *Le baston noueux est plané!*'" —"The knotty club has been planed!"[47] Some Parisians openly celebrated Louis's death, saying, "Blessed be he who struck the blow!"[48]

The king was mad, his brother was dead, and the murderer had fled the city, leaving France without a leader, but the people did not yet realize that a body cannot live without a head — or that the death of one tyrant often begets another.

12

The Justification

———◄◦►———

WITHIN DAYS OF John's hasty escape from Paris, tempera-
tures plunged across Northern Europe, and a fresh snowfall blocked the roads, imprisoning people in their towns and
villages. It was to be the worst winter in living memory, with a
great freeze locking everything in ice for over seventy days.
"Wine froze on the table; ink froze on the desk," water froze
right to the bottom of wells, and rock-hard bread had to be
thawed by the fire before it could be eaten. "It became possible
to walk over sea from Flanders to Zeeland, and all the rivers of
north-west Europe froze over."[1] As the gates of Paris remained
closed against robbers and wolves, food grew scarce, and prices
soared. Cattle froze in their stalls, people froze in their homes,
and even birds starved to death, unable to find any food "on
account of the thick snow and ice covering all the fields, trees,
and streams."[2]

Safe in his Flemish territories, with the terrible winter roads
helping to shield him from reprisals, the Duke of Burgundy
busied himself by gathering support from his family, friends,
and allies. A fugitive from justice who was guilty by his own
admission and yet completely unrepentant, John was embark-
ing "on a novel and audacious course of action: the justification
of his own crime."[3] He summoned his brothers, Anthony and

Philip, to a conference at Lille that began on December 3, exactly a week after his escape from Paris. Along with representatives from John's towns and territories, the men heard "a detailed account of the assassination in both French and Flemish."[4]

John next traveled to Ghent, fifty miles away by harsh winter road, where he convened an assembly of the three estates of Flanders—his principal knights, clerics, and burgesses. Also present were his brother-in-law, John of Bavaria, and other high-ranking nobles. Burgundy's chancellor read out "a formal justification of his crime"—an early draft of what would become a much longer, more elaborate legal defense.[5] Similar proclamations were made in other Burgundian towns and territories, including Bruges and Ypres.[6]

A chronicle by a monk at Ghent preserves the gist of John's initial defense. The monk, Jean Brandon, wrote that John's spokesmen accused Louis of having "opposed the reunification of the Church, saddling the people with onerous taxes, persecuting widows and orphans, violating highborn ladies, virgins, and nuns, causing the king's illness, and plotting to kill the Duke of Burgundy."[7] Despite these scandalous allegations, however, there was as yet no attempt to dignify Louis's murder as justifiable "tyrannicide." That would come later.

All this time, John kept up a stream of correspondence with his agents in Paris, to which he dispatched several more officials, including his chancellor, to strengthen his representation.[8] He also began exchanging letters with the royal dukes in Paris, aiming to return to the capital and rehabilitate himself by defending his crime before the king.

While John was busily rallying support, Louis's widow, Valentina Visconti, was also preparing to descend on Paris. Louis's funeral had fallen exactly on the birthday of his eldest son and

heir, Charles, who had just turned thirteen.[9] By the time a courier brought word of the murder to Château-Thierry, where Valentina was staying at the time, the duke's funeral was over.[10]

On hearing the horrible news, Valentina had "torn her hair and clothing, filling the air with her cries."[11] After two weeks in mourning, she finally pulled herself together and ordered her servants to prepare for a journey, despite the forbidding winter weather. "With a large retinue and all dressed in black," she rode to Paris as fast as she could in the cold and the snow, taking along two of her three sons.[12]

On Saturday, December 10, as Valentina approached the city with her entourage, the Dukes of Anjou, Berry, and Bourbon rode out to meet her with "a great number of men and horses" and escorted her back to the city.[13] This apparent show of solidarity by the lords of France gave Louis's widow reason to hope that she would find not only sympathy for her loss but also support for the vengeance she had come to demand.

King Charles, enjoying an interlude of sanity, personally welcomed the duchess to court. All in black, now in tears and with her sons in tow, Valentina "threw herself down on her knees before the king and raised a most pitiable complaint about the cruel murder of her husband and lord."[14]

In front of the hushed assembly, she tearfully recalled the horrible murder scene as it had been described to her—Louis's shattered head, his many stab wounds, his severed hand, and his body thrown insultingly on the mud. She likened his murderer, John of Burgundy, to the arch-traitor Judas Iscariot, and she implored Charles to avenge the crime that had widowed her and left her children without a father: "Use your power to bring the guilty to justice!"[15]

This was the first time Charles had laid eyes on Valentina since she had been forced to leave the court ten years earlier amid rumors that she had bewitched him.[16] The king, moved to "tears" himself by Valentina's grief, raised her to her feet and "kissed her," promising that he would take up her case with his royal council.[17] Thus reassured, Valentina left the palace to lodge at the nearby Hôtel of Orleans.

The following week, Valentina had another audience with the king, this time before his council.[18] With her were Louis's chancellor and "many knights and squires, all dressed in mourning." The king received her with his own chancellor, along with the three royal dukes—Anjou, Berry, and Bourbon—who had informed Charles of Burgundy's guilt on the day of John's flight from Paris.

Valentina broke down again, "weeping profusely" as she renewed her appeals for justice.[19] Then, on her behalf, Louis's chancellor itemized the case against the murderers, clearly using information collected by Guillaume: how the assassins had spied on Louis beforehand and lain in wait for him, how they had tricked and betrayed him with a false message from the king, how they had murdered him at a certain time and place, how this murder was tantamount to regicide, and how the king was now duty-bound to avenge his brother's death on behalf of the duchess and her children—his own nephews—for the sake of family blood ties and also his own sovereign majesty.[20]

Once this brief had been read out, the king's chancellor responded formally for Charles, affirming that "the king will do good and expedient justice as quickly as he can." Then Charles himself spoke, saying, "Let it be known to all that the case here presented touches us"—*nous*, the royal "we"—"as though it were committed against our own proper person."[21] This was a public declaration that the king regarded Louis's murder as nothing less than high treason and an attack on the throne.

Two days later, just before Christmas, the king sat in state with his Parlement at the old royal palace in La Cité to decree a new arrangement for the succession.[22] Since Louis had been empowered as regent to rule in case of the king's incapacity, his death left the future of the realm uncertain. Charles now placed the underage dauphin in the queen's protection, authorizing his coronation no matter how young and granting him the power to rule in the event of both the king's and the queen's incapacity. Without any direct mention of him in these proceedings, John of Burgundy, the dauphin's father-in-law, was thus excluded from the government of France.

Right after New Year's—when nobles at court traditionally exchanged golden drinking vessels, jewelry, and other lavish gifts known as *étrennes*—Charles held yet another audience.[23] The king granted to Valentina and her children all the rights and lands that normally would have reverted to the king on her husband's death, thus assuring her eldest son and her other children of their inheritance.

Together, these various royal acts and edicts assured Valentina that she would have the king's justice and that the slaying of her husband would be properly avenged. Shortly afterward, the duchess left Paris with her children, apparently fearing Burgundy's imminent return.[24] Later the same day, Charles had a relapse of his illness and fell back into madness.[25] Rumors spread that Valentina herself was the cause and that once again she had been practicing sorcery on the king.[26]

---◦►---

Although the royal dukes had welcomed Valentina to Paris with great fanfare and had personally witnessed the king's promises to her, once Charles fell ill again and they again took charge, they chose a different course. Rather than pursuing justice against John or confronting him with his crime, they instead continued the negotiations with him that had begun in December.

The crisis caused by Louis's assassination and its stunning aftermath, far from uniting the royal family into an outraged bloc against Burgundy, had "shattered and demoralized them."

While some, like Valentina, sought revenge, others "wished to pardon John," mainly because of the very real threat of civil war.[27] Although John formally owed fealty to France, he ruled what was virtually a rival kingdom—the adjoining duchy and county known as "the two Burgundies," plus many rich territories in Flanders.[28] Now safe in his own lands, he would never give himself up, and the royal family could hardly take him by force. As the dukes all recognized, the fierce veteran of Nicopolis "really knew how to use an army," and from his many walled and well-armed towns—Bruges, Ghent, Antwerp, and Dijon—he could march a forest of steel to Paris in a matter of days.[29] To reunite the royal family and prevent further bloodshed, perhaps some sort of settlement would be best.

Around the time of Valentina's arrival in Paris, the royal dukes had dispatched an emissary, Count Waleran of Luxembourg, to offer John a deal. At Lille, Waleran had told John that the royal family was prepared to offer him immunity if he would simply hand over the assassins. John had indignantly rejected the offer, insisting that his deed had nothing criminal about it, and he therefore required no such amnesty. In addition, he refused "to betray those whom he had agreed to protect."[30]

Faced with John's refusal, the royal dukes tried another tack. In late December, while Valentina was still in Paris obtaining the king's assurances of justice, Anjou and Berry secretly arranged to meet with John for talks during the third week of January.[31] The proposed venue, Amiens, was more than eighty miles north of Paris but only twenty miles or so from the border of Artois, sufficiently close to John's own territory to tempt him to show up. To smooth the way toward a reconciliation, the royal dukes also paid John a substantial sum, restoring his suspended annual pension of thirty-six thousand francs and thus appeasing him on one of the most divisive issues over which he had quarreled with Louis—money.[32]

Other royals—including the queen—also sought to placate John. Isabeau was rumored to have been sleeping with Louis at the time of his murder, and of course, two years earlier, she had conspired with Louis to remove the dauphin from Paris. But now, alert to a change in the political winds and apparently eager to forge a new bond with the man who had ordered her alleged lover's death, Isabeau sent Burgundy an *étrenne,* a conciliatory New Year's gift—perhaps a jewel or one of the gold drinking vessels traditionally exchanged at this time of year.*[33]

Only one ranking member of the royal family refused to countenance Burgundy. This was the elderly Duke of Bourbon, the last of the royal dukes to learn of John's guilt and the first to ask why the others had not arrested him instead of letting him escape. Indignant at the prospect of his murderous nephew's rehabilitation and return, the old duke left Paris and retreated to his own estates in the duchy of Bourbon.[34]

—◇—

By mid-January, plans for the meeting at Amiens were set. With a small army as escort, John crossed back into French territory, while Berry and Anjou made their way north from Paris with their own retinue. The great winter freeze had not yet broken, and the two royal dukes depended on "large numbers of peasants with shovels to clear the snow off the road in front of them."[35]

John arrived at Amiens on January 20, accompanied by his two brothers and a troop of 261 knights and squires.[36] At his lodgings in town, he displayed over his doorway a painted banner depicting a sharp lance of war and a blunted lance of peace. In chivalric tradition, the one symbolized mortal combat, the

---

* The nature of the gift is not recorded, nor is that of John's *étrenne* to Isabeau two years later, but some years after that he would give her a cut diamond in an enamel setting.

other a friendly joust. The clear message was that Burgundy would give the royal dukes whatever they wanted: war or peace.[37]

What Berry and Anjou hoped to obtain at the conference was an apology from John for his crime that might enable them to reconcile the fractured royal family and appease Louis's vengeful relatives.[38] But during the ten-day conference, they made no progress at all toward this goal. John, flanked by his lawyers and advisers, behaved "in a proud, arrogant manner," defiantly insisting that killing Louis had been a case of justifiable homicide.[39] In support of this claim, John ordered yet another public reading of his defense of Louis's murder, and, more alarmingly, he declared that he would now go to Paris to justify his cause in person before the king.

For the two frustrated royal dukes, the council was a defeat. For Burgundy, it was a victory, although his projected return to Paris to defend his crime would inevitably inflame the Orleanists and push France closer to civil war. The only thing Anjou and Berry managed to extract from John was a promise that he would enter Paris with no more than two hundred men-at-arms.[40]

———◆———

As the chilly conference broke up at Amiens, the great winter freeze also came to an end. But initial relief at the warming weather quickly turned to fear, as thawing snow flooded farms and villages, and loosened ice wreaked havoc on the waterways. "On the larger rivers," wrote an eyewitness, "I saw huge white ice floes three hundred feet long, like enormous blocks of stone."[41] Raging floodwaters swept away houses and mills, drowning "many men, women and children" and a great deal of livestock.[42] Boats and barges were smashed to bits, and bridges torn from their pilings and wrecked. In Paris, many low-lying streets along the Seine flooded, and acres of ice carried downstream by the currents piled up behind the Pont Saint-Michel, a newly built bridge lined with shops and houses. As horrified crowds watched, the huge weight of the accumulated ice separated the bridge from its supports and raised it up into the air like an apparition contrary to nature, causing it to break apart and tip the hastily emptied houses into the frigid river.[43]

———◄◦►———

In mid-February, soon after the great thaw, John assembled an army of eight hundred men-at-arms and set off from Amiens. On February 25 he stopped at Saint-Denis, a few miles north of Paris, and heard Mass at the royal chapel filled with the tombs of French kings.[44] There he was met again by the Dukes of Berry and Anjou, who had summoned their own troops to Paris and ridden out to caution John not to enter the city with more than two hundred men, as he had earlier promised. John defiantly ignored their warning.

Three days later John led his army into Paris through the Porte Saint-Denis, the same gate through which he had fled the city not so long before. The other royal dukes made no attempt to stop him, apparently resigned to John's return and wishing to avoid an armed confrontation. Enthusiastic Parisians "poured out of their houses" into the streets to welcome Burgundy, and "even little children" shouted "Noël!"—a popular cry generally reserved for greeting the birth of a royal heir or a king's return to the city.[45] As an eyewitness described it, "He made his entry in full armor, to the great astonishment of all, as though returning in triumph from a victory over the enemies of the realm. He was escorted by eight hundred knights and squires divided into three corps and armed head to foot, with only their heads bared."[46] Everywhere the cry went up: *"Vive le duc de Bourgogne!"*[47] It was an auspicious return for a man who had so recently fled the city as a confessed murderer and hunted fugitive.

John immediately went to pay his respects to the dauphin, Louis, his eleven-year-old son-in-law, since the king was again "absent."[48] Then he took up residence once more in his imposing stone palace, the Hôtel of Artois, where he had sheltered the assassins after Louis's murder and whose premises he had departed in haste a few days afterward.

Despite the warm popular welcome greeting his return, John took no chances with his life, for he was still officially persona non grata and had many enemies, both open and secret. "Two companies of crossbowmen" were soon "escorting him through the streets to ensure his personal safety."[49] John's menacing retinue "greatly alarmed the other princes and the royal council. But no one dared to say or do anything that would annoy him, because he was very popular with the people, and he always had with him a strong troop of soldiers and kept his palace well garrisoned."[50]

To make his palace even more secure, John immediately set about improving its fortifications. The Hôtel of Artois stood astride the old city wall of Philip-Augustus, incorporating a half dozen of its tall round watchtowers and surrounded by a high, sturdy wall.[51] The wall bristled with battlements and machicolations (parapets jutting from the top that were pierced with holes so projectiles could be dropped on attackers below). But John now ordered the construction of an even more secure redoubt within his heavily defended palace: a new stone tower, ninety feet high, from which he would rule his domain.

The tower, whose construction actually began several weeks before John's return, would take three years to complete.[52] Built entirely of quarried limestone and costing fourteen thousand francs, it had walls two feet thick, pierced by arrow slits in case of siege. A narrow spiral stairway inside the tower was guarded by a portcullis, a heavy iron grate that could drop down in an instant to prevent ambush from within. At the top of the tower was the duke's private bedchamber, equipped with its own latrine to save him the trouble and danger of exiting. Below was a council chamber where John conducted business. Under these, and from the central pillar of a larger, more decorative staircase, sprouted a stone tree with intricately carved foliage representing John's lineage:

chestnut leaves for his father, hawthorn for his mother, and hops for John himself. But no amount of ornament could disguise the paranoia that built this medieval panic room. Its main purpose, wrote a chronicler, was to let John "sleep there in safety at night, as it was perfectly constructed to safeguard his life."[53] A personal refuge and a symbol of power, the tower was also a declaration that John meant to stay in Paris, justify his deed, and defend himself against all enemies.

Duke John's tower. Bristling with fortifications, the tower also had fireplaces, a latrine, and a carved stone stairway.

———◄○►———

Scarcely a week after his return to Paris, and almost three months to the day after Valentina had tearfully denounced him at the royal court and called for vengeance, John orchestrated another, even more grandiose, public defense of his crime. The highlight of his return to Paris and a spectacular piece of political theater, it was the largest and most elaborate presentation so far of what came to be known as the Justification. All previous performances were mere rehearsals that paled by comparison.

For the Paris performance of the Justification, John picked as his spokesman a noted scholar and celebrated orator named Jean Petit, a leading member of the legal team that had been preparing Burgundy's defense over the past several months. Petit, forty-five, held a doctorate in theology from the University of Paris and had been employed by the Burgundy family for over twenty years.[54] A Norman by birth and combative in the extreme, he had taken part in all the leading intellectual disputes of the day. His vigorous attacks on the Avignon pope in particular had brought him into favor with Philip the Bold and into the duke's stable of loyal scholars and clerics. Petit now served the son as he had the father. John assigned him the key task of delivering the Justification, not only for his prowess at argument and debate but also for his vocal endurance: Petit could speak for hours on end without flagging.

John chose his venue as carefully as he chose his rhetorical champion.[55] The court first offered him the Louvre, which he rejected, and then the old royal palace in La Cité, which he also refused, insisting on the Hôtel Saint-Pol, the king's main residence. The Hôtel Saint-Pol was synonymous with royal power and prestige as well as with the sanctity of the king's own person. By dragging his bloody crime and his defiant defense of it into the midst of the royal court, John had already won another symbolic victory.

On March 8, a Thursday, "between six and seven o'clock" in the morning, the invited guests began arriving at the king's palace.[56] Their destination was the Grande Salle, an ornate and cavernous room that could accommodate an audience of many hundreds.[57] In an irony that Burgundy must have savored, since it added a macabre force to his case against Louis, this was the same room where the disastrous Bal des Ardents had taken place fifteen years earlier.[58]

The most important guests arrived first, beginning with Louis the dauphin, standing in for the king, who was still "confined by illness."[59] Escorting the dauphin were "Louis of Anjou, the Dukes of Berry and Brittany, the Duke of Bar, the counts of Alençon and Tancarville," and other royals.[60] But this time, not even the greatest lords entered the king's palace in the manner to which they were accustomed. For security reasons, John had ordered that all the invited guests be listed by name in advance — making it a "ticketed event" — and that all entrances to the hall be closed and guarded except for one door-like window,* facing the courtyard, through which everyone had to enter and leave.[61] "One by one," the dauphin and the other nobles, all colorfully berobed, stepped through the carefully guarded window; they were followed by other members of the royal council, representatives of the Parlement and the university, and many city officials, as well as "a great number of common people."[62]

Meanwhile, John himself was riding to the palace on horseback "with a brilliant entourage."[63] Three great lords, including the Duke of Lorraine and the cardinal of Bar, rode on his right, and four others on his left, with many others trotting along "ahead and behind." John's mounted retinue was so long

---

* In all likelihood, this was a French window, or *porte-fenêtre*, perhaps opening onto a terrace that was reached by way of a temporary wooden staircase built in the courtyard below.

that "as the last of them were leaving his *hôtel,* the first of them were arriving at the royal palace," a distance of a mile or so, and "the streets in between were filled with Burgundy's horses."[64] As this grand procession wound through the city, John nodded this way and that in his saddle, greeting "the huge crowds of people" packing the streets and cheering him "from their windows." The adoring crowds, grateful to John for having saved them from Louis's tyranny, loudly "prayed to God that He would help the duke achieve his just and true ambition."[65] By the time John arrived at the royal palace, he was in "a very good humor."[66]

By now the great hall was packed, and most of the invited dignitaries had taken their seats. John let his entourage precede him through the one well-guarded window, and then he himself entered last, "all alone."[67] As he stepped over the sill, all could see that he wore "his customary black hat" and a vivid scarlet robe "trimmed with fur and covered with golden fleurs de lis," the royal insignia.[68] But beneath his elegant robe glinted the woven steel rings of a mail vest, "which all could see whenever he lifted an arm," another sign that despite his defiant attitude, John lived in mortal fear of assassination. As soon as he entered the room, the window was secured behind him.

The great lords were already seated together on the dais at the front of the hall. John turned to face them, his bright red robe aswirl, and doffed his hat in a show of respect.[69] Then he went over and joined them, sitting down between the Dukes of Berry and Brittany—purposely near the dauphin, who sat on the other side of Berry.

———◦———

Also seated at the front of the hall, carefully watching everything, was Guillaume de Tignonville, who had been invited in his capacity as provost of Paris. Guillaume sat with his sergeants on "a scaffold having six rows of seats" that flanked the dais "to the right."[70] With him on the same scaffold were the king's chancellor and other members of the royal council. Opposite Guillaume, on a similar scaffold to the left, sat Jean Petit, flanked by Burgundy's chancellor, lawyers, and advisers.

Guillaume could hardly have refused to attend what was, in a sense, an official legal hearing about Louis's murder. But he must have been painfully aware that this was no honest tribunal like the royally appointed one over which he presided at the Châtelet. Rather, it was a bold mockery of justice. Charged by the royal dukes to find those responsible for Louis's murder, he had faithfully done his duty, mobilizing his army of sergeants and clerics to investigate the crime, ransacking the city for evidence and witnesses, and ultimately tracking the arch criminal to his lair and even prompting him to confess—after which the lords of France had simply let him get away. Now he had to watch in impotent silence as Burgundy, a confessed murderer and fugitive, was allowed to orchestrate his own rehabilitation, abetted by growing popular support and the cowardly submission of the same royal dukes who had given Guillaume his charge to pursue justice and the truth.

Seated at the front of the hall in full view of everyone, Guillaume must have felt betrayed on all sides—by the indecisive royal family, by the fluctuating court, by the fickle people—and he doubtless seethed with indignation as Burgundy publicly thumbed his nose at him and began an ostentatious defense of his treacherous and bloody deed.

As Guillaume himself had once written, "There is no shame in doing justice."[71] Was there now to be no shame in publicly defending a heinous crime?

◄◦►

Once Burgundy took his seat on the dais at the front, an expectant hush fell over the cavernous hall.

Jean Petit, wearing his clerical robes, rose and went to the lectern. He turned to the lords seated behind him and knelt, saying that he did not wish to incur their displeasure but that he was bound to say what he was about to say "as the servant of my lord the Duke of Burgundy."[72]

Rising again, Petit began his speech proper.[73] First he cited his scriptural text, "Covetousness is the root of all evil," a familiar passage calculated to indict Louis's greed and luxurious style of living.[74] Then, following well-worn academic custom, Petit stated his thesis, which took the classic form of a syllogism:

Major: It is permissible and meritorious to kill a tyrant.
Minor: The Duke of Orleans was a tyrant.
Conclusion: Therefore the Duke of Burgundy did well to kill him.

This piece of sophistry must have astounded many people in the room that day. Private acts of vengeance had been defended in the past, and the law sometimes excused them. But a personal vendetta had never been justified in the name of the king or the safety of the realm. The stunning audacity of Petit's argument was to elevate a murder ordered in cold blood and treacherously carried out for manifestly personal reasons to the level of raison d'état.[75]

In keeping with academic tradition, much of the argument that Petit put forward over the next several hours to support his preposterous thesis depended heavily on written sources, or "authorities."[76] From the great universities and well-stocked monastic libraries down to the humblest parish church with little more than a mass book, certain ancient texts reigned supreme. Petit, a doctor of theology well versed in such materials, accordingly marshaled a vast array of quotations—from scripture, the Church fathers, canon law, civil law, and other sources—to vindicate his thesis. He cited no fewer than a dozen precedents "in honor of the twelve Apostles," a kind of sacred symmetry that appealed to an age when numerology enjoyed an almost mystical status.[77] One of the twelve precedents, clearly chosen to put Burgundy's sanguinary deed in the best possible light, was the example of the archangel Michael, "who without a command from God or any other but wholly out of natural love, defeated and sent to everlasting death the tyrant and traitor Lucifer, who had plotted against his king and sovereign lord God in order to usurp his honor and lordship."[78] Louis, the logic went, was demonic, while John, his righteous foe, was allied with the angels.

But the most riveting part of Petit's speech was the lengthy catalog of poisonings, witchcraft, treason, and other crimes he alleged against Louis as "evidence" that he had secretly sought to harm his brother the king. As a chief example of Louis's supposed treachery, Petit told the following story, preserved in all of its lurid details by his own script, which survives, and also in the notes of a cleric employed by John of Burgundy to keep a careful record of the proceedings:

> The duke made the acquaintance of an apostate monk, a knight, a squire, and a servant who knew how to go about the devil's own work. He ordered them to do a thing that would destroy the king, and to accomplish this he gave them the use of a castle at Lagny-sur-Marne called Montjoy. He also gave them a sabre, a sword, and a gold ring.
>
> One morning at dawn these four men left the castle and traveled a quarter of a league to a field where there was a thicket. The monk told the other three to wait there until he called for them and then went a little way off by himself, carrying the sabre, the sword, and the ring. The monk drew a figure on the ground and placed the sword inside it on the right, the sabre on the left, and the ring in the middle. Then he stripped himself to his shirt and began reading aloud from a book. Soon a devil

appeared. It picked up the sabre and put it down again. Then came another devil, wearing red. It picked up the sword, swung it around, broke off the tip, and told the monk that the thing was done. After this the monk returned to the other three men, and they all went back to the castle.

The following night, the four men left the castle again and went to the gibbet at Montfaucon, where they cut down the corpse of a newly hanged man and put it in a sack on the back of a horse. Since day was breaking, and they were ten leagues from the castle, they agreed to take the dead body to the knight's house in Paris and put it in the stable. Afterwards they placed the ring in the corpse's mouth and passed the sword and the sabre into its anus. Then they said to each other: "It is done." After this they went to the Duke of Orleans and told him that shortly there would be some news.

Soon afterwards, when the king was at Beauvais, he fell gravely ill, so that his hair and nails fell out. And very soon after this the king went to Meaux on pilgrimage, and he was so tormented by his illness that it was a great pity to see. And in his illness he cried: "Save me from the sword-strokes of my brother Orleans! Kill my brother Orleans, for he is killing me!" And from that time on the king was ill, as is known throughout the whole realm, which is a pity. And it is well-known to everyone that the Duke of Orleans was to blame for this illness.[79]

After telling this sordid tale—a carefully crafted piece of folklore meant to appall the audience and ruin whatever was left of Louis's reputation—Petit elaborated on Louis's alleged plots against his brother the king.[80] He claimed that the same apostate monk had provided Louis with a cherry branch dipped in the blood of a red rooster and a white hen that could be used to injure the king; that Louis had conspired with his father-in-law, the Duke of Milan, to do away with Charles; that several times he had tried to poison the king and the dauphin; that he had made a secret pact with Henry Bolingbroke to usurp their respective thrones; that he had tried to force Queen Isabeau and her children out of France; that he had plotted with the Avignon pope to make himself king; that he had posted troops to different castles in France in order to seize power; and that he had levied heavy taxes on the people in the name of national defense while actually using the revenues to fund his own designs on the throne.

And there was also the infamous Bal des Ardents. Louis was to have joined the wild men himself, said Petit, but he had refused at the last second, saying his costume did not fit. Nonetheless, just minutes later, Louis carried a lit torch into the midst of the dancing revelers, asking which one was the king "in order to set fire to his clothing."[81] Madame Burgundy had helped save the king from disaster by throwing her mantle about him.[82] Some of the nobles attending Petit's speech in the Grande Salle had personally witnessed the disaster in the same room fifteen years earlier, and they may have been surprised to learn of Madame Burgundy's central role in saving the king— a story that Petit seems to have invented for the occasion.

Winding down, Petit returned to his theme that the Duke of Burgundy had faithfully served the king and the realm by killing the king's brother and thus removing the tyrant and traitor Louis from their midst. As a result, there was to be no question of prosecuting or punishing him. Rather, Petit urged, the Duke of Burgundy should receive a royal pardon for his loyal service to the king and be rewarded with "love, honor, and riches."[83]

——◁◦▷——

Petit had begun speaking at ten in the morning, and when he finished it was two in the afternoon.[84] The audience had sat through the whole four-hour performance in complete silence. There was only one interruption. During the story about the swords enchanted by devils, the young dauphin—Burgundy's son-in-law—piped up and asked one of the other lords on the dais whether his uncle Louis had really tried to kill the king.[85] But apart from this brief commotion, everyone in the hall sat still for the entire production, a feat of collective endurance almost as astonishing as the remarkable endurance of the speaker himself.

When Petit finally finished, he knelt again and asked Burgundy to make an avowal, a public acknowledgment that everything in the speech had been said at John's express command. Petit, having acted as Burgundy's spokesman, wished to absolve himself of any guilt should his claims find disfavor with the court.

John rose from his seat on the dais, removed his hat, and said loudly so that everyone in the great hall could hear, *"Je vous avoue"*—"I acknowledge you."[86]

"Thank you, my lord!" Petit replied, and he stood up again, his services as a kind of devil's advocate concluded for now.[87]

Witnessing all of this from the dais at the front of the hall, Guillaume de Tignonville must have found Petit's speech very ominous and disturbing. The University of Paris was hardly the first—or last—academic body to betray the truth and further an injustice. But seeing the university's power and prestige thus marshaled, Guillaume must have realized that his own days as provost were numbered.

———◄○►———

By that evening, the contents of the Justification had been reported throughout the city. Louis's partisans were outraged, privately calling the accusations against him "false and deceptive, while the Burgundians maintained the contrary."[88] But no one dared to openly criticize John or his defense of tyrannicide in the king's name. The speech delivered that day by Jean Petit on Burgundy's behalf has been called by a leading scholar of

the period "one of the most insolent pieces of political chica-
nery and theological casuistry in all history."[89] But for the
moment, at least, it seemed to have silenced nearly all
opposition.

Taking advantage of the momentum, Burgundy, a master of
propaganda, at once began a pamphlet war, ordering his scribes
and clerics to copy out and disseminate the Justification in the
form of numerous paper and parchment booklets to be sent
around France and throughout Europe.[90] He also commissioned a number of deluxe illuminated copies as gifts for his
friends and relatives. Several of these presentation copies survive; its painted frontispiece sums up John's defense of tyrannicide in a single image.[91] It shows a fierce lion (John) clawing
a wolf (Louis) who has seized a crown in its jaws—a political
allegory for Burgundy's self-proclaimed defense of the king
and the realm.[92]

<hr />

As soon as the Justification had been presented at the royal palace, John pressed for an audience with the king, who had not
attended. Charles, scarcely recovered from his latest bout of
insanity, was still in a vulnerable state, a fact that John was
doubtless counting on.[93]

On March 9, the very next day, John rode again with great
pomp to the Hôtel Saint-Pol and was received there by Charles
as the rest of the royal family and the lords of France looked
on.[94] Preying on the feebleminded king's paranoia, John had a
cleric summarize the allegations about Louis's treacherous plots,
presenting highlights from the much longer speech delivered
the day before. Charles, who not so long ago had tearfully
embraced the widowed Valentina and solemnly promised to
avenge her husband's murder with royal justice, did not raise a
single question about the charges against Louis, however preposterous. At once he "mildly and gently" pardoned John for

ordering the murder and signed a letter declaring that "he had removed all 'displeasure' from his heart."[95]

Charles then signed a second letter, doubtless prepared in advance by Burgundy, which granted John the right to pursue anyone who tried to "dishonor" him.[96] In effect, the king was giving Burgundy carte blanche to punish his enemies and detractors as he saw fit, an opportunity that John would waste no time in exploiting to the fullest.[97]

Before Burgundy left the palace, the king warned him to beware of any traps his enemies might set, advice that Charles might better have given to his own brother a few months earlier.[98]

John — despite his mail vest, his bodyguards, and the great stone tower in progress betraying his own dread of assassination — arrogantly replied, "I fear no one."

13

Amende Honorable

————◁○▷————

AFTER HIS TRIUMPHAL return to Paris and his astounding royal pardon, Burgundy, riding a wave of popular support, began to strike out at his enemies. The royal court had feared just such a backlash, and a hasty exodus from Paris began. The queen, who had tried to appease John even before his return, left the capital on March 12, only three days after his royal pardon.[1] Isabeau took all of her children with her, including the dauphin, apparently afraid that Burgundy would try to assume control of his son-in-law, the heir to the throne. The Dukes of Anjou and Berry soon followed her, joining the queen at Melun. There, on March 18, they held a meeting of the royal council.[2] Charles was conspicuously absent. The day after he pardoned John, he had fallen ill again, "speaking in strange and marvelous languages." His condition was worse, people said, than it had been at any time during the past ten years, and for now he remained in Paris with Burgundy.[3]

Burgundy's reprisals were not aimed at the royals, however, but at various royal servants who had incurred his hatred. These he now drove from office, replacing them "with those who pleased him."[4] One of his main targets was Louis's loyal knight Clignet de Breban, who had set off in pursuit of John with an armed troop after Burgundy's escape from Paris.

Clignet reportedly had aimed to avenge Louis's death by capturing and killing John. Now John revenged himself on Clignet, taking advantage of the fact that as admiral of France, a royal appointment, Clignet could be summarily dismissed at the king's pleasure.* Using his new influence over the dithering and afflicted king, who had been almost completely abandoned for the moment by the rest of the royal family, John had Clignet sacked from his post on April 23 and replaced by one of his own picked men.[5]

Burgundy's chief target for revenge, however, was the provost of Paris, Guillaume de Tignonville, the diligent man of law who had forced his confession and sudden flight from the city. Guillaume, too, had been at the royal council meeting on March 18, a gathering of the anti-Burgundian faction that "had greatly displeased" Duke John.[6] The provost, like the admiral, was a royal appointee who served at the king's pleasure, so Guillaume's position was vulnerable too. And Guillaume's continuing quarrel with a third party would give Burgundy just the lever he needed to pry him from his official post.

———◄◊►———

In the wake of Louis's sensational murder and John's flight from Paris, many people had forgotten the controversial execution of the two self-professed clerics at Montfaucon. Both of the hanged men had claimed clerical benefits, only to be disavowed by the university. But following student protests, the university had reversed itself and complained to the king that the provost had overstepped his authority and violated the university's rights.[7] On November 18, less than a week before Louis's murder, the royal council met at the Louvre to hear the case, the dauphin presiding in the king's place.[8] Also present was John of

---

* As admiral of France, Clignet had also been responsible for the attack on English shipping in October 1407 that had angered Burgundy.

Burgundy, whose paid assassins were making their final plans to kill Louis just days later. Burgundy had no idea at the time how useful the two hanged men would eventually prove to be.

All through December and during the long winter freeze, the executions continued to occupy university officials. By Christmas, the university had called a general strike, suspending classes in protest and also placing a moratorium on public preaching by its clerics, thus depriving Parisians at large of essential spiritual benefits.[9]

When John returned to Paris two months later to defend himself, the university was still pressing its case against the provost. The university had already sent letters and emissaries to the duke complaining that the provost had "scandalized" the clergy and the Church and asking for Burgundy's help against their mutual enemy.[10] Now having an eager, powerful ally in the university, John seized on the quarrel to take revenge against the provost.

Even before Burgundy's return, Guillaume seems to have anticipated the duke's next move. On February 10, the day after work on John's new tower began and the same day that the Parlement got word of John's imminent return, the imperiled provost addressed the high court, saying he had received reports of bodies stolen from the Montfaucon gibbet by "certain criminals or sorcerers."[11] Perhaps foreseeing an attempt by the university to remove the two clerics from Montfaucon, Guillaume painted this sort of meddling with the law as nothing less than the Devil's work. That case was over, he implied, and those who hoped to revive it were of a dark and sinister sort.

◄◦►

The University of Paris, the most prestigious school of any kind in Europe, where Thomas Aquinas and other luminaries had taught, jealously guarded its rights and privileges.[12] The famous university attracted students and masters from every nation, bringing wealth and prestige to the city, conferring an aura of learning on the kings of France, making Paris a great hub of book production, and enriching shopkeepers and tradespeople by its consumption of goods and services.[13] However, the university brought conflict as well: The students—all male, in those days—were often at odds with the city, whether over the jurisdiction of a legal case or the prices charged by shopkeepers in the Latin Quarter.[14] Tensions between town and gown, a social division dating from this time, often led to violence, as with the brawl that began in 1365 when "some sergeants turned up on the Left Bank to collect tax on the sale of horses," and the "battle and strife" between the butchers of Sainte-Geneviève and some students in 1395.[15]

The university had its own royal charter and was independent of secular law. If it felt that the city had trampled its rights, it could appeal to the king and censure the offenders.*[16] In 1304, the provost convicted and hanged five clerics for various crimes, one of whom turned out to be innocent. The university complained to the king, and the Church excommunicated the provost. He was forced to walk to Montfaucon to "unhang" the innocent cleric; he cut down the body and accompanied it across the city, stopping at every street to lay his hand on the bier, confess his error to the crowd, and ask them to pray for the deceased.[17]

More recently, another provost who ran afoul of the university had nearly been burned at the stake. Hugh Aubriot, appointed provost in 1367 by Charles V, had not only paved streets and refurbished ports to improve the city's commerce but also energetically attacked its vices.[18] But he made many enemies with

---

* In 1229, a student was killed in a riot in the Latin Quarter, and the university faculty, obtaining no redress, left Paris for more than a year, returning only as a result of the pope's intervention.

his harsh sentences against offenders. Soon after the king died in 1380, the bishop of Paris, with the university's collusion, had Hugh arrested and charged with heresy. After a secret trial in a Church court, he was convicted and condemned. He escaped the stake only by kneeling before the bishop and performing an *amende honorable* in front of Notre-Dame, although he ended his days under house arrest.

The Dukes of Burgundy had long been allied with the university, and John, like his father, Philip, had busily recruited able scholars and clerics from its ranks to staff his sprawling administration and serve the Burgundian cause. One who had repaid his hire many times over with loyal service was Jean Petit, the theologian and orator who had so ably served as John's mouthpiece at his Justification. As Petit had shown, a university man could twist logic and rhetoric to serve any convenient cause, however base or disreputable—and the disorderly students who populated the Latin Quarter, punctuating their studies with drunken brawls and debauchery, did not exactly argue for a close tie between education and morality.[19] Nor did the fact that university men brought up on criminal charges often escaped prosecution or serious punishment by claiming benefit of clergy—a benefit unavailable to poor commoners dragged off to the scaffold or the gibbet.[20]

"At the university," said a chronicler, "were some Norman students well-disposed toward the Duke of Burgundy, and they knew that the duke was eager to have the provost removed from office and to replace him with someone more favorable to himself."[21] The Normans, who claimed one of the two hanged men as their own, enlisted the university chancellor and the powerful bishop of Paris, Pierre d'Orgemont, to buttress their complaint to the king that the provost had "insulted" the university by trampling on its time-honored rights and privileges.[22]

On April 6, King Charles became personally involved, issuing a letter addressed to Guillaume and his lieutenant on behalf of the Church and the university. Guillaume had already lost his most powerful ally with Louis's death, and he realized he had lost the support of the other royal dukes when they let John get away with murder. Now he lost the king's protection as well. The royal letter had the force of law and affirmed the university's suspension of teaching and preaching, forbidding the people to assemble at any church in Paris.[23] Just like that, the public, who had once admired the provost's even-handed justice—including his prosecution of the two thieves whose hangings had come back to haunt him—turned against Guillaume, blaming him for the university strike now depriving them of spiritual benefits.[24]

On April 30, by another royal decree, Guillaume was stripped of his office, his seal, his hat, his robes, his post at the Châtelet, his annual salary, his hundreds of sergeants and clerics, and also his personal bodyguard, the Twelve.[25] (Had he not owned a house in the Rue Béthisy, he would have lost his home as well.) Guillaume's lieutenant, Robert de Tuillières, who had helped to direct the investigation and track down Louis's killers, was also dismissed.[26]

In addition to being sacked, Guillaume was also excommunicated.[27] The bishop of Paris declared him to be "contumacious and rebellious" for violating the Church's rights and privileges and also accused him of "perjury and other disgraceful crimes." Guillaume was denied the sacraments, and his sentence of excommunication was read out and announced by writ "at the doors of all the churches in Paris." Even worse than losing his post in this world, Guillaume was now at risk of damnation in the next.[28]

There was one way out. The bishop would absolve him if Guillaume performed an *amende honorable,* a public ceremony of penance tantamount to a confession of guilt and a request for pardon.[29] The terms of the *amende* were very specific and similar to those inflicted on one of his predecessors more than a century earlier: Guillaume was to go to Montfaucon with the Paris executioner and in a procession of clergy to *dépendre*—"unhang"—the two clerics.[30] All of this pomp and ceremony could not actually resurrect the dead, of course; its purpose, according to the penal logic of the age, was to punish the provost and purify the city by "exactly reversing" the original offense.[31] After the bodies had been cut down, he was to escort them back to the city, restore them to the bishop of Paris, and see to their honorable burial. Thus would the Church and the university punish the man who had dared to challenge their authority—and God's—in the name of justice.

———◦———

Early on the morning of May 16, Guillaume appeared at the Porte Saint-Denis to perform his *amende,* taking his place in a long procession of clergy, university officials, and officers from the Châtelet in front of "a huge crowd of spectators, both men and women."[32] It was only a little over six months since he had left the city by the same gate, also in procession, to hang the two clerics at Montfaucon. But this time things were very different. Stripped of his rich robes, Guillaume wore ordinary clothes.[33] No longer in command of the one hundred and twenty sergeants in the procession, he had been demoted in the eyes of all.[34] Once responsible for punishing others, he was now being punished himself. Even the executioner had a different role that day. "Dressed like a priest in a surplice" and riding a horse before a cart carrying two empty coffins, the executioner was uncharacteristically going to "unhang" two men.[35]

The procession marched through the gatehouse and over the drawbridge, and the noisy crowd of spectators followed behind. Beyond the city wall, as the road turned east, away from Montmartre, the sun was rising in the sky over the hill topped by the great stone gibbet. When the cart carrying the two coffins finally reached the top of the hill, "it had just struck eight o'clock in the morning."[36] One of the sergeants from the Châtelet unlocked the sturdy gate, and the executioner entered the enclosure, followed by several university officials on hand to help identify the bodies. In keeping with the terms of the *amende,* the executioner pointed out for all to see "where the two bodies were hanging near the gibbet's second pillar." One of the university officials then "climbed a ladder" propped against the pillar and examined the corpses to confirm their identity.

After the bodies had been identified, the executioner "and his assistant" went up the ladder and cut them down, handling the stinking and desiccated remains as respectfully as possible and placing them in the "wooden coffins" on their cart.[37] As a sign of respect, they also "cut away the bindings" from each dead man's hands and covered the bodies with "a black cloth."[38] Guillaume stood by, watching.[39] The procession then formed up again and began descending the hill, and Guillaume accompanied the cart carrying the bodies back to the city.

After entering the city again at the Porte Saint-Denis, the cavalcade headed down the long straight street all the way "to the Châtelet" and filed through the passageway running beneath the old fortress.[40] They exited the Châtelet at the other end, and everyone marched onto the Grand Pont behind it and crossed over to La Cité. Then, turning east, they headed for the Cathedral of Notre-Dame "in a grand and solemn procession."[41]

By now, the whole city of one hundred thousand or so would have been alerted to these events, for "the bells of all the churches" in Paris were tolling.[42] A large crowd had already gathered in front of the cathedral, where the two massive bell towers loomed over the *parvis,* the cathedral square, the bells adding their great bronze reverberations to the general din. Here friars preached, bakers sold their bread, beggars pleaded for alms, prostitutes plied their trade, and the Church excommunicated its enemies.[43] Here Guillaume now had to complete his public humiliation.

Waiting for him on the cathedral steps was the bishop of Paris, Pierre d'Orgemont, arrayed in his white miter and vestments, holding his crosier and flanked by dozens of priests and clerics in their black robes.[44] The assembled dignitaries included berobed university officials who had refused to acknowledge the two felons while they were alive but who now waited to welcome back the corpses as their own.

The procession wound into the square, and Guillaume escorted the cart to the cathedral steps, where it finally drew to a halt. The executioner and his assistant removed the coffins and placed them on two trestles set up "before the great door of the cathedral" so that "one trestle stood within the bishop's jurisdiction, and the other within that of the city."[45]

The tolling of the bells died away.[46] Then, in accord with the terms of the *amende,* Guillaume leaned over each coffin and kissed the decomposing corpse on the mouth—if a mouth could even be found after more than six months of exposure.[47]

Officially, this was a kiss of peace, meant to seal a truce between two hostile parties, like that exchanged by John and Louis in church a few days before Louis's assassination. But seldom did such a kiss join the living with the dead.[48] Of all the humiliating moments that day for Guillaume, it must have been the worst and the one he most dreaded.

After this wretched ritual, Guillaume kneeled on the pavement before the bishop, "asking to be pardoned for his offense."[49] The bishop ordered the bodies to be taken away for burial. Guillaume stood and resumed his journey, as the procession now became a funeral march, with full honors for the two dead criminals. As the assemblage left the cathedral square, "the sergeants and others carried lighted wax candles," and the church bells resumed their ringing.[50]

Just west of the square, the group turned south and crossed the river again at the Petit Pont, following the Rue Saint-Jacques into the heart of the Latin Quarter. By now "all the mendicant orders and all the parish priests in Paris" had joined the grand procession of flickering, moving lights.[51] People lined the streets to watch, many of them wearing the robes and hoods that marked them as university men.

The rehabilitated clerics were to be buried at the Church of Saint-Mathurin, fronting the Rue Saint-Jacques about a quarter of a mile south of the river. Mathurin was a fourth-century saint celebrated for his powers of exorcism, and his church, which preserved some of his relics, had close ties to the university.[52] Now the university sought the saint's blessing on another, vindictive sort of exorcism.

When the procession arrived at the church, Guillaume "rendered the bodies to the university rector."[53] Then the two coffins were brought into the sanctuary and placed before the main altar, where they would remain overnight for the customary vigil kept by priests and mourners.

The next day, May 17, the two clerics were "honorably interred in the cloister."[54] Two carved stone effigies were eventually added to their tombs, along with a Latin epitaph naming them as scholars who had been unjustly executed. An engraved copper plate on the wall told their story in French, concluding, "The provost and his lieutenant were dismissed from office as a result of the university's lawsuit, as stated more fully in letters patent and other documents about this case. May God pardon them for their sins. Amen."[55]

As a final penance, Guillaume was forced to pay for much of this pomp, although the king, who seems to have had a soft spot for the provost, helped defray the costs with a gift of one hundred *écus* in gold.[56] At Montfaucon, "alongside the road to Paris," Guillaume also had to raise "a tall stone cross" bearing the carved images of the two clerics.[57] And at Saint-Mathurin, he had to endow "two chapels for the souls of the deceased."[58]

———◄○►———

Guillaume's successor had been named on April 30, the same day that de Tignonville was sacked.[59] Pierre des Essarts was formally installed on May 5, appearing before the Parlement of Paris to swear his oath of office.[60] He helped preside over his predecessor's *amende honorable,* standing on the cathedral steps with the bishop of Paris and the university officials to watch Guillaume's humiliation, even reading out a brief proclamation in his capacity as the new city provost.[61]

Unlike Guillaume, who refused "to relax the demands of justice," des Essarts, a nobleman who "belonged to the Duke of Burgundy's entourage," was "less recalcitrant" and more pliable, apparently willing to go along to get along.[62] His appointment, like his master's return to power and the rehabilitation of the two executed felons, inaugurated an ominous new era in Parisian law enforcement. From then on, the king's justice would be firmly in the hands of one of Burgundy's own creatures. No matter what future crimes Duke John might commit in pursuing his lofty ambition to rule France without rival, no investigators would ever follow him home, threaten to search his house, or force him to flee the city.

Barely six months after Louis's murder, Burgundy had taken possession of the capital, seized the reins of power, and driven his enemies from office. He had restored his finances, garrisoned the city with his army, and was building himself a great new tower from which to rule his domain. He enjoyed the support of the university and the people, who "saw him as the one strong man who could save the country."[63] "As master of Paris and of the whole realm, he might well have rejoiced in a political triumph he had purchased at a bargain price—the death of just one man."[64] But the bargain would prove to be a very costly one for John and all of France.

14

Civil War

———◄○►———

THAT SUMMER, HAVING secured control of Paris, Burgundy marched off to help put down the long-simmering revolt in Liège that Louis of Orleans had helped to foment in the final months of his life. Liège, a principality bordering Luxembourg on the river Meuse, belonged to Burgundy's brother-in-law, John of Bavaria. Until now, Burgundy had been too busy with Louis's murder and its aftermath to do more than send money. Now, finally free to add his own military might to the effort, he left Paris on July 5, headed for Ghent. With his two brothers, Burgundy set about raising an army—in all, nearly five thousand men—to reinforce John of Bavaria and his brother William in their fight against the rebels.[1]

On September 23, after weeks of mustering troops, organizing supply trains, and marching here and there, the allies met the rebels in a pitched battle near Tongres, one of the renegade towns.[2] Burgundy, commanding one wing of the allied army, led the charge. The veteran of Nicopolis, according to an eyewitness, displayed "bravery and coolness" as he "moved on a small horse from one part of the army to another, exhorting and encouraging his men....And although he was frequently hit by arrows and other missiles, he did not, on that day, lose one drop of blood."[3] After a hot, fierce fight lasting an hour and

a half, the allies prevailed. Burgundy had ordered that no prisoners be taken for ransom, and the allies killed some eight
thousand of the enemy while losing only a fraction of that
number themselves. They marched to the town of Liège,
encamped outside its walls, and contentedly watched as the
ringleaders of the revolt, two knights and fifteen townsmen,
were brought out to have their heads cut off, one by one.[4]
Inside the town, Burgundy's troops rounded up the renegade
priests who had supported the rebellion and drowned them in
the river Meuse. At Huy, another rebellious town, nineteen
townsmen were beheaded and many clergy were drowned,
including some nuns. The victors received as a present the head
of the rebel leader, who had been killed in the battle; they had
it stuck on a lance and displayed it for all to see.

To celebrate his victory, Burgundy commissioned a tapestry
showing the highlights of the Liège campaign in five large pan-
els, including a panoramic battle scene measuring twenty-four
feet by seven and glittering with costly gold and silver thread.[5]
John's triumph also earned him his famous sobriquet. From this
time on he was known as Jean sans Peur—John the Fearless—
no doubt in part for his dauntless leadership in battle, but also
for his share in the brutal reprisals afterward.[6]

———◦———

While John was grimly enhancing his brutal reputation far
from Paris, the royal family apparently thought better of letting
Louis's murderer off so easily. At the queen's urging, Charles
canceled his earlier pardon, claiming that he had been misin-
formed about the details of the crime.[7] Isabeau also enlisted a
surprising ally: Louis's widow, the exiled Valentina.

Valentina had been promised that the king would take up
her cause, so she had been outraged to hear of John's royal pardon and of the scandalous accusations laid at her husband's

tomb by Jean Petit. Now Isabeau evidently sent word to Valentina that she finally would receive justice at court.[8] Of course, Louis had allegedly maintained a close, even adulterous liaison with the queen. But now that Louis was dead, Isabeau, probably fearing John's designs on the dauphin, made an alliance with her former rival against their common enemy. Valentina ordered her lawyers to draw up a refutation of Petit's arguments.

In late August, Valentina returned to Paris, dramatically entering the city "in a litter draped in black, drawn by four horses also covered in black, at the hour of vespers, accompanied by a long train of black carriages filled with noblewomen and ladies in waiting, and many dukes and counts and men-at-arms."[9] After making "a sad and solemn procession" through the city, the duchess lodged at the Hôtel de Bohême, just north of the Louvre and only a few streets away from Burgundy's own palace.[10] On September 11, she went to the Louvre, where the queen presided over a large audience of royals and courtiers as an abbot presented a lengthy refutation of Petit's argument.[11] Many of those present had witnessed the Justification earlier that year, but this new hearing was just as one-sided as the other had been, with no one present now to speak for John. After Petit had been refuted in absentia, Valentina's chief lawyer stood up and read aloud a list of demands calculated to bankrupt and humiliate Burgundy and force his exile from France:

> *First, the Duke of Burgundy shall humbly confess his guilt and ask pardon of the duchess of Orleans and her children, in public, at the Louvre, the Palais, the royal hôtel of Saint-Pol, and, finally, on the spot where the murder was committed, kneeling there to ask God's pardon and kissing the earth. . . .*
>
> *Second, all the buildings in Paris owned by the Duke of Burgundy shall be destroyed, and the ruins left for all time. On*

the site of each building a stone cross shall be raised with an inscription recording the cause of the demolitions.

Third, a similar cross shall be erected on the spot where the murder took place, and the house in which the assassins hid shall be pulled down.

Fourth, the Duke of Burgundy shall, at his own expense, found, build, furnish and maintain, at the place where the murder was committed, a collegiate college for six canons, six vicars and six chaplains. . . .

Fifth, a similar church, but twice the size, shall be established by the Duke of Burgundy in the town of Orleans. . . .[12]

On and on it went, a catalog of churches, chapels, priests, prayers, and endowments that John of Burgundy was to found and maintain, including shrines in both Jerusalem and Rome, all to expiate his crime and honor the memory of his slain victim. In addition, all of John's lands were to be confiscated and sold; he was to be imprisoned until every demand was met, after which he was to be banished from France for twenty years.

Swayed by these speeches and emboldened by Burgundy's absence, the royal council resolved to proceed against John with "all the rigor of the law," and, if he did not submit, to raise an army and march against him.[13] The king, barely lucid and pressured by the royal family, again revoked his pardon of Burgundy. Valentina asked for, and got, the revocation in writing. Then, having apparently won the royal court to her cause, she returned once more to Blois.

———◄◦►———

Shortly after this delusory court pageant, however, news arrived in Paris of John's stunning victory in Liège. The court heard a "point-by-point" account of how Burgundy and his allies had avenged themselves on the ringleaders in the rebel-

lious towns with beheadings, drownings, and other brutali-
ties.[14] Reports of John's ferocity on and off the battlefield struck
terror in the royal court, and "many who had been all ready to
treat the duke with the utmost rigor began to hang their heads
and retreat from their previous opinion."

Near the end of October came the alarming news that John,
by now informed of Valentina's success in mobilizing the court
against him, was on his way back to Paris. The prospect of
Burgundy's return threw everyone into a panic. The court was
"terrified as much by the horrors of a possible popular revolt in
Paris, as by the approach of John the Fearless."[15] Almost at once,
another unseemly royal exit began.

On the night of November 2, while Paris slept, a stealthy
caravan of royals slipped out of the city, heading for Tours, a
hundred miles to the south.[16] The fugitives included the king,
the queen, and the dauphin, as well as the Dukes of Anjou and
Berry—all of the highest-ranking Valois—along with many
courtiers and servants. The feebleminded Charles seems to
have been carried off against his will. According to one report,
he was bundled out of the palace and into a boat on the Seine
amid his cries of protest.[17]

The next morning, Parisians—still fond of their king despite
his long illness—were outraged to learn of his virtual abduc-
tion by the court, and city officials declared a state of emergency.[18] The new provost ordered the great iron chains to be
hauled out of storage and installed at street crossings throughout the city. City officials wrote to Burgundy—a popular hero
after his victory at Liège, and the king's protector in the eyes of
the people—informing him that the queen and many of the
peers had fled the capital, taking Charles and the dauphin.

John returned to Paris on November 28, leading some two
thousand men-at-arms "in beautiful battle array" through the
Porte Saint-Denis to a victor's welcome.[19] Parisians thronged
the streets and squares again to greet the hero of the Liège

campaign. Just as they had cheered John's return in February and beseeched God's blessing on his Justification, once more the crowds "loudly shouted 'Noël!' " over the clatter of marching steel boots and iron-shod hooves.

But John knew that even with popular support, he had a tenuous grasp on the government of France as long as the king and the dauphin, who together embodied royal power, remained out of reach. Lodged again at the Hôtel of Artois, now fronted by his partly completed tower, John dispatched ambassadors to open negotiations with the royal family at Tours.[20]

A week later, an unforeseen event helped speed the embassy's work. On December 4, Valentina suddenly died.[21] The supposed cause of her death was "anger and disappointment at being unable to obtain justice for her husband's murder." After an elaborate funeral, Valentina's body was interred at Blois, where she had spent many years in exile. Her embalmed heart was sent to Paris and buried at the Celestine priory in her husband's tomb.

John of Burgundy may have feigned grief for Valentina, just as he had publicly mourned her murdered husband a year before, but her death reportedly made him "very glad."[22] For the past year, Louis's widow had been his most bitter and obstinate foe. Now, at a stroke, her unforeseen passing removed a major obstacle to reconciliation within the royal family and peace in France.

Valentina's death left four orphans — three boys and a girl. The eldest, Charles, the new Duke of Orleans, was just fourteen. With his twelve-year-old brother, Philip, he now had to bear the burden of representing their slain father's cause against the powerful and dangerous Duke of Burgundy. On her deathbed, still wearing black for her slain husband, the duchess had called her children around her to bequeath a heavy legacy, urging them "never to cease their pursuit of their father's murderer."[23]

A few days after Valentina's death, the king ordered young Orleans to leave the quarrel with Burgundy to him.[24] In January the king announced that John would once again have to ask his pardon for Louis's murder, and now the pardon of Louis's children as well. Charles of Orleans reluctantly agreed to the reconciliation, as did John, although he refused to perform an *amende honorable,* and he spent several weeks haggling over the exact wording of what he would say to Louis's sons.[25]

The ceremony was set for Chartres, acceptably neutral ground for both parties.[26] On the morning of Saturday, March 9 — a year to the day after his first royal pardon — Burgundy and a retinue of six hundred mounted men-at-arms clattered into town.[27] The king, the queen, and the dauphin, as well as the Orleans brothers, were already there and inside the church.[28] Before entering the cathedral grounds, John dismissed all but one hundred of his men, as previously agreed, to match the number in the Orleans retinue.

The great cathedral, soaring to dizzy heights on its massive stone piers and lofty flying buttresses, was guarded that day by a special "peace-keeping force of 400 men-at-arms and one hundred archers."[29] The western portal, where a regal Christ presided over the Last Judgment, remained shut, and the two dukes, Burgundy and Orleans, entered separately by the north and south transepts, passing between rows of well-armed soldiers and watchful stone saints. Once inside, each party waited in a chapel hung with brilliant tapestries, out of each other's sight. John's bodyguard was reduced to twenty knights.[30] As a precaution, John most likely wore a mail coat, for now "he always wore armor beneath his robe."[31]

A short while later, they were ushered into the vast and echoing nave crowded with nobles, clerics, and troops. Light streamed in through row upon row of tall, pointed Gothic windows luminous with images of patriarchs and saints, knights and kings — Moses and Thomas à Becket, Roland and Charlemagne — all robed in red, green, or gold or clad in armor, and all haloed by the brilliant Chartres blue.[32] The magnificent cathedral, a hymn of praise in stone and glass to the Virgin, was also a symbol of the orderly moral universe created and ruled by God.*[33]

At the crossing where the nave met the transept, carpenters had raised a large wooden palisade. The king and queen sat here, enthroned on high, attended by the dauphin, the Dukes of Anjou and Berry, several Valois counts, and many others. The Duke of Bourbon was also present, having finally agreed to countenance John of Burgundy nearly a year and a half after Louis's murder.[34] Behind the king sat Charles of Orleans and his brother Philip.[35]

At the king's command, Burgundy mounted the scaffold, accompanied by his spokesman, John of Nieles. Burgundy knelt before the king, with Nieles, who asked the king to withdraw his anger from Burgundy and restore him to his good favor. Then Burgundy himself spoke, as previously agreed, saying, "Sire, I entreat this of you."[36]

But the king, perhaps tired or distracted or already feeling a flutter of the madness that would soon descend upon him again, failed to say his lines on cue, remaining silent.[37]

The Duke of Berry, still sharp at sixty-eight, quickly stepped forward and asked Burgundy to withdraw a few paces. He then knelt before the king and held a whispered conference, as the dauphin and Louis of Anjou joined him.

"Sire," said Berry, "we beg you please to receive the prayer and request of your cousin Burgundy." The king replied: "We wish it and grant it out of love for you."

---

* The relics enshrined at Chartres included the tunic worn by the Virgin at the time of the Annunciation, one of the most precious objects in Christendom.

Burgundy then approached again, and the king said to him, "Good cousin, we grant you your request and we pardon you for everything."

The whole ceremony had nearly come to naught because of the ailing and unpredictable king. And the most difficult part still lay ahead.

Burgundy and Nieles now approached Charles of Orleans and his brothers, who stood behind the king "weeping loudly."[38]

Nieles said, "My lords, here stands the Duke of Burgundy, who begs you to banish any feelings of hatred or revenge that you may hold in your hearts on account of the deed perpetrated against the person of my lord of Orleans your father, and that from now on you will become and remain good friends together."

Then John said, "I beg this of you."

Again, the ceremony came to a halt, now because Louis's sons failed to say their lines.[39] This time it was the king who did the prompting, "ordering his nephews to honor their cousin's request."

"Sire," they answered, "since it pleases you to command us, we will grant his request and relinquish all of our ill feeling toward him. For we do not wish to disobey you in anything."

As soon as they uttered these crucial words, a cardinal in red glided forward with an open mass book.[40] John placed his right hand on the sacred page, as did Louis's sons. Then they all swore to keep the peace.

The king sealed the oaths by commanding Orleans and Burgundy to conduct themselves on friendly terms from now on and forbidding them to do any harm or mischief to each other or show any hatred to each other or any other person friendly to either party—"except for those guilty of the aforementioned homicide, who are now and forever banished from our realm."[41] Since the man guilty of ordering the homicide in question was standing right there, freshly pardoned by the king, these words must have had a bitter taste for the Orleans brothers.

The Peace of Chartres, as it came to be known, was largely a sham: "The Duke of Burgundy demanded, without desiring, pardon, which the Duke of Orleans, without forgiving, granted."[42] This elaborate piece of political theater, complete with a royal cast and a magnificent stage, did nothing to heal the hatred and loathing that still dangerously divided the Valois.[43] But it did silence at least for the moment the grieving heirs of John's assassination victim, who quietly retreated to Blois.

◦

The following year, 1410, Orleans and Burgundy abandoned their promise of friendship as the forced pretense it had been and mobilized their troops. Young Orleans had by now gained a new and powerful ally in the Duke of Berry as well as in Count Bernard of Armagnac, a ferocious warrior whose daughter Charles married that year to seal their alliance.[*44] In August, the rival armies took up positions around Paris, behaving in the usual fashion of soldiers as they foraged in the local farms and villages, terrorizing peasants and seizing crops and cattle: "Everything was devastated for twenty leagues round about....For more than a month, a bushel of good flour cost four-and-a-half or five francs, so that poor people in the town fled away in despair; many of them were set upon and killed."[45] The new provost kept the city on high alert, "riding all over the town, in full armor, with a strong body of troops" and making "the inhabitants of Paris keep the most careful guard every night," with "big fires kept up in all the streets till daylight."[46] But eight thousand Burgundian troops billeted in the city frightened Parisians almost as much as the Orleanist army outside the walls.[47] In September, the Parlement's chief clerk, Nicolas de Baye, "walled up the entrance to the turret of his

---

* Charles married Bonne of Armagnac a year after his first wife, Isabelle, the king's daughter, died in childbirth.

house to keep the troops out." Worse yet, a new tax imposed by Burgundy on Parisians to pay for his troops, and the severity of the tax collectors, recalled the tyrannical exactions of Louis.

As the rival armies held Paris hostage, "no bread came into the city by land or water except what was fetched by force of arms."[48] The king, in a rare show of royal will, finally managed to force the hostile parties to the negotiating table. The resulting treaty required all the princes "to swear not to commit aggression one against the other in word or deed, between now and Easter 1412."[49] While the treaty sent the armies home and averted civil war for the time being, it would not last nearly until its overly optimistic expiration date.

—◦—

The next year, 1411, Charles of Orleans began mustering troops again, despite the king's orders.[50] He wrote to the University of Paris, long a Burgundian ally, demanding that it formally condemn Jean Petit's justification of Louis's murder. Burgundy, now residing in Flanders in accord with a royally ordered withdrawal of troops from Paris, responded by calling up his own knights and men-at-arms.

That summer Orleans and his brothers sent Burgundy a letter known as a *défi*—a traditional challenge to a duel, often taken as a formal declaration of war.[51] The letter accused John of "the very horrible and treacherous murder" of their father as well as "great treason, disloyalties, dishonors, and crimes" against the king, and it warned Burgundy that they would make war on him.[52] John replied with characteristic ferocity, saying that the *défi* brought "great joy to his heart," and calling the Orleans brothers "false and disloyal traitors, malicious, rebel and disobedient felons" whom he would oppose with all his might. Orleans had thrown down the gauntlet, and Burgundy had picked it up, signaling a trial by combat that soon would engulf all of France.

In July, the king slipped into madness again, so a royally brokered peace was out of the question for the moment.[53] During John's continued absence from Paris, the city remained loyal to him, but its people increasingly feared an attack from the Orleanist army marauding around the capital, especially after Orleanist troops came up to the Paris walls on the north side near the end of August.[54]

At this time, the military captain of Paris—the man in charge of garrisoning and defending the city—was Burgundy's cousin Count Waleran of Luxembourg.[55] Under his leadership, the citizens lit watch fires and patrolled the streets at night, and all strangers entering or leaving Paris were searched to prevent weapons or secret letters being passed between Orleanists inside and outside the city. At both ends of the city, heavy iron chains were stretched across the Seine to forestall surprise attacks from the river.[56] As John's deputy, however, Waleran scandalized many Parisians by recruiting his agents and enforcers from among the butchers, skinners, and tanners, a large and powerful bloc of guildsmen who were bribed into John's service with abundant gifts of Burgundian wine.[57] Their daily work amid the violence of the abattoirs and the stench of offal accustomed these brawny, uninhibited men to the casual, efficient spilling of blood. And their skills and tools—mallets, knives, and cleavers—were readily adapted from pigs and cows to their fellow humans.

The royal butcher Thomas Le Goix and his three sons, along with a flayer named Simon Caboche, were the ringleaders of this gang of thugs—some five hundred in all—who policed Paris, calling themselves the royal militia. The Cabochiens, as they came to be known, threatened, roughed up, and ran out of town all those suspected or accused of Orleanist sympathies. They committed "terrible and horrible murders, robberies, and pillage . . . against those said to be of the Orleanist party."[58] Whoever incurred their hatred was "put to death or at least thrown into prison and stripped of his property, which at the first opportunity they freely pillaged without asking any-one's permission. Many rich and respectable people were thus reduced to the most frightful misery."[59]

In October, the provost—Pierre des Essarts—ordered all city officials to wear blue vests or tunics marked by the St. Andrew's cross, one of Burgundy's symbols, with the royal fleur-de-lis at its center. Out of loyalty to Burgundy or fear of being branded Orleanists, thousands of ordinary Parisians fol-lowed suit, and tailors hastened to supply the surging demand for the new city uniform. "Within a fortnight," wrote an eye-witness, "there were more than a hundred thousand people in Paris, children and adults, wearing this cross both back and front, for no one went out of the city without it."[60]

While the butchers in Burgundy's pay conducted a reign of terror in Paris, the Orleanist army had marched away from Paris into the Somme valley, about fifty miles to the northeast. There they began raiding towns just over the border of Artois, in John's own territory.[61] In August, John and his brother Anthony marched east from Douai with an army of ten thou-sand.[62] Archers and crossbowmen led, followed by a long war train of "one thousand" horse-drawn carts and wagons bearing provisions and pulling "ballistas and catapults of an extraordi-nary size" as well as "siege-engines of all sorts."[63]

These siege engines included "a large number of gunpow-der weapons."[64] John, an early gunpowder enthusiast, kept an extensive inventory of cannons and liked to watch field tests of newly forged guns.[65] Unlike the trebuchet, the mangonel, and other catapults that lofted boulders over town walls and rained down destruction on the buildings within, the great bombards could knock down the walls themselves.[66] Some of John's mas-sive bronze guns weighed up to eight tons and fired projectiles—generally balls of stone or lead—weighing as much as eight hundred pounds.[67] To maneuver, load, and fire these behe-moths required big teams of draft horses and crews of specially trained men.*⁶⁸ "That devilish instrument of war," as one observer called the new gunpowder artillery, would revolutionize how men fought and killed each other, allowing them to breach once impregnable castles and greatly multiplying the mortality rate on battlefields.⁶⁹

John led his army south toward the occupied town of Ham, on the Somme, around which his troops took up positions in early September.⁷⁰ The town had a garrison of five hundred men-at-arms commanded by Bernard d'Albret, "a valiant man of arms" and cousin to Charles d'Albret, the constable of France, who had ordered the investigation of Louis's murder.⁷¹ John's great guns were dragged into firing position, foreshadowing the mechanized artillery that would blast and pound the same area, the Somme, into a vast graveyard of shell holes almost exactly five hundred years later.

The next morning, John's troops sent a continuous hail of cannon fire and projectiles into Ham. "The enormous stones which they hurled with their machines threw panic among the townspeople and destroyed the towers and steeples of churches, especially those of the cathedral as well as the highest houses in the town."⁷² The thunderous barrage went on "day and night" until finally the huge gun stones breached the main town gate, destroying it and part of the adjacent wall.⁷³ The defenders filled up the breach with wood and rubble and held out against a "cruel and sharp" assault for three more hours, until night fell, but Bernard d'Albret told his men that they could not hope to last another day, and that night he led his soldiers and many townspeople to safety through an unguarded postern gate.

---

* Figures for earlier years are scarce, but a 1474 inventory specifies three horses for pulling a large serpentine, a type of gun weighing up to 1,500 pounds, and two horses to pull a smaller one weighing about 300 to 500 pounds. By this measure, an eight-ton gun would require at least sixteen horses. A cart carrying five large powder casks took four horses, as did a cart carrying forty gun stones. One 1475 Burgundian artillery train required 5,245 horses.

Siege of a fortified town. Archers shoot arrows into the town as cannons poke from behind wooden shields (lower left).

The next day, Burgundy and his brother, seeing the town undefended, ordered their troops in. They "slaughtered a great number of unarmed citizens and even clerics, without regard for age or station, and forced their way into houses, pillaging every room and setting fires everywhere, gorging themselves afterwards on plunder to the point of satiety."[74] John had the ruined town decorated "with 3,000 banners which had been specially painted in Cambrai."[75] The pillar of smoke rising from Ham could be seen from afar. Several nearby towns, fearing the same fate, surrendered to John, their emissaries "dressed in black" and kneeling before him to proffer the town keys.[76]

Near the end of September, Charles of Orleans and his allies brought their armies close to John's at Montdidier, between the Somme and Oise Rivers.[77] But the Orleanists could not agree on a strategy of attack, and then Burgundy suffered the sudden loss of the Flemings, who claimed to have fulfilled their military obligation and marched home. As a result, the pitched battle that many had expected never took place. The Orleanists soon decamped to the south, deciding to concentrate their forces on the biggest prize in France: Paris.

In early October, the Orleanists reached Saint-Denis, again threatening the capital, and their troops began besieging the walled town and looting nearby farms and villages: "They did as much damage as Saracens would have done; they hanged people up by the thumbs or by the feet, they killed or took for ransom, they raped women, and started fires. Whoever it was that did these things, everyone said, 'It is the Armagnacs,' and no one would stay in the villages but them."*[78]

On October 11, Saint-Denis capitulated, and three days later the Orleanists captured Saint-Cloud, which controlled a strategic bridge on the Seine just downstream from the capital.[79] All this time, they continued terrorizing the region around Paris, which supplied the city with grain, meat, and wine; many men went to war in search of riches and plunder, and they saw the area as ripe for looting and kidnapping for ransom.[80] Orleanist troops, unchecked by their leaders, put their captives in halters, leading them "like 'vile slaves' either to ransom or to drown in the water," or "putting their hands and feet to hot iron" and "torturing and then killing them if they did not buy back their own lives."[81]

As the Orleanist noose tightened around Paris, people began to panic. The enemy had their camps only a mile or so outside the city on Montmartre, a hill over four hundred feet high, from which "they could see right into the city and tell who was going in and out."[82] Weeks had passed without fresh news of Burgundy, and "it was thought that he was dead."[83] In fact, Burgundy was on his way back to Paris but had narrowly escaped assassination during a stop at Pontoise, about twenty miles to the north. A stranger with a knife hidden in his sleeve

---

* "Armagnacs," a common name for the Orleanists, after Count Bernard of Armagnac.

had been admitted to his presence one day, and John, suddenly growing suspicious, seized a nearby bench as a shield while his attendants subdued the man and found the weapon. (The would-be assassin, very likely an Orleanist or an accomplice in their pay, was beheaded in the town square.) Soon afterward, on October 23, lookouts on the Paris walls sighted John's approaching army, and they were not alone, for marching with them were some two thousand English troops.[84]

—◦—

John had "ridden all night in arms to reach Paris," making a great loop to the southwest from Pontoise and crossing the Seine at Meulan before turning sharply east toward the capital.[85] At the unexpected sight of Burgundy's army, a cry went up throughout Paris that relief was at hand, and "there poured out of the city a great host of militia, including an array of well-armed butchers leading the provost from the Châtelet." Along with "many princes and great lords and captains," including Burgundy's brother Philip and members of the royal council, the welcoming party rode several miles out to greet the duke "with great honor and reverence, as though he were the king of France just back from a long journey abroad."[86] When Burgundy's army, his English allies, and his Parisian escort entered the city, overjoyed people thronged the streets, cheering the troops with cries of "Noël" at every crossing. As it was late in the day, "a great number of torches, candles, and lanterns were lit in all the streets."[87]

The English mercenaries—about two hundred mounted men-at-arms and eighteen hundred archers under the command of Thomas Fitzalan, Earl of Arundel—now tipped the military balance in Burgundy's favor.[88] On November 8, Burgundy led a daring overnight raid from Paris to retake Saint-Cloud. The English and Burgundian troops captured the town and put some six hundred enemy soldiers to the sword.

Burgundy "had the drawbridge set on fire, so that at least three hundred were drowned in their panic and haste to get into the tower." It was "one of the finest assaults seen in a long time," wrote an observer.[89] Almost immediately, the badly beaten Orleanists decamped from Saint-Denis and the vicinity of Paris.[90]

The next day, after a solemn procession to the cathedral square at Notre-Dame, priests formally excommunicated the Orleanists "by bell, book and candle."*[91] They read out the names of the Duke of Orleans, Count Bernard, and all their confederates, condemning them as "rebels, felons and enemies of the realm," excluding them from the rolls of the faithful, and denying them holy communion.[92] Their banishment was also formally declared "by sound of trumpet in all the public squares of Paris."[93]

◄◦►

Although they received a warm Parisian welcome, the English troops opened a disastrous new phase in the French civil war that would damage the divided kingdom for decades to come. John had not always been so friendly with the English. As recently as 1406, he had mobilized troops for a march on Calais as part of a joint assault, with Louis of Orleans, on English strongholds in France. And at John's Justification, Jean Petit had alleged a secret conspiracy between Louis and Henry IV to usurp their respective nations' thrones. But the English were John's most important trading partner, and since becoming duke in 1404, he had been in almost constant negotiations with them to ensure safe shipping in the Channel and thus the security of the wool trade so vital to his finances.[94] John was also

---

* In a ritual dating back to the eighth century, "after reading the sentence, a bell is rung, a book closed, and a candle extinguished. From that moment the excommunicated person is excluded from the sacraments and even from divine worship."

hoping to betroth his daughter Anne to the English crown prince, although he was twenty-five and she was barely seven.[95] In late September, a month before returning to Paris with his English mercenaries, John had met with Henry IV's ambassadors at Arras for talks about a more durable Flemish-English alliance, one to be sealed by a royal marriage. A note on the back of the instructions to the English ambassadors, which still survive, says that they were to try "to discover if John would help King Henry recover the former English possessions in Guyenne"—a relic of the Aquitaine, a jewel of which English kings still dreamed.[96] A few thousand troops, sent to help Burgundy fight the Orleanists, was a small price for Henry to pay if John held the key to reconquering France. Henry would not live to see the dream fulfilled, or even the launching of the attempt, but he would bequeath the tantalizing prospect to his hugely ambitious son.

———◦———

In 1412, after a winter's respite, the civil war in France resumed.[97] Hostilities broke out this time near Bourges, a beautiful old cathedral town on the Loire where the Orleanist leaders, now joined by the Duke of Berry, had gathered for a spring war council.* Charles of Orleans, Bernard of Armagnac, and the Duke of Berry decided to counter Burgundy by seeking their own alliance with England, further entangling outsiders in the French civil war. Like Burgundy, the Orleanists bargained away part of France in exchange for English aid, offering "to restore the duchy of Guyenne to Henry IV if he sent them troops."[98] Henry, still in talks with John about a royal marriage, held off on striking a deal with the Orleanist

---

* Bourges was Berry's ducal seat, and after he retreated there from Paris and joined the Orleanist league, he began minting coins that were exact duplicates of the king's in order to pay his own troops.

warlords. But when King Charles—then between bouts of madness—got wind of the Orleanist bid for English support, he angrily called for an expedition, vowing to lead it himself, with the dauphin and the Duke of Burgundy as his lieutenants. Charles may have been driven by paranoia related to his illness, since a military campaign offered "a focus for his persecutory delusions."[99] Burgundy, always eager to wrap himself in the royal banner, readily took to the field with the unstable king and the underage dauphin. Doubtless aware that he was the de facto commander and reinforced by royal troops, he could pursue and harass his own enemies while looking like a patriot in the king's service. In May, the king led his army out of Paris and was soon joined by John's army. By early June they were encamped before Dun-sur-Auron, a smaller town guarding the approaches to Bourges.

For the campaign, John had brought a new bombard, christened Griette, whose field trials he had supervised that spring. An eyewitness to the siege described the gun's effect: "Nearly twenty men were required to handle it. When it was fired, the thunderous noise could be heard four miles away and terrorized the local inhabitants as if it were some reverberation from hell. On the first day, the foundations of one of the towers were partly demolished by a direct hit. On the next day, this cannon fired twelve boulders, two of which penetrated the tower, thus exposing many of the buildings and their inhabitants."[100]

After Dun-sur-Auron surrendered, the royal army moved on to Bourges, fortified by thick stone walls and garrisoned by many hundreds.[101] The king and the Duke of Burgundy began hurling great stone balls into the town and against its walls, and the Orleanists fired back with their own guns, also sallying forth in a surprise raid—only narrowly repulsed—with the aim of capturing the king and killing Burgundy. As the siege dragged on, however, disease swept through the royal army. The alleged cause was poisoned wells on the city's outskirts, but it was more likely dysentery, a wartime scourge that often carried off more soldiers than the battles did.[102] Because of the oppressive heat, horses in the besieging army died in great numbers, and "the stench of their carcasses much infected the camp."[103] As both sides recognized their weakening positions, negotiations began. By mid-July, a treaty had been signed by the king and Burgundy on one side, and the Orleanists on the other.[104] Both sides had to renounce any alliance with England, and all royally confiscated property was to be returned. To John's satisfaction, the treaty also forbade any legal prosecution of Louis's murder. It even called for a Burgundian-Orleanist union between one of John's daughters and Philip of Orleans. A marriage between the hostile parties, it was hoped, would reunite the Valois and cleanse the royal family of Louis's bloodstains.

The treaty was solemnized on August 22 at Auxerre in the Church of Saint-Germain, richly hung with tapestries and gold cloth for the occasion, amid clouds of incense and Gothic splendor reminiscent of the Peace of Chartres. To swear their oaths of peace, the Dukes of Orleans and Burgundy placed their right hands "on the holy gospels, a piece of the True Cross of Our Lord, and other holy relics from the cathedral church."[105] As if in silent protest, Charles of Orleans and his brother "were dressed in mourning."[106]

Afterward, in a show of mutual affection, "the Duke of Orleans and the Duke of Burgundy rode together with the other lords, the two of them sharing a single horse"—an unlucky echo of Louis's assassination, when two of the duke's squires had similarly shared the same mount.[107] A royal decree outlawed the terms *Orleanist* and *Burgundian,* as if banishing dangerous words from the realm would help to keep the peace.[108]

—◄◦►—

Unsurprisingly, the Orleanists chafed at the terms of the treaty, and the following year, 1413, they mustered their troops and threatened to make war again.[109] That spring, the Cabochiens had their last hurrah in Paris: several blood-soaked days when angry mobs surrounded the Bastille — not for the last time in French history — broke into the dauphin's palace, and ran riot in the streets, hunting down and slaughtering alleged traitors and throwing the bodies into the Seine, all with Burgundy's tacit approval.[110]

But many Parisians now felt like hostages in their own homes, and the riots were bad for business. Amid a growing public backlash and the urging of opposition leaders, the king — aided by the dauphin, now sixteen and increasingly opposed to Burgundy — acted through his council to curb John's power and that of his lawless henchmen.[111] In a showdown at court, Burgundy was forced to hand over the keys of the Bastille in front of the king, the dauphin, and a large crowd, a gesture he could not refuse to make without seeming a warmonger.[112] The king even invited the Orleanist leaders to Paris, the last thing in the world that Burgundy wanted.[113]

By August, Orleanist partisans were swarming back into the city, and "there were more of them in Paris than you could count."[114] The Cabochiens saw their popular support evaporate, and "they fled Paris in all haste for fear of being arrested and punished as they deserved for their evil deeds."[115] Among the fugitives were the ringleaders, Simon Caboche and the Le Goix brothers. Others were caught and arrested, including several chamberlains in Burgundy's household.[116] Burgundy tried to put a good face on things, even entertaining the ambassadors of the Duke of Orleans at the Hôtel of Artois, but his palace was being watched by night, and he began to fear his own arrest — or worse.[117]

———◄◦►———

During this time, a notorious handbill appeared around the city, pasted up overnight at churches, cross streets, and other public places where the literate few might read it aloud to the illiterate multitude.[118] The text, composed in the form of a letter and doubtless put up by Orleanist partisans, began as follows:

> *Lucifer, emperor of the deep Acheron, king of hell, duke of Erebus and Chaos, prince of the Shadows, marquis of Barathrum and of Pluto, count of Gehenna, master, regent, guardian and governor of all the devils in hell and of those mortal men alive in the world who prefer to oppose the will and commandment of our adversary Jesus Christ, to our dearest and well-loved lieutenant and proctor-general in the West, John of Burgundy.*[119]

The letter went on to implicate Burgundy in Satan's plot to destroy Christendom, citing the many shrines and churches already ruined by John's rampaging armies. As a reward for John's loyal service, Satan would crown him "king of Turkey, emperor of Constantinople," and "king of Jerusalem, Babylon and Carthage and of several other kingdoms." The letter closed with mordant humor, saying that Satan had personally sealed it "with our very horrible signet" as several troops of devils stood witness, "in our most dismal consistory...in the year of our doleful reign six thousand six hundred and six."*

Just as John had once spread propaganda about Louis's resorting to witchcraft, so his enemies now used the same weapon against him. According to an old rumor, John was spared at Nicopolis because a Saracen magician predicted that one day Burgundy would kill more Christians than the Ottomans themselves.[120] And John himself had confessed to ordering Louis's death "by the tempting of the Devil." Now his own words came back to haunt him, as his enemies dubbed him "the Devil's lieutenant."[121] The letter from Lucifer purported to show

---

* The year 6606 probably is meant to echo the biblical "number of the beast," 666, associated with Satan (Rev. 13:18).

that the short, ugly duke—not his murdered cousin—was the real warlock or necromancer.[122]

———◄○►———

On August 23, Burgundy, seemingly nonchalant, rode out from Paris arrayed for the hunt with "a brilliant entourage of knights and squires."[123] But this was a ruse, the same one adopted years earlier by Louis of Orleans and the queen to cover a hasty departure from Paris. Soon John had spurred his horse into a gallop and was racing toward his own territories "as quickly as if he was being pursued by his most mortal enemies."[124]

To ensure his escape, John sent orders ahead that his troops were to seize and secure the bridge over the river Oise at Pont-Sainte-Maxence, the same bridge (now rebuilt) that he and his men had destroyed after crossing it in late November 1407.[125] It was only a little over five years since Burgundy had first fled Paris fearing for his life. Again the hunter had become the hunted, and again Burgundy's precipitous flight took the city by surprise, "astonishing many people."[126]

A week later Charles of Orleans and his allies rode into the city "to the sound of trumpets" and with "a huge escort of knights and squires." People turned out to cheer them as enthusiastically as they had once cheered Burgundy. As the troops passed through streets "lined with townspeople," a man hired to do so "excited the crowd to even louder acclamations by throwing silver coins here and there."[127]

John had lost Paris and the support of its fickle people along with nearly everything else he had gained since Louis's murder. Like many great lords, he had been cast down by Fortune, a goddess blind to human ambition. "Fortune," wrote a Parisian observer during the tumultuous summer of 1413, "kept chopping and changing in this kingdom."[128] But as had been the case more than once since John's crime, this latest and most unexpected reversal was not the last.

15

The Scourge of God

———◄◦►———

T HE BLOODSHED UNLEASHED by Louis's assassination plunged
France into "a great deal of suffering and strife lasting for
a very long time," wrote a chronicler, "so that the whole realm
was left desolate and impoverished."[1] But as John of Burgundy
fled Paris for a second time in the late summer of 1413, put to
flight by hostilities he had ignited himself, the civil war was
setting the stage for an even larger calamity that would soon
engulf the nation. A new challenger now approached the field,
a foreign enemy who would exploit the turmoil in France to
the fullest for his own advantage, greatly prolonging the people's misery with a ruthless strategy of total war, terror tactics,
and devastating artillery sieges.[2]

In the spring of 1413, Henry IV of England had died and
been succeeded by his warlike son Henry V. Almost from the
day he was crowned, at the age of twenty-six, Henry—using
his ancestral claim to the French throne to divert attention
from the throne usurped by his father—began arming England.* The new king busied himself "buying bows, bow strings

---

* The dispute originated in 1066 when William the Conqueror, Duke of Normandy
and thus a vassal of the French king, became king of England. When Edward III, Henry
V's great-grandfather, refused to pay homage to the French king in 1337 for his French
territories, Philip VI seized the Aquitaine, prompting Edward to claim all of France.

and arrows, while guns were being founded at the Tower and at Bristol, and gun powder and gunstones manufactured in large quantities.* He also purchased, or had manufactured, siege towers, scaling ladders, battering rams and other tools for demolishing and breaching walls, and collapsible pontoon bridges. Timber, rope, mattocks, picks and shovels were stock-piled, together with every other conceivable necessity for siege warfare—from caltrops to iron chains, from sea-coal to wood-ash."[3]

As he laid in supplies of all sorts, Henry recruited troops from all over Britain, including mounted knights and infantry, archers, pikemen, and corps of knife-wielding Welshmen known for "their courage, their ferocity and their propensity to commit atrocities."[4] The invasion would cost a great deal of money as well, much of which Henry raised through loans, pawning his own jewels and "even his crowns."[5]

In August 1414, Henry opened negotiations with the French, not to make peace but to show the world their intransigence and thus justify his inevitable invasion. His list of demands was one that the French were sure to refuse: all of Normandy, Anjou, Maine, Touraine, and Poitou, plus most of Provence, the whole of the Aquitaine, and "the hand of Charles VI's daughter, Catherine, with a dowry of two million crowns"—well over two hundred million dollars today. The French countered by offering the Aquitaine and a dowry of six hundred thousand crowns. Henry rejected the proposal, now having exactly the pretext for war he wanted.

On Sunday, August 11, 1415, after more than two years of stockpiling supplies, recruiting soldiers, and raising money,

---

* As an example of the quantities, ten thousand gun stones were delivered to the Tower in October 1414 at a cost of sixty-six pounds, thirteen shillings, and four pence—about forty-five thousand dollars today.

Henry embarked from Southampton, the colorful sails of his armada catching the wind and suddenly blooming in the Channel.[6] His invasion fleet of fifteen hundred vessels large and small contained some ten thousand soldiers: two thousand men-at-arms and about eight thousand archers. With them sailed numerous "armorers, smiths, farriers, surgeons, cooks, chaplains, engineers, carpenters and masons," as well as fletchers and bowyers to supply his archers and even a band of pipers and fiddlers. To ensure fresh meat for the king's army once in France and to augment its foraging there, the ships also carried hundreds of live pigs, cows, and sheep, which made for noisy, smelly transit.

The English landed near Harfleur, Henry's first objective, and promptly laid siege to the town with a thunderous barrage from their guns. "Stone shot as big as millstones knocked wide holes in the walls."[7] But the heavily fortified town managed to hold out for more than a month, and "the bloody flux"—dysentery—struck the English camp, killing two thousand men and sending almost as many back to England, too ill to fight.[8] The bombardment continued, augmented by fire arrows, and the English brought up scaling ladders for a general assault. Finally, in late September, to Henry's relief, the starving town surrendered.[9]

It was an inauspicious start to the campaign, as the siege had cost Henry a great deal of time and a third of his troops. But on October 6, he marched from Harfleur and headed for the great English fortress at Calais, intent on further conquest along the way. "The English slew and looted as they went, their passage announced by columns of black smoke from burning farmhouses."[10] At Fécamp, farther up the Normandy coast, they set fire to the abbey, and women who had sought refuge there "were dragged out and raped." A ruthless warlord and a man of severe piety, Henry accounted the suffering of the French as their rightful punishment for withholding his inheritance, announcing, "I am the scourge of God." "War without fire," he also liked to say, "is like sausages without mustard."*[11]

But as Henry marched north, he found his way repeatedly blocked, since the French held nearly all the fords on the rivers.[12] Then a drenching downpour began, lasting for days, while dysentery continued to weaken many soldiers.[13] On October 24, Henry's hungry, sick, and sodden army sighted a great French host awaiting them near a farming village known locally as Azincourt. The French army, with as many as thirty thousand troops, outnumbered Henry's by at least four to one. The French reportedly spent that night feasting and "dicing for the English lords they expected to capture" and hold for ransom.[14]

The next morning, October 25, the two very unevenly matched armies faced off across a soggy field sown with new corn.[15] Henry's eight hundred men-at-arms stood in a ragged line, backed by his five thousand archers, while the far more numerous French infantry stood about six hundred yards away in three dense ranks fronted by two corps of mounted knights eager for the glory of the cavalry charge.

That French army was thick with Orleanist nobility, including Louis's heir, Charles of Orleans, now twenty and temporarily distracted from seeking vengeance against John of Burgundy by the English invasion.[16] Burgundy himself hung back, having promised the king that he would join the defense of France, but then retreating all the way to his ducal seat in Dijon by the day of the battle.[17] John's younger brother Philip, however, was in

---

* Total war is ancient, not modern, and was common in the Middle Ages. In 1300, a cleric named Pierre Dubois presented Philip IV of France with a treatise, *Doctrine of Successful Expeditions and Shortened Wars,* urging the king to avoid wasteful sieges and risky pitched battles and instead destroy the enemy's ability to make war by attacking his farms and villages. The strategy was refined over the next century or so, as the Burgundians and the Orleanists used it against each other, and the English employed it against the French.

the French ranks, and his other brother, Anthony, was hastening to the field.

Another knight present at the field that morning, armed and ready for battle, was Guillaume de Tignonville, the former provost of Paris.[18] Now about fifty, Sir Guillaume was still loyal to his king and to France, despite his humiliating treatment by the French lords and the ingratitude of the people. Like his fellow nobles, Guillaume was there to defend France against the foreign invader—and no doubt also to earn a share in the glory of the expected victory.

The two armies stood facing each other for four hours under a steady drizzle as the English waited for the French to attack.[19] Finally, Henry ordered his bowmen to advance within range, "barefoot because of the mud," and begin shooting. The first high volleys fell almost as harmlessly as the rain on the French, repelled by their steel caps and heavy plate armor. Then the front rank of French infantry began advancing, eight thousand strong, "roaring hollowly from inside their close helmets," as five hundred mounted men-at-arms charged the English on each flank.

But the French infantry soon got mired in the mud, and English arrows stung the French horses into a frenzy, driving them back to trample their own troops.[20] Trudging "grimly on, often sinking knee-deep into the mud on account of their weight," the French infantry eventually collided with the English front line, knocking them back several paces with the impact. But "the French were so packed together that they could not raise their arms to use their weapons, while those in front were pushed over by those behind." In the chaotic scrum that followed, "many drowned in the mud or were suffocated by the bodies above." The lightly armored English foot soldiers, thin enough on the ground to move about freely, seized the advantage, clambering over their immobilized enemies and dispatching them with "swords, hatchets, mallets, axes, falconbeaks," or any weapon to hand, even sharp wooden stakes torn out of the mud, where they had been planted to impale the French cavalry. The slaughter lasted "for three long hours."[21] Lying helpless in the mire, crushed by their own comrades, hundreds of fallen French soldiers were finished off with daggers thrust through the eye slits of their helmets. It was a rout, a debacle, a disaster for the French that exceeded even the humiliating defeats inflicted on them by English armies at Poitiers more than half a century earlier and at Crécy before that.

In the end, the English casualties, amazingly, numbered only about five hundred, while the French lost nearly ten thousand men in the muddy melee, including three dukes, nine counts, ninety-two barons, fifteen hundred knights, "and countless gentlemen."[22] In an infamous episode during the battle, Henry ordered many French prisoners killed. But hundreds more were captured and spared—one report says fourteen hundred and another as many as twenty-two hundred.[23] In subsequent weeks and months, many of the English victors grew rich on ransoms, profiting hugely from the battle that came to be called Agincourt.

Burgundy profited too, despite his failure to join the fray, for Henry had conveniently slaughtered hundreds of Orleanist nobles. John was also indebted to Henry for capturing a prize prisoner—Charles of Orleans, Louis's principal heir and Burgundy's archenemy. Refusing to ransom the young duke, Henry sent him back to England, where Charles was to spend the next twenty-five years as a prisoner in the Tower of London and other castles.[24] Unable to pursue his quest for justice against Burgundy and avenge his murdered father, forced to leave his inherited cause to others, he turned his plight as a prisoner into pages and pages of mournful poetry.

By failing to appear at Agincourt, John had escaped capture or death, but he did not escape a reckoning of sorts. Among the casualties on the field were both of his younger brothers, Anthony and Philip, who for years had loyally supported their older brother's blood-spattered cause. (Anthony, arriving late for the battle, had rushed onto the field with his armor unbuckled and was almost instantly slain.)[25]

Another casualty of Agincourt was the former provost, who appears in a list of slain French nobles as "le seigneur de Tignonville."[26] We have no idea how Guillaume died—whether he was struck by an arrow during the initial charge, crushed to death in the ensuing melee, or finished off in the carnage that followed. In any case, he clearly was not among those who surrendered at sword point and purchased their lives and freedom by paying ransom. So while his old enemy John of Burgundy sat out the battle in perfect safety far from the field, Guillaume risked all for his nation and gave the last full measure of devotion.

———◄◦►———

Without Henry's stunning upset at Agincourt, what we now call the Hundred Years' War would have ended far short of a century. Henry's risky invasion renewed the suspended war, and his unexpected victory greatly prolonged it. But it was Louis's assassination and the resulting civil war between the Orleanists and the Burgundians that crippled France for decades to follow in the face of the new English onslaught.[27] A popular medieval fable tells of two dogs fighting over a bone, which they both lose to an interloping bird of prey.[28] The rival factions in France likewise fought each other to the great advantage of their common foe.

The following year, 1416, John met with Henry at Calais to discuss an alliance, first taking elaborate precautions for his own safety, including a hostage exchange.* At the great castle

---

* The hostage was Henry's brother the Duke of Gloucester. By prearrangement, Burgundy met Gloucester in no-man's-land, at a ford across a river. Greeting each other in midstream, they shook hands and embraced, then each crossed to the opposite bank and went under guard to the other's camp; they returned to the ford three days later and crossed over again.

on the seacoast, the two lords talked alone until nightfall, and "John agreed in a secret treaty to recognize all Henry's claims, promising that as soon as the English had conquered enough French territory he would pay homage to Henry as his sovereign."[29] After abandoning France in its time of need, John apparently had no scruples about striking a deal with its mortal enemy, noncommittally waiting to see if Henry's ambitions would be crowned by success.

In 1417, Henry returned to France to launch what has been called "the Norman Conquest in reverse," beginning with the brutal siege and capture of Caen.[30] Henry's guns and engines rained ruin on the town day and night, until finally the walls were breached. The English "herded all the population they could find, civilian as well as military, regardless of sex, into the market place where, on Henry's orders, they massacred at least 2,000 of them. Blood ran in streams along the streets. The king only ordered the killing to stop after coming across the body of a headless woman with a baby in her lap still sucking at her breast."[31]

The autumn and winter of 1418 saw the terrible siege of Rouen. For six months, Henry slowly strangled the town, reducing its desperate inhabitants to eating "dogs, cats, mice, and rats."[32] He also let loose his Irish cavalry on the surrounding country. Fierce men, fifteen hundred strong, wearing saffron cloaks and armed with knives and javelins "raided far and wide to their heart's content, riding back with severed heads and even babies dangling from their horses' necks." The beleaguered town sent repeated appeals to Paris—and to Burgundy himself—but no relief came. Around Christmas, amid the freezing winter rains, the defenders turned out twelve thousand "useless mouths"—old men, nursing mothers, and children, who slowly starved to death or died of exposure in the great muddy ditch around the town. Henry's pity was limited to allowing infants born in the ditch to be raised up in baskets and baptized by his priests before being lowered back down to die.

After Rouen fell, Henry marched his army farther up the Seine and deeper into France, capturing one fortified town after another. By July 1419, the English had reached Pontoise, only twenty miles from Paris and the last stronghold guarding the approaches to the capital. Just before dawn on July 31, a Sunday, English troops crept through the outlying vineyards up to the town and hid in the dry moat encircling the walls. There they raised scaling ladders and swarmed over the ramparts in a surprise attack. "The town was horribly sacked, its citizens losing everything they possessed—not to mention the atrocities to which their women were subjected."[33]

Later that morning, as Parisians were going to Mass, a few desperate, terrified refugees from Pontoise straggled up to the Porte Saint-Denis. Soon "great crowds were coming, men, women, and children, some of them wounded, some stripped, another carrying two children in his arms or on his back. Some of the women had no hoods, others had but a wretched petticoat or shift.... As they came along they wept, moaning and crying and exclaiming, 'Lord, by thy grace, keep us from despair! This morning we were living happily in our own homes; now by midday we are like exiles begging our bread....' Some pregnant women gave birth during the flight and quickly died."[34]

At the sack of Pontoise, panic swept through Paris. But rather than besieging the capital, Henry contented himself for the moment with devastating the surrounding region. "In those days," wrote a chronicler, "the only news one heard was about the ravages of the English in France every day; they took towns and castles, spread ruin throughout the entire realm, sending everything, loot and prisoners, back to England."[35] Barrels of wine, horses, armor, weapons, furniture—whatever could not be used on the spot was shipped home. "A particularly vile practice was the kidnapping of boys and girls, to be sent across the Channel and sold as indentured servants."[36]

By this time, Paris was again Burgundian. The Orleanists had dominated the city since John's departure in 1413, even orchestrating John's solemn excommunication in front of Notre-Dame on the tenth anniversary of Louis's murder—November 23, 1417.[37] But John, despite the English invasion imperiling France, was determined to retake the capital for himself. In May 1418, his partisans in Paris secretly opened the Porte Saint-Germain-des-Prés after nightfall, and John's waiting troops seized the sleeping city along with the king. In the bloody coup that followed, hundreds of Orleanists were massacred in the streets, their bodies "heaped up in piles in the mud like sides of bacon."[38] One of the victims was Count Bernard of Armagnac, who had led the Orleanists since the capture of their duke at Agincourt.[*39] After Bernard's murder, the Orleanists regrouped around the dauphin, who had fled Paris during the coup and established a court in exile at Bourges.[40] The dauphin was no longer Louis, Burgundy's son-in-law, who had died, nor Louis's younger brother John, who had succeeded him and then died as well, but Charles, a third royal heir, just sixteen years old.[41]

Burgundy, now fearing that Henry would besiege Paris and conquer the rest of France, had begun negotiating with Charles the dauphin about an alliance against the English.[42] The dauphin had reason to seek a truce in the civil war as well, for he stood to lose his kingdom and his crown. But his closest advisers included many high-ranking Orleanists who were still spoiling to avenge their murdered duke against Burgundy.[43]

---

* Burgundy's partisans also killed Robert de Tuillières, Guillaume de Tignon-ville's former lieutenant, seizing his house in the Rue Arbre-Sec, evicting his widow and children, and dividing his goods among themselves.

In September 1419, a little over a month after the fall of Pontoise, the dauphin met with Burgundy at Montereau, forty miles south of Paris, where the river Yonne joins the Seine. They held a parley on a bridge, each accompanied by ten picked men and backed by their armies on opposite banks. A sturdy wooden stockade had been built on the bridge for the occasion. When John entered it, several Orleanist nobles in the dauphin's entourage attacked him, braining him with an ax and finishing him off with a sword through the belly.[44] Reports say that they also cut off one of John's hands in retribution for his cousin's murder.[45]

Louis of Orleans had finally been avenged, twelve years after the fact. But his avengers destroyed any chance of a truce that might have saved France, driving the outraged Burgundians into an alliance with the English that prolonged the war for decades and greatly multiplied the sufferings of the French. Louis's assassination had virtually decapitated the nation, plunging it into civil war. And the retaliatory ax blow to John's head, in a celebrated phrase, made "the hole through which the English entered France."[46]

—◁◦▷—

The following year, King Charles surrendered Paris, gave his daughter to Henry in marriage, and signed a treaty disinheriting the dauphin.[47] Within two years of this capitulation, Charles VI and Henry V were both dead.[48] At Henry's death, in 1422 — probably from dysentery contracted during a siege — his infant son, Henry VI, became the nominal king of an occupied France under a regency formed by his uncles.[49] But the teenage dauphin refused to relinquish his claim to the French throne, and the war that had already outlasted many kings raged on, like a fire or a pestilence impossible to contain.

As it did so, the misery of the French worsened. Towns and

villages saw their wealth drained off by heavy new taxes.[50] Everyone—nobles, clergy, and commoners alike—had to swear oaths of allegiance to England.[51] Nobles who refused were forced from their castles and made to forfeit their lands. Some took to the forests, living as outlaws and leading guerrilla raids against the English, who in turn hunted them down as "brigands."[52] Men convicted of brigandage were hanged—or, if they had broken their oaths, they were drawn, beheaded, and quartered. Convicted women were buried alive, a customary punishment meant to preserve their modesty. Peasants, as always, suffered terribly, caught in the pincers of war and killed, raped, and plundered by both sides.[53]

In August 1424, the French suffered another terrible defeat at the battle of Verneuil, said to be "a second Agincourt."[54] That same month, an anonymous artist in Paris began work on a great mural in the city's largest cemetery, the Holy Innocents, in the Rue Saint-Denis. The cemetery featured a sculpture, *The Three Living and the Three Dead,* said to commemorate the murdered Louis of Orleans.[55] Now, near a charnel house piled with bones, a new memento mori gradually spread along one of the four walls enclosing the cemetery until it stretched to over one hundred and twenty feet. The vast and frightening scene, soon to be copied and imitated all over Europe, was finished by Lent of the following year, and people flocked to see it.

The mural showed the Danse Macabre—the Dance of Death. A dozen life-size skeletons or cadavers alternated with figures of the living and formed a human chain, dancing along the length of the wall on their way to the grave. Here was a king, there a merchant; here was a knight, there a beggar.[56] All were joined together in the same dance, for all would come to the same end, as some verses beneath this "homily in pictures" also warned: *Mort nespargne petit ne grant*—"Death spares neither high nor low."[57]

Danse Macabre. Death summons a priest and a laborer.

In 1429, the Dance of Death became the backdrop to another spectacle, a violent religious outburst from the people expressing their desperation. In April of that year, a Franciscan friar came to Paris and preached every morning in different parts of the city, including the Cemetery of the Holy Innocents. In his gray robe and cowl, he spoke to crowds of several thousand for four or five hours on end "with his back to the charnel-houses...near the Danse Macabre."[58] Brother Richard, as he was known, urged people to turn away from worldly things and rekindle their devotion to God. One day his preaching "so moved and so stirred up" the crowd that in a penitential frenzy, they lit over one hundred bonfires throughout the city and began to destroy their worldly vanities. Into the purifying flames they threw "chess and backgammon boards, dice, cards, balls and sticks, and every kind of covetous game." Women "burned in public all their fine headgear." The bonfires blazed through the night and into the next day, smoke rising toward Heaven like holy incense meant to please God.

As Death stalked the land, and as famine, plague, conquest, and war galloped everywhere with apocalyptic fury, desperate people threw themselves into all sorts of religious frenzies, seeking signs and wonders that might predict the future or reveal God's will and gathering around holy men or women who could explain their suffering and lead them to salvation.

"There was at this time," wrote a chronicler shortly after the bonfires had lit up Paris, "a Maid in the Loire country who claimed to be able to foretell the future." This virgin, still in her teens, was also unusual in that she wore armor, rode a war-horse, and claimed to have been sent by God to save France from its enemies.[59] Lowborn and unlettered, she had seen visions and heard voices. Some said she was mad, like the late king. Some said she was possessed by the Devil. Then, in May, word reached Paris that she had raised the siege of Orleans. On June 12, she led a victorious assault on Jargeau, a nearby town held by the English. Six days later, the French swept to victory at Patay, completely routing the English and killing over two thousand of the enemy. Soon came word that the Maid was marching to Reims to have the dauphin crowned as the new king of France. The reports had a sensational effect throughout the nation.[60] Had God finally heard the people's cries of distress? It was the first truly hopeful news for France in a very long time.

Epilogue

———◁◦▷———

T HE MYSTERIOUS FRIAR in the red hood who orchestrated
the mayhem in the Rue Vieille du Temple on Saint Clement's Day was a Norman knight named Raoul d'Anquetonville.[1]
One unconfirmed story says that Louis had seduced Raoul's
wife and that Raoul took his revenge by serving as ringleader
of Louis's assassins.[2] Another says that Raoul lost everything at
dice to Louis, who offered him a chance to redeem his estate
by killing John. Raoul, the story goes, confessed the plot to
John, who then hired him to kill Louis.

Rumors aside, records show that Raoul was a notorious
scapegrace repeatedly cited for unpaid debts and even for embezzling a large sum from the queen.[3] He had been arraigned for
debt at the Châtelet in 1401 and again in March 1407, when de
Tignonville was provost; Guillaume may have presided over
the tribunal in person. According to historian Léon Mirot,
who a century ago tracked down many surviving records of
Raoul's activities, the Norman's "constant need for money,
complete absence of morality, and lack of any scruples seems
sufficient to explain his crime."[4] In August 1407, after the friar
first approached the rental agent about a house, Raoul met with
John at Lille, where John paid him one hundred *écus* "for various expenses" doubtless connected to the plot against Louis.[5] It
was Raoul, says Mirot, "who planned the attack, who rented
the House of the Image of Our Lady where the assassins lay in

wait for Louis of Orleans; and it was he who, after the crime, arranged the escape."

It was also Raoul who profited the most from Louis's murder. A surviving Burgundian account book even specifies the amount of blood money he was paid. On August 12, 1408, Raoul was granted a yearly pension of twelve hundred francs "in consideration of his noble services to the king and the Duke of Burgundy"—wording that suggests yet another attempt to justify murder for hire as loyal service to France.[6] Thomas de Courteheuse, who had beguiled Louis into the fatal trap, was also paid off.[7] All of the conspirators were convicted and banished in absentia, but only one of them, an obscure Breton who does not even seem to have been at the scene of the crime, was ever caught and executed.[8] Raoul lived out his days in Bruges, enjoying his ill-gotten gains until his death, in 1413. John even compensated the family of Jacob de la Merré, the loyal valet killed during the attack on Louis, giving his relatives one thousand crowns as *prix de sang,* or restitution, and declaring his "violent sorrow" over the valet's unintended death.[9]

◄○►

When Guillaume de Tignonville was sacked in 1408, the king, evidently not wanting to lose this valuable administrator, put him in charge of his chamber of accounts.[10] Later that year, Guillaume went to Liège as part of a royal embassy charged with dissuading Burgundy from fighting the Liègeois and also to inform him of the king's new resolve to see justice done for Louis's murder.[11] Guillaume probably witnessed the ferocious battle of Othée before carrying the duke's intransigent reply back to the court.[12]

Guillaume's new post in the chamber of accounts—and perhaps his bold journey to Burgundy's camp with unwelcome news—again made him a target for the vindictive duke. In October 1409, de Tignonville was arrested at Amiens and thrown into prison as part of a Burgundian purge of "corrupt" officials, one of whom spectacularly went to the block perched on a cart and dressed in his own livery.[13] But after a short time, Guillaume was released.

The following year, 1410, Burgundy actually approached Guillaume to ask his help in prying the Duke of Berry away from the Orleanist camp. Remarkably, Guillaume agreed to help and went to Poitiers as part of an embassy—certainly not for love of Burgundy, or even out of fear, but doubtless in order to help broker peace for France.[14] Despite his diplomatic skill, however, the embassy failed, and that summer saw the first open hostilities in the French civil war.

<o>

It is tempting to suppose that as a man of letters, Guillaume had a hand in the notorious "Devil's Letter" that seems to have hastened Burgundy's second flight from Paris, in 1413, much as his diligent investigation had prompted John's first departure five years earlier. But as a friend of poets and the author of a respected book, Guillaume was not likely to have taken pride in an anonymous political libel. The work on which he staked his reputation, *Moral Sayings of the Philosophers,* would proliferate in manuscript copies all over Europe, followed by numerous printed editions over the next several centuries, assuring him an afterlife of modest literary fame.[15] Surprisingly, Philip of Burgundy, son of de Tignonville's old enemy, owned at least four copies.[16] But it would have surprised Guillaume even more to be remembered today for a minor, nonliterary work—the investigation report contained in the thirty-foot scroll.

The report shows in practice the ideals of truth and justice set forth in Guillaume's moral treatise. As provost, Guillaume certainly had judicial torture at his disposal, and he almost certainly used it, or allowed its use, in other cases. But his long, detailed investigation report does not so much as hint that he or any of his officers resorted to "the extraordinary way"—forced confessions—to solve Louis's murder, despite the crime's magnitude and the urgency of the situation.[17] Instead, de Tignonville diligently examined the crime scene, collected evidence, deposed witnesses, and deduced the truth from the information thus obtained, enabling him to flush the arch villain from hiding. As a knight, a courtier, and a diplomat, Guillaume may have been thoroughly a man of his age. But in his police work, he seems to have been rather ahead of his time.

Apparently Guillaume was already a widower when he rode off to meet his fate amid the mud and blood of Agincourt, although the cause of Alix's death goes unrecorded.[18] But his daughter survived him and married a nobleman, Jean de Monceau.[19] Their second son, Guillaume de Tignonville, inherited not only his grandfather's name and estate but also his politics and his literary bent, serving the Orleans family in many prestigious posts and writing poetry on the side.[20] The so-called Bastard of Orleans, Jean de Dunois, born of the notorious veiled mistress and raised by Valentina as one of her own, grew up to become a French national hero.[21] While his half brother Charles sat out the war, a captive in England after Agincourt, Jean threw himself into battle, fighting beside Joan of Arc at Orleans, helping to lead many other campaigns, and living to see the English finally defeated and expelled from France in 1453. One of Guillaume's later descendants, Jeanne du Monceau de Tignonville, became a mistress of Henri IV (1553–1610), who affectionately called her "La petite Tignonville."[22]

Today the site of Louis's murder can still be seen in the Marais—an unmarked spot in the narrow, bustling Rue Vieille du Temple just north of where it crosses the Rue des Rosiers, although the old wooden houses that once flanked the street there are long gone. (The historical marker that places the murder in an alley just off the nearby Rue des Francs Bourgeois is wrong.)[23] And Duke John's fortified tower still frowns over the second arrondissement, the sole relic of the imposing Burgundian palace where he hatched his plot and sheltered the assassins after the crime. The Châtelet where Guillaume directed the investigation was demolished soon after the Revolution; only its name, given to the decorative fountain and the busy Métro station located there now, survives.[24] And Guillaume's original investigation report, a tattered parchment scroll, lies far from Paris in a distant corner of France.[25] The scroll, although fragile and faded and once more almost forgotten in its provincial resting place, endures.

The Rue Vieille du Temple today. The approximate site of Louis's murder, just north of the Rue des Rosiers.

Besides providing a record of Guillaume's diligent sleuthing, the scroll preserves the only lasting trace of dozens of ordinary Parisians otherwise lost to history. The events of November 1407 lit up their lives like a flash of lightning, and the provost's scribes briefly captured their excited and worried voices, which then fell into silence and near oblivion. Theirs is a story of everyday life and an extraordinary crime. Centuries later, they speak to us: the baker and the broker, the water carrier and the florist, the interrogator and the carpenter's apprentice—and, of course, the provost himself.

A Note on the Depositions

<hr />

THE LEGAL DEPOSITIONS in the provost's report are used in chapter 4 to detail the prelude to the assassination, in chapter 5 to recount the murder and the killers' escape, and in chapters 6, 8, and 9 to reconstruct the investigation. Since the depositions use indirect (third-person) quotations, here they have been put back into direct (first-person) form, reflecting how the witnesses actually spoke. Legalese clearly added by the scribes is often omitted, and run-on sentences are shortened to amplify the spoken voice; a few clarifications have been silently added. But the dialogue is otherwise intact, preserving its flavor and enabling modern readers to learn from the people directly involved what a crime investigation in medieval Paris was like.

The method may be illustrated from the testimony of Jacquette Griffard, the shoemaker's wife who saw the murder from her upstairs window. For example, Jacquette's deposition contains the following phrase: "Si fut tellement esperdue qu'elle ne savoit que faire ne que dire" (literally, "she was so upset that she did not know what to do or say").[1] In chapter 8, this appears in first-person form, as Jacquette certainly spoke it, a bit abbreviated so as to suggest her excited frame of mind: "I was so upset, I didn't really—" The scribe wrote next, "Toutesfoiz elle dit que cellui qui avoit ledit chapperon vermeil et qui emmena les autres comme dit est, estoit le plus grant d'eulx tous comme il lui semble fermement" ("All the same, she said that the one who had the said red hood and who led the others, as is said, was the tallest of them all as it clearly seemed to her"). This has been trimmed of legalese and rendered more colloquially: "Well, the man in the red hood who was in charge, he was definitely the tallest of them"; *Toutesfoiz* becomes "Well," and *fermement,* "definitely."

We are lucky to have so much vivid testimony in the vernacular. But it is not always clear whether a certain word or phrase was original to the witness or added by the scribe. Here the scribe clearly added *ledit* ("the said") and *comme dit est* ("as is said"), but *fermement* ("clearly, definitely") could be Jacquette's own term or the scribe's inserted assessment of her claim. The exact event often remains shadowy and elusive amid the tangle of textual report.

Acknowledgments

———◄○►———

M ANY PEOPLE HELPED to make this book a reality, and I am grateful to them all. At Little, Brown and Company, Geoff Shandler enthusiastically acquired the book and edited the text with great care, hugely improving it with his sharp eye and shrewd advice. Crucial support also came from publisher Michael Pietsch and many others at Little, Brown—altogether a superb publishing team. Special thanks to Geoff's assistants, Brandon Coward and Allie Sommer; production editor Ben Allen; copyeditor Tracy Roe; jacket designer Julianna Lee; indexers Anne Holmes and Rob Rudnick; and map editor Jeffrey L. Ward. My savvy literary agents, Glen Hartley and Lynn Chu, placed the book brilliantly and have looked after my interests with dedication and painstaking care. As always, I owe much to Peg—my wife, closest reader, and consigliera—who helped me reshape the book's narrative flow with a careful early reading, took high-resolution photos of the provost's scroll while we were in France, and welcomed the ghosts of the medieval Parisians who often haunted our table talk. My father, Marvin, also read the manuscript thoughtfully at an early stage. And two generous colleagues, Henry (Andy) Kelly of UCLA and Michael Hanly of Washington State University, vetted the finished manuscript, giving me the benefit of their wide and deep knowledge of things medieval. Pierre-Jean Riamond of the Bibliothèque Nationale de France kindly provided access to manuscripts and photos of a rare document; Louis de Carbon-nières of the University of Lille and the Institut d'Histoire du Droit lent his expertise on medieval law. Other colleagues to whom I am indebted include Richard and Mary Rouse (UCLA), Anne D. Hedeman (University of Illinois, Urbana-Champaign), Elizabeth (Peggy) A. R. Brown (CUNY), Renate Blumenfeld-Kosinski (University of Pittsburgh), Deborah McGrady (University of Virginia), Cecilia Gaposchkin (Dartmouth), and Thomas Kren (the J. Paul Getty Museum). For unfettered access to the unique parchment scroll, I thank the Archives départementales des Pyrénées-Atlantiques, in Pau, France, especially Anne Goulet (directrice), Catherine Bertrand, Alain Bérard, and Monique Vanderplaetsen. And for tracking down elusive images, I am grateful to Jennifer Belt and Peter Rohowsky of Art Resource, New York. Special thanks to David Lehman for the epigraph; to Janet Shirley, translator of *A Parisian Journal,* for helpful information about maps; to Serge Heuga and his family, proprietors of Chez Olive, in Pau, for their generous hospitality; to Danny Galbraith of Geoscience Australia for celestial data; and to Andrew Zinn, of Zinn Photography, for an expert author photo. Finally, since many old, fragile documents have not yet been digitized (and may not be for decades to come), I am grateful to the UCLA Academic Senate for funding a research trip to the archives in France.

Notes

Abbreviations

Atlas de Paris	Lorentz et al., *Atlas de Paris au Moyen Âge*
Boucicaut	*Le livre des faicts du mareschal de Boucicaut*
CUP	Denifle et al., *Chartularium universitatis parisiensis*
DENF	Morlet, *Dictionnaire étymologique des noms de famille*
DMA	Gauvard et al., *Dictionnaire du Moyen Âge*
"Enquête"	Raymond, "Enquête du Prévôt de Paris"
Famiglietti, *RI*	Famiglietti, *Royal Intrigue*
Fierro, *HDP*	Fierro, *Histoire et dictionnaire de Paris*
Plan de Paris	Leuridan et al., *Plan restitué de Paris en 1380*
RSD	Religieux de Saint-Denis, *Chronique*
Vaughan, *JF*	Vaughan, *John the Fearless*

Introduction

1. Pau, Archives départementales des Pyrénées-Atlantiques, MS. Série E 56, famille d'Albret, année 1407. Although a copy was made at Pau in 1666 and sent to the royal library in Paris (MS. Languedoc Doat 9), the report remained little known until Pierre Bonamy presented a paper to the royal academy in 1748 and published excerpts in 1754 ("Mémoire"). Another century went by before Paul Raymond published his full transcript of the original scroll in 1865 ("Enquête").

2. Lehman, *The Perfect Murder,* 27–28, discusses Sophocles's play as an early detective story.

3. A. M. Stein, quoted in ibid., 55. Also mistaken is the historian who claims that Louis's assassination "had nothing of a police mystery about it"—"rien d'une énigme policière" (Garcia, "Comment la nouvelle," 98).

4. Gauvard, *"De grace especial,"* 186.

Chapter One: The Provost

1. *CUP,* 4:147 (no. 1840); de Baye, *Journal,* 1:205n; Hillairet, *Gibets,* 41, specifying Wednesday, October 26, 1407. Porte Saint-Denis: *Atlas de Paris,* 51 (lower sketch, also showing gatehouse and drawbridge).

2. Favier, *Paris au XVe siècle*, 20; and 53–54 for population comparisons with other large European cities ca. 1400.

3. *Atlas de Paris*, 55, 57, and 217 (map also showing Montfaucon). The vintage varied, but four years later (1411), *A Parisian Journal*, 55, specifies "the middle of the vintage" as early October. See also Fierro, *HDP*, 452–53; and Favier, *Paris au XVe siècle*, 289.

4. Villon, "Frères humains," 209, probably based on Montfaucon, describes "rotting" corpses dried "black" by the sun and devoured by magpies and ravens. See also Champion, *Villon*, 1:318–20; Batiffol, "Le Châtelet," 63: 280–81; Hillairet, *Gibets*, 31–39 (noting the wind-carried odor from the "north east," 35); and Burl, *Danse Macabre*, 26–27.

5. Burl, *Danse Macabre*, 27. Procession and personnel: Hillairet, *Gibets*, 37. Hangman: *CUP*, 4:155 (no. 1852), citing a *bourellus* present on May 6, 1408, who had participated on October 26.

6. *A Parisian Journal*, 39; Geremek, *The Margins of Society*, 25.

7. Hillairet, *Gibets*, 37, cites the *cordeliers*, or Franciscans, also known as Gray Friars because of their gray cloaks.

8. Cousinot, *Geste des nobles*, 120 ("furent trainez et penduz au gibet"). The condemned might walk, ride in a cart, or be dragged behind a horse (Hillairet, *Gibets*, 36–37). Carts were common (see, e.g., *A Parisian Journal*, 51, 73).

9. Batiffol, "Le Châtelet," 61: 258 ("they attended executions").

10. RSD, 3:725, specifies a "public" hanging "in broad daylight," which "the crowd ran to see."

11. Monstrelet, *Chronique*, 1:75 ("loudly and clearly"). On the cloth and color of clerical garb, see Hodges, *Chaucer and Clothing*, 160–61, n. 3.

12. Burl, *Danse Macabre*, 26, with "the cawing of crows" from Hillairet, *Gibets*, 38.

13. Burl, *Danse Macabre*, 26. Hillairet, *Gibets*, ch. 3, describes the gibbet in great detail, including its periodic whitewashing (35).

14. Hillairet, *Gibets*, 33, says the capacity was "48 to 60" bodies. However, in one five-day period in 1431, sixty-two thieves were hanged at Montfaucon (*A Parisian Journal*, 258).

15. Le Grix White, *Forgotten Seigneurs*, 51. "Chamber of horrors" and chained "delinquents": Champion, *Villon*, 1:318; Burl, *Danse Macabre*, 26.

16. Cohen, *The Crossroads of Justice*, 136.

17. On Montfaucon's association with devils and magic, see Veenstra, *Magic and Divination*, 60–61.

18. For biography, see Demurger, "Guerre civile," 294–95; Eder, "Tignonvillana inedita," 852–73; and Bozzolo and Loyau, *La Cour amoureuse*, 1:60.

19. Batiffol, "Le Châtelet," 61: 233, listing the provost's many responsibilities; *Atlas de Paris*, 186 ("le premier magistrat de police").

20. Gauvard, *"De grace especial,"* 948–49.

21. From a 1364 royal ordinance on the Paris night watch (*guet*), quoted in Lespinasse, *Les métiers et corporations,* 1:46. *A Parisian Journal,* 48, mentions a 1405 decree that townsmen buy armor for the city's defense. Contamine, *War in the Middle Ages,* 73, lists some of the weapons likely borne by the lower classes.

22. *A Parisian Journal,* 48, 52–53.

23. Fierro, *HDP,* 45–46.

24. Eder, "Tignonvillana inedita," 856–68 (examples with dates of legislation). On leper hospitals, see *Atlas de Paris,* 181–83; and Fierro, *HDP,* 957–58.

25. Batiffol, "Le Châtelet," 61: 258–64; *A Parisian Journal,* 39; and Geremek, *The Margins of Society,* 24–25 (estimated figures).

26. *A Parisian Journal,* Introduction, 39.

27. Geremek, *The Margins of Society,* 23–24; Burl, *Danse Macabre,* 26. Fiddlers: *A Parisian Journal,* 124 (for the year 1418), as paraphrased by Geremek, 27.

28. Juvénal, *Histoire,* 446. On his personal integrity and aggressive law enforcement, see also de Baye, *Journal,* 1:229; and Gauvard, *"De grace especial,"* 232, 274.

29. Juvénal, *Histoire,* 447.

30. Eder, "Tignonvillana inedita," 853, putting Guillaume's birth "between 1360 and 1370."

31. Bozzolo and Loyau, *La Cour amoureuse,* 1:60 (with device). Guillaume's personal seal: Demay, *Inventaire des sceaux,* 2:242, no. 8897.

32. Belleval, *Azincourt,* 259. Tignonville served under Pierre de Villaines, probably in the Guelders expedition; see Vaughan, *Philip the Bold,* 98–99.

33. Demurger, "Guerre civile," 294–95, and Bozzolo and Loyau, *La Cour amoureuse,* 1:61 (no. 33), enumerate his various appointments.

34. Eder, "Tignonvillana inedita," 853–54 (Rome, Avignon), 858 (Milan).

35. Dessalles, *Histoire du Périgord,* 2:346.

36. Favier, *Paris au XVe siècle,* 413–15, lists provosts by name and dates of tenure.

37. One manuscript originally containing an image of Tignonville has lost the leaf in question (Chantilly MS. 1680, cataloged by Aumale, *Chantilly, le cabinet des livres,* 2:83).

38. Cousinot, *Geste des nobles,* 121.

39. RSD, 4:345 (unusual praise from the same monk who criticizes Guillaume for prosecuting clerics). On the monk of Saint-Denis, now identified as Michel Pintoin, see B. Guenée's introduction in RSD, vol. 1.

40. Demurger, "Guerre civile," 295; G. Tyl-Labory, "Guillaume de Tignonville," in Bossuat, *Dictionnaire des lettres françaises,* 1:647.

41. Juvénal, *Histoire,* 446, referring to Guillaume as both *chevalier* and *clerc.*

42. Champion, *La librairie,* xi, 13. For bindings of leather or rich cloth, see the several inventories printed by Champion (lxix–lxxiv).

43. See, for example, Raynaud, *Les cent ballades,* lxii–lxiii, 211–12, and refs. in Eder, "Tignonvillana inedita," 854.

44. De Tignonville, *The Dicts and Sayings,* 216–18.

45. Ibid., 162/30; Eder, "Tignonvillana inedita," 971 ("Nulz ne doit auoir honte de faire justice"); cited in Gauvard, *"De grace especial,"* 274.

46. Bozzolo and Loyau, *La Cour amoureuse,* 1:60–61. On Deschamps and Christine de Pizan, see refs. in Raynaud, *Les cent ballades,* lxii. For the literary quarrel and two letters from Christine to Guillaume, see Hult, *Debate,* letters no. 17 and 26. Hindman, *Christine de Pizan's "Epistre Othéa,"* 5, cites Guillaume's legal aid to Christine.

47. Eder, "Tignonvillana inedita," 874 (family tree, with daughter's name given as "Philippe" on chart but as "Philippa" on 872); Bernois, "Aveu," 75.

48. Vallet de Viriville, "Assassinat," 257, n. 2, notes that the house had once belonged to the counts of Ponthieu. Hillairet, *Rues,* 2:255, gives its precise location.

49. Several chronicles recount the case, including RSD, 3:722–25; Juvénal, *Histoire,* 444, 446–47; Monstrelet, *Chronique,* 1:75–76; and Cousinot, *Geste des nobles,* 120–21. RSD claims that confessions were extracted from the two men by torture, but Monstrelet and Juvénal do not mention torture, and Cousinot, a lawyer in the Parlement at the time (*CUP,* 4:147, no. 1840) and in a good position to know, offers quite a different account. The names of the two clerics, appearing variously in the sources, here follow RSD's usage.

50. Ducoudray, *Les origines du Parlement,* 593–600; Geremek, *The Margins of Society,* 136–47.

51. See Favier, *Paris au XVe siècle,* 199–235.

52. Gauvard, *"De grace especial,"* 274, citing a 1406 complaint by de Tignonville.

53. Cousinot, *Geste des nobles,* 120. Provost's right to appeal to Parlement: Batiffol, "Le Châtelet," 61: 250. The Parlement similarly sided with the provost in 1381 when the bishop of Paris claimed jurisdiction over a "sham clerk" accused of robbery and murder (Geremek, *The Margins of Society,* 62).

54. Cousinot, *Geste des nobles,* 120; "infamous evildoers," RSD, 3:727. See also Juvénal, *Histoire,* 444 ("disreputable and dishonorable").

55. RSD, 3:725.

56. Hillairet, *Gibets,* 33 (noting wall and "une porte solide").

57. Ibid., 36.

58. Ibid., 37, noting that confessions began to be permitted in 1396.

59. Burl, *Danse Macabre,* 27.

60. *A Parisian Journal,* 221–22, describes a contemporary hanging. Cohen, *The Crossroads of Justice,* 189–90, discusses ritual elements.

61. E.g., *A Parisian Journal,* 222 ("hanged and strangled"). The 1486 hanging: Tuetey, "Une exécution," 60.

62. Hillairet, *Gibets,* 35. Villon's ballade "Frères humains" describes the bones of the dead turned "to ashes and dust," and eyes "pecked out" by birds (209). On *revenants,* see Cohen, *The Crossroads of Justice,* 135–36; and Jean-Claude Schmitt, "Revenant," in *DMA,* 1205–6.

63. Jean Fouquet left a vivid view of Paris as seen from high ground to the north (ca. 1450) in "Miracle de Dagobert endormi" (BnF MS. 6465, f. 57), reproduced in Avril, *Jean Fouquet*, 223, and *Atlas de Paris*, 6. White buildings free of industrial soot appear in images by the Limbourgs and Fouquet (e.g., *Atlas*, 11, 55, 86–87, 90) and among restored buildings of the period (e.g., *Atlas*, 15, 81, 94, 109).

64. Gascar, *Charles VI*, 18, cites "le rêve du palais d'ivoire," originally biblical in inspiration.

65. Favier, *Paris au XVe siècle*, 53–54, cites estimates from 80,000 to 200,000. Gascar, *Charles VI*, 19, suggests up to 300,000, which is probably a bit high.

Chapter Two: The Châtelet

1. Batiffol, "Le Châtelet," 61: 236.

2. Woolgar, *The Great Household*, 87, detailing breakfast in the noble English household "before the fifteenth century," when the fare was probably similar to France's. In some households, breakfast was taken "in a small group." Fish and other items were added by "the end of the fifteenth century." On chaplains and religious life in noble households, see ibid., 176–78.

3. Major routes were five to eight meters wide, and smaller ones just two or three, not always paved. On paving, see *Atlas de Paris*, 213; Favier, *Paris au XVe siècle*, 22; and Fierro, *HDP*, 1057, citing dimensions from 1296 and 1415 edicts. A 1371 law required householders to pave the streets by their own homes (Desmaze, *Le Châtelet de Paris*, 65). By 1407, the Rue Vieille du Temple was paved with *carreaux* ("Enquête," 225–26, 232–33).

4. The definitive scholarly map of medieval Paris is the *Plan restitué de Paris en 1380*, cited hereafter as *Plan de Paris* and used throughout, along with local maps in the *Atlas de Paris*.

5. *Atlas de Paris*, 16.

6. Ibid., 83 (map of the old *palais*), 86–87 (Limbourg image), 11 (Fouquet image).

7. On the urban landscape of Paris in general, see Favier, *Paris au XVe siècle*, 13–51; and Guenée, *Un meurtre*, 121–31.

8. Guenée, *Un meurtre*, 125 ("le coeur de la capitale").

9. Shennan, *The Parlement of Paris*, 106, and Guenée, *Un meurtre*, 53, describe the furniture of a *lit de justice*, or royal audience.

10. *Atlas de Paris*, 40–43, details its topography and functions.

11. Ibid., 44–48.

12. Shennan, *The Parlement of Paris*, 108; Dohrn–van Rossum, *History of the Hour*, 135, enumerates other public clocks in France around this time.

13. *Atlas de Paris*, 22–23, also details the number and location of water mills. On water mills, see also Fierro, *HDP*, 1000–1001; and *A Parisian Journal*, 148, on grinding "corn" (grain) into flour for bread.

14. On this bridge and its money changers, see Fierro, *HDP*, 759–60.

15. For its history and layout, see Batiffol, "Le Châtelet," 61: 229–32; Claude Gauvard, "Châtelet," in *DMA,* 277–80; and *Atlas de Paris,* 21, 23 (Viking attacks), 186 (map).

16. Hillairet, *Gibets,* 158.

17. Hillairet, *Évocation,* 185. Hillairet, *Gibets,* 158, describes the windows.

18. *Atlas de Paris,* 213, states that "it caused rampant disease in the neighboring streets." Blood and offal: Crossley-Holland, *Living and Dining,* 92.

19. Hillairet, *Gibets,* 167–68.

20. Batiffol, "Le Châtelet," 63: 46–52; Hillairet, *Gibets,* 161–62.

21. Note on money adapted from Sumption, *The Hundred Years War,* 2:592–93.

22. Hillairet, *Gibets,* 162–63.

23. Shennan, *The Parlement of Paris,* 71, n. 1.

24. De Tignonville, *Ditz moraulx,* in Eder, "Tignonvillana inedita," 919, cited by de Carbonnières, *La procédure,* 247.

25. Hillairet, *Gibets,* 162.

26. Batiffol, "Le Châtelet," 61: 241–45 (*auditeurs* and tribunal room); 245–50 (*examinateurs*); 255–57 (*notaires, greffier*).

27. Batiffol, "Le Châtelet," 63: 268. The floor of the Grande Chambre in the old royal palace was also tiled: Shennan, *The Parlement of Paris,* 107.

28. Batiffol, "Le Châtelet," 63: 268.

29. Ibid., 61: 257–58. On false tonsures, see Geremek, *The Margins of Society,* 137–38. Barbers and surgeons: Fierro, *HDP,* 772, s.v. "chirurgien."

30. Batiffol, "Le Châtelet," 63: 266–73, details the customary legal procedure.

31. Peters, *Torture,* 44–54, with a discussion of methods, 67–69. See also Ducoudray, *Les origines du Parlement,* 506–19. Torture "commonly used at the Châtelet": Geremek, *The Margins of Society,* 50.

32. Cohen, *The Crossroads of Justice,* 154.

33. Soman et al., "Le Châtelet de Paris au début du XVe siècle," 577. Geremek, *The Margins of Society,* 47–53, analyzes the 1389–1392 ledger.

34. Batiffol, "Le Châtelet," 63: 268–71. Hillairet, *Gibets,* 160, offers a summary.

35. Batiffol, "Le Châtelet," 63: 270–71.

36. Duplès-Agier, *Registre criminel du Châtelet de Paris,* 1:231–39, cited in Batiffol, "Le Châtelet," 63: 271.

37. For various types of records, see Gauvard, *"De grace especial,"* ch. 1; and Clanchy, *From Memory to Written Record,* 74–76. For examples of content, see Duplès-Agier, *Registre criminel du Châtelet de Paris,* and Soman et al., "Le Châtelet de Paris au début du XVe siècle."

38. Cohen, *The Crossroads of Justice,* 68.

39. On writing technology and book storage, see Clanchy, *From Memory to Written Record,* chs. 4–5; and Powell, *Medieval Studies,* 49–58, noting that paper mills appeared in France after 1300.

40. Fierro, *HDP*, 309.

41. RSD, 3:724, describes Guillaume as "in jure civili eruditus."

42. Favier, *Paris au XVe siècle,* 54, compares Venice, Genoa, and Florence.

43. Basin, *Histoire de Charles VII,* 1:17.

44. Guillebert de Metz, "La description de la ville de Paris," 232–33 (written over several decades up to 1434). Favier, *Paris au XVe siècle,* 294, thinks these figures somewhat exaggerated.

45. Crossley-Holland, *Living and Dining,* 80–85; Fierro, *HDP,* 453–54.

46. Geremek, *The Margins of Society,* 21. City walls, gates, and other defenses: *Atlas de Paris,* 49–51; Favier, *Paris au XVe siècle,* 23–26.

47. *Atlas de Paris,* 49, gives a height of seven meters, not counting the *levée* forming its foundation, while Fierro, *HDP,* 844, says thirteen meters, perhaps including the *levée.*

48. *A Parisian Journal,* 162.

49. Geremek, *The Margins of Society,* 82–86, citing the Cemetery of the Holy Innocents in particular as "a meeting-place for prostitutes, profiteers, vagabonds and idlers of every description" (86).

50. Ibid., 107–8, noting the lack of pockets and easy pickings in crowds.

51. See Fierro, *HDP,* s.v. "heure," esp. 925–26.

52. Ibid., s.v. "guet," 915–16, noting that church bells sounded the curfew at 8:00 p.m. in summer, 7:00 p.m. in winter. See also Geremek, *The Margins of Society,* 26–28; and *A Parisian Journal,* Introduction, 39 (noting that there were two watches).

53. Thomas, *Religion and the Decline of Magic,* 606–14 (elves, goblins); Robbins, *The Encyclopedia of Witchcraft,* 254–59 (incubi), 490–92 (succubi).

54. Geremek, *The Margins of Society,* 26.

55. Ibid.,158–59, cites laws forbidding students "to carry swords or arm themselves with staves," which suggests how common it was to carry weapons.

56. Ibid., 14–17.

57. Ibid., 16.

58. *A Parisian Journal,* 51.

59. Ibid., 128 (for 1418).

60. Sumption, *The Hundred Years War,* 1:10, describing France in 1328 but still true nearly a century later.

61. Estimated at twenty to twenty-three million ca. 1300 for the area of "present-day France" but perhaps only half that by ca. 1390 (Duby, *France in the Middle Ages,* 261, 269). See also Braudel, *The Identity of France,* 2:157–61.

62. Seward, *The Hundred Years War,* 25–26, gives figures for the 1330s, adjusted here (by a 5:1 ratio) in proportion to those given above for France.

63. Sumption, *The Hundred Years War,* 1:9–14, gives a snapshot of France in 1328, and Duby, *France in the Middle Ages,* 269–87, fills in the picture for the next century or so.

64. Lodge, *A Sociolinguistic History of Parisian French,* 63 (dialect map of France).

65. Sumption, *The Hundred Years War,* 2:385–91, 393–95, portrays the situation in mid-fourteenth-century France.

66. Ibid., 3:223–24, dates the decisive role of gunpowder artillery against castles from the siege of Saint-Sauveur in 1375. Smith and DeVries, *The Artillery,* 13–14, cite the 1377 siege of Odruik.

67. Low rates of literacy persisted into early modernity, especially among rural laborers. At the end of the sixteenth century in Beziers and Narbonne, for example, "agricultural labourers were 97 per cent illiterate, small farmers 90 per cent and the bourgeoisie a mere 7 per cent" (Houston, "Literacy and Society," 271, with refs.).

68. Boyer, "A Day's Journey," 604. See also Autrand, *Charles VI,* 48–51.

69. Seward, *The Hundred Years War,* 139, 142, notes that Richard's death "meant the revival of the War." Richard was deposed on October 1, 1399, and died on February 14, 1400 (Van Kerrebrouck, *Les Valois,* 115–16), at a time when the start of the calendar year was often figured from the vernal equinox in March.

70. Van Kerrebrouck, *Les Valois,* 115–16, gives dates of her birth, marriage, and widowhood. On Isabelle's return, finally "settled" on May 27, 1401, see Vaughan, *Philip the Bold,* 51.

71. Seward, *The Hundred Years War,* chs. 1–3, including the origins of the war and the battles of Crécy and Poitiers. The definitive history is Sumption, *The Hundred Years War,* now up to volume 3.

72. Nordberg, *Les ducs et la royauté,* 149, cites a record at Bruges that dates the attack to "the end of October 1407." On vessels and tactics, see Sumption, *The Hundred Years War,* 3:125–26, 138–39.

Chapter Three: The Mad King's Brother

1. Guenée, *La folie,* 293–98, the most detailed chronology of the king's spells. See also Autrand, *Charles VI,* ch. 18, and Famiglietti, *RI,* ch. 1, with detailed notes and references to earlier studies.

2. Autrand, *Charles VI,* 30–31.

3. Pius, *I commentarii,* 6.4, 1:1055–57; Pius, *The Commentaries of Pius II,* 425.

4. RSD, 2:405; Famiglietti, *RI,* 5.

5. Brachet, *Pathologie mentale,* 635–36; Famiglietti, *RI,* 7; Guenée, *La folie,* 37.

6. Gascar, *Charles VI,* 127.

7. Famiglietti, *RI,* 6; Autrand, *Charles VI,* 316–17.

8. Van Kerrebrouck, *Les Valois,* 233–41, gives birth date, titles, territories, etc. On Louis's intelligence, learning, eloquence, and physique, see Autrand, *Charles VI,* 181.

9. Guenée, *Un meurtre,* 144.

10. Ibid., 143.

11. RSD, 3:189, cited by Vaughan, *JF*, 30. See also de Baye, *Journal*, 1:207 ("gouverneur à ce royaume"); and Famiglietti, *RI*, 36.

12. De Baye, *Journal*, 2:288, notes a proclamation (July 1404) threatening to punish anyone posting libels against Louis; cited in Vaughan, *JF*, 30.

13. Bozzolo and Loyau, *La Cour amoureuse*, 1:61 (no. 33), note Guillaume's tenure since 1391.

14. Juvénal, *Histoire*, 447. Tournelles had been owned by Louis since June 7, 1404 (Héraut Berry, *Chroniques*, 21, n. 6).

15. Champion, *La librairie*, xi, 13.

16. Demurger, "Guerre civile," 294.

17. Nordberg, *Les ducs et la royauté*, 231–32, notes the regent's power to appoint law officers.

18. Sellier, *Quartier Barbette*, 42, citing RSD, 1:359, on a particular artist. Gowns that "exposed the neck": Gibbons, "Isabeau of Bavaria," 65, citing the poet Deschamps on court fashions and the friar Jacques Legrand's censures of Isabelle and her ladies (RSD, 3:268). On Louis's reputation for scandalous affairs, see Guenée, *Un meurtre*, 144. Hillairet, *Rues*, 1:389, citing Brantôme, locates Louis's "cabinet de portraits" at the Hôtel de Bohême.

19. Famiglietti, *RI*, 298, n. 84, briefly sketches de Chauny's (or de Canny's) career. On de Chauny and his wife, see also Van Kerrebrouck, *Les Valois*, 440, n. 3; and Johnson, as cited below in the note on Delacroix.

20. RSD, 3:741.

21. Eugène Delacroix, *Louis d'Orléans Showing His Mistress*, in Johnson, *The Paintings of Eugène Delacroix*, 1:97–98.

22. On the Craon affair, see Froissart/Buchon, *Chroniques*, 13:48–87, partly translated in Froissart/Brereton, *Chronicles*, 392–401. Summary and analysis in Autrand, *Charles VI*, ch. 16; Famiglietti, *RI*, 2 (with notes); and Henneman, *Olivier de Clisson*, 153. Crowns to dollars: Barker, *Agincourt*, xv, 354.

23. Froissart/Buchon, *Chroniques*, 13:89–95; RSD, 2:2–23. See also Autrand, *Charles VI*, 289–95; Famiglietti, *RI*, 2–3 (with notes), for a sifting of the sources; and, for the date, Guenée, *La folie*, 28, and "Annexe," 294, no. 1.

24. Queux de Saint-Hilaire, *Le livre des cent ballades*, 238. Eder, "Tignon-villana inedita," 853, does not specifically place Guillaume at Le Mans in August 1392 but says that earlier that year he was appointed the king's special envoy to the Duke of Brittany.

25. Froissart and RSD (as cited above) list the principal nobles on the expedition, including Philip. Schnerb, *Jean sans Peur*, 63, states that Philip's son John was also present.

26. Froissart/Brereton, *Chronicles*, 393, with details of the king's clothing.

27. RSD, 1:564; Famiglietti, *RI*, 13.

28. RSD, 2:21, identifying the victim as "the bastard of Polignac," adding that four others were also killed. Famiglietti, *RI*, 3 and 207–8, n. 15, sifts the casualty reports.

29. Ibid., 2:21.

30. Guenée, *Un meurtre,* 143.

31. Froissart/Brereton, *Chronicles,* 395.

32. RSD, 2:21.

33. Froissart/Brereton, *Chronicles,* 396.

34. Famiglietti, *RI,* 3 and 210, n. 27.

35. RSD, 2:25.

36. Ibid.

37. Froissart/Lettenhove, *Chroniques,* 15:82–83.

38. Famiglietti, *RI,* 29; Van Kerrebrouck, *Les Valois,* 233.

39. On the Bal des Ardents, see RSD, 2:65–71; Froissart/Buchon, *Chroniques,* 13:140–46; Froissart/Johnes, *Chronicles,* 2:550–53; and Autrand, *Charles VI,* 299–303.

40. Froissart/Johnes, *Chronicles,* 2:550.

41. RSD, 2:67.

42. On Jeanne de Berry, see Van Kerrebrouck, *Les Valois,* 261 (b. 1378, married June 5, 1390). As Jeanne's exact birth date is not known, she may still have been fourteen at the time of the ball, in January 1393.

43. Froissart/Buchon, *Chroniques,* 13:144; Froissart/Johnes, *Chronicles,* 2:550.

44. Froissart/Buchon, *Chroniques,* 13:144 ("trop en volonté de savoir qui ils étoient").

45. RSD, 2:67 ("quasi in ictu oculi").

46. Ibid., 2:69.

47. Autrand, *Charles VI,* 301.

48. RSD, 2:66, says only that *someone* threw a torch; evidently, it was assumed to be Louis. Years later, mention of the ill-fitting costume appeared in Jean Petit's Justification (1408), along with the claim that Louis asked one of the revelers "by a secret sign" which one was the king (Thierry le Roy, "Rapport," 20). The abbé de Cérisy admitted that Louis had intentionally tried to burn the king, but only as a youthful joke (see Veenstra, *Magic and Divination,* 91–92).

49. RSD, 2:87–89, with other details of the king's second, much longer spell, including, "His mind descended into such dense shadows."

50. Ibid., 2:405; Autrand, *Charles VI,* 311–12.

51. RSD, 2:87, and 405, detailing the king's attempts to erase his own emblem.

52. Guenée, *La folie,* 293–98 (chronology), with an analysis of the evidence in ch. 2.

53. Famiglietti, *RI,* 7–21. Guenée, *La folie,* 61–62, surveys various modern diagnoses. Famiglietti, *RI,* 9, cites a possible hereditary cause, but Autrand, *Charles VI,* 306, rejects this thesis.

54. Guenée, *La folie,* ch. 4.

55. Ibid., 37–38, giving instances of the king's confinements.

56. Famiglietti, *RI*, 5; Guenée, *La folie*, 37.

57. Monstrelet, *Chronique*, 1:228; Autrand, *Charles VI*, 309, 311.

58. Isabeau, born in 1371; Charles, born December 3, 1368; married July 17, 1385 (Van Kerrebrouck, *Les Valois*, 114–15). Four-day courtship: Froissart/Brereton, *Chronicles*, 256–58.

59. RSD, 2:89.

60. Ibid.; Juvénal, *Histoire*, 394; Guenée, *La folie*, 92–95.

61. Guenée, *La folie*, 76. See also Jean-Patrice Boudet, "Sorcellerie," in *DMA*, 1346–48.

62. Robbins, *The Encyclopedia of Witchcraft*, 330–337 ("Maleficia"); see also 85–88 ("Charms") and 392–98 ("Possession").

63. Guenée, *La folie*, 92, and Veenstra, *Magic and Divination*, 84, note allegations of poison or sorcery.

64. Van Kerrebrouck, *Les Valois*, 438.

65. Froissart/Lettenhove, *Chroniques*, 15:260.

66. Ibid., 15:260–61. Collas, *Valentine de Milan*, 224–25, citing various versions of the poisoned-apple story, identifies the child as Louis, born May 26, 1391, and close in age to Charles the dauphin, born February 6, 1392. Van Kerrebrouck, *Les Valois*, 116, 234, confirms these dates. Louis died in September 1395, not long before Valentina's "exile."

67. Veenstra, *Magic and Divination*, 83, also cites the rumors about the divining mirror and the Italian magician.

68. Famiglietti, *RI*, 238, n. 183, citing Collas, *Valentine de Milan*, 227. Guenée, *Un meurtre*, 147, notes the queen's dislike for Valentina.

69. Froissart/Johnes, *Chronicles*, 2:607; Froissart/Lettenhove, *Chroniques*, 14:354. Louis's reaction: Durrieu, "Jean sans Peur," 213, quoting Froissart on Louis's resulting "melancholy."

70. Autrand, *Charles VI*, 181. See also Veenstra, *Magic and Divination*, 59–67.

71. Hedeman, "Pierre Salmon's Advice for a King," 117.

72. Veenstra, *Magic and Divination*, 25–28.

73. RSD, 2:542–47; Veenstra, *Magic and Divination*, 64–67. Augustinians wore black robes (see, e.g., Chaucer, "The Canon's Yeoman's Prologue," 557, *Riverside Chaucer*, p. 270).

74. Veenstra, *Magic and Divination*, 67.

75. Van Kerrebrouck, *Les Valois*, 353; Vaughan, *JF*, 1–2.

76. Keen, *The Penguin History of Medieval Europe*, 284–88; Vaughan, *Philip the Bold*, 45–47 (impact on France).

77. Vaughan, *Philip the Bold*, 47. Philip behind the rumors: Veenstra, *Magic and Divination*, 81–85.

78. Vaughan, *JF*, 30–31, says that Louis was "firmly in power in France within months of Philip the Bold's death."

79. De Baye, *Journal*, 1:206; Van Kerrebrouck, *Les Valois*, 233–34 (a more complete, documented list).

80. Harmand, *Pierrefonds,* 42.

81. Famiglietti, *RI,* 39, with an itemized list; see also Vaughan, *JF,* 3. The dollar figure is derived from the exchange values in Sumption, *The Hundred Years War,* 2:592–93, and Barker, *Agincourt,* xv, 354 (crowns to dollars).

82. Famiglietti, *RI,* 39.

83. RSD, 3:233.

84. Jorga, *Philippe de Mézières,* 505. On Louis's piety, see Guenée, *Un meurtre,* 143–44.

85. Champion, *La librairie,* vii–xvi.

86. Laborde, *Les ducs de bourgogne,* 3:69 (5558ᵃ), 120 (5714); cited in Darwin, *Louis d'Orléans,* 136–37 (and 235n).

87. Biver and Biver, *Abbayes, monastères et couvents,* 49, 50.

88. Ibid., 47–59, notes Charles V's patronage, 49, 50–51.

89. Ibid., 49, citing Le Fèvre, *Description des curiosités,* 65, on Louis's cell as a later tourist attraction.

90. "Testament," in Beurrier, *Histoire du monastère,* 301.

91. Jorga, *Philippe de Mézières,* 506.

92. Beurrier, *Histoire du monastère,* 285, putting Louis's dream "a few days before his death." See also Biver and Biver, *Abbayes, monastères et couvents,* 49; and Jorga, *Philippe de Mézières,* 506.

93. Beurrier, *Histoire du monastère,* 285; Biver and Biver, *Abbayes, monastères et couvents,* 49.

94. Biver and Biver, *Abbayes, monastères et couvents,* 49.

Chapter Four: The House in the Rue Vieille du Temple

1. Hillairet, *Évocation,* 102–7; *Atlas de Paris,* 109.

2. RSD, 3:285 (in 1409). But Famiglietti, *RI,* 227, n. 25, disputes the idea that Isabeau had grown fat.

3. Isabeau bore seven children between July 1393 and November 1407: Van Kerrebrouck, *Les Valois,* 116–18.

4. RSD, 6:487; Autrand, *Charles VI,* 415–18; Van Kerrebrouck, *Les Valois,* 129, n. 69.

5. RSD, 3:269 (sermon by Jacques Legrand, May 27, 1405); Famiglietti, *RI,* 41–42.

6. Vaughan, *JF,* 30: Isabeau "suspected by many of being [Louis's] mistress as well as ally." Seward, *The Hundred Years War,* 138, describes Isabeau as the king's "beautiful, sluttish wife." Famiglietti, *RI,* 42–45, disputes that Louis and Isabeau were lovers, arguing that the rumors of their adultery arose decades later. Gibbons, "Isabeau of Bavaria," 66, notes that Cousinot, *Geste,* 109, attributes rumors about Louis and Isabeau (ca. 1402) to Philip of Burgundy.

7. *Atlas de Paris,* 207–9, details materials, roofing, height, etc. The ground floor was typically stone, with wooden upper stories, often plastered to reduce fire danger.

8. Examples in ibid., 209; and Crossley-Holland, *Living and Dining,* 15.

9. Geremek, *The Margins of Society,* 81 ("typical...at this time").

10. *Atlas de Paris,* 37–39, details the old wall of Philip-Augustus, "between 6 and 8 meters high," and the Porte Barbette, a smaller "postern" gate. Guard towers: Fierro, *HDP,* 844.

11. Hillairet, *Rues,* 2:636–37; Bonamy, "Mémoire," 521.

12. Bonamy, "Mémoire," 522–23; Sauval, *Histoire,* 3:629.

13. Mesqui and Ribéra-Pervillé, "Les châteaux de Louis d'Orléans," 300–301, 332, also noting (341, n. 45) that Fouchier had supervised work on the Parlement's latrines in 1404 (de Baye, *Journal,* 1:92–93).

14. "Enquête," 219–21 (Marie Fouchier). Empty for nearly six months: "Enquête," 223–24 (Perrin Labbé). Geremek, *The Margins of Society,* 79, says that twenty livres a year was normal but cites rents as low as twelve.

15. "Enquête," 230–31 (Driette Labbé). Driette, deposed on Thursday, November 24, says the man in the white coat came by "a week before yesterday"—i.e., Wednesday, November 16. Collas, *Valentine de Milan,* 331, notes that Driette ("Driete" in the record) is short for Andrée.

16. "Enquête," 219–21, with some details from 223–24 (Perrin Labbé). Marie Fouchier puts the visit on "one day in the previous week," "either Tuesday or Wednesday"—that is, November 15 or 16—making the latter date most likely in view of Driette's evidence.

17. Ibid., 219 ("elle qui parle répondi que il feust le bien venu").

18. Crossley-Holland, *Living and Dining,* 15, floor plan of a Parisian house showing the front entrance (a) near the hall (b); *Le Ménagier,* xl–xli, describes the hall (*la salle*); *Goodman of Paris,* 138 ("the hall").

19. Perrin Labbé, "Enquête," 223, states that the client asked about having the house until this date in the following year.

20. Clanchy, *From Memory to Written Record,* 88, 181, and plate 8, illustrating tally sticks (introduced into England from France).

21. "Enquête," 221. On personal seals as signatures, see Clanchy, *From Memory to Written Record,* 244–46.

22. "Enquête," 231.

23. Ibid., 224 (Perrin's testimony); *Le Ménagier,* xli (*Goodman of Paris,* 28), describes a *dressoir* in the hall used for storing spoons and drinking cups and where wine was poured for guests.

24. "Enquête," 231 (Driette).

25. Ibid., 238–39, with the name altered from "Cayn," following *DENF,* 156–57, s.v. "Cagne."

26. "Enquête," 241 (Simon's wife).

27. Ibid., 228; "Griffart" altered to "Griffard" (*DENF,* 481); and "Jaquete," probably for the regional variant "Jacquet" (*DENF,* 532), is here modernized as "Jacquette."

28. "Enquête," 231.

29. Ibid., 247 (Girard Lendouil), gives his comrade's name as Tixerrant (see *DENF*, 930, s.v. "Tissandier").

30. *Atlas de Paris,* 217–19, details the city's water supply. On water carriers, see also Fierro, *HDP,* 1096.

31. Eder, "Tignonvillana inedita," 857 (citing a 1404 edict from the provost). Fierro, *HDP,* 1096, says that drawing water was forbidden along part of the Left Bank, but *Atlas de Paris,* 217, states that Parisians "customarily" used river water throughout the Middle Ages.

32. The "fontaine de l'Apport Boudoyer," as shown in *Atlas de Paris,* 219 (map).

33. *Dictionnaire raisonné universel,* 3:554–55 (s.v. "porteur d'eau"), defines a *voie* as thirty-six pints, or eighteen pints per bucket (*seau*). The Paris pint was nearly an English quart (*A Parisian Journal,* Introduction, 35), but a *voie* of thirty-six English quarts, or nine gallons, would require two buckets holding nearly five gallons each and together weighing over eighty pounds, very awkward to carry any distance. Using the smaller, English pint gives a bucket capacity of about two and a half gallons, or five gallons per *voie,* with a total load of just over forty pounds.

34. *Dictionnaire raisonné universel,* 3:555 (s.v. "porteur d'eau"), citing delivery carts that carried "two *muids,*" about seventy-two gallons, weighing just over six hundred pounds, using the above equivalences.

35. No cart appears in the deposition, but in all likelihood the three water carriers used one. If not, each man had to carry a pair of buckets four times from the river to the Fouchier house, a round trip of two-thirds of a mile and a total of nearly three miles per man—an unlikely expenditure of time and effort.

36. *Atlas de Paris,* 209, 213; Favier, *Paris au XVe siècle,* 22, with details of paving, gutters, mud, and ordure; Fierro, *HDP,* 885 (s.v. "fosse d'aisances").

37. A straight line north from the riverbank to the Rue des Rosiers, near the Fouchier house, is almost five hundred meters (*Plan de Paris*), and the actual route is longer.

38. "Enquête," 231–32 (Driette).

39. Solar and lunar data from Geoscience Australia (online), calculated for Paris (latitude 48° 52' N; longitude 2° 20' E), where November 23, 1407 (Julian) = December 2, 1407 (Gregorian).

40. "Enquête," 230 (Gilet le Sellier).

41. Monstrelet, *Chronique,* 1:156; Greimas, *Dictionnaire de l'ancien français,* s.v. "brun."

42. Crossley-Holland, *Living and Dining,* 25; Chaucer, "The Book of the Duchess," line 293, *Riverside Chaucer,* p. 334 ("in my bed al naked").

Chapter Five: A Cold, Dark Night

1. *Atlas de Paris,* 215; Fierro, *HDP,* 835–36; and Hillairet, *Évocation,* 20 ("only three lights" in Paris). On the night of November 23, one shopkeeper

said he could "see quite well by the light of several candles" still burning "in the street" after curfew, although when pressed for details, he also said "it was very dark" ("Enquête," 229–30).

2. On November 23, a month before the winter solstice, the city was apparently still on "summer hours," since one witness (Jean Porelet) refers to the events occurring "around eight o'clock at night and after curfew sounded" ("Enquête," 237).

3. Cousinot, *Geste des nobles,* 116; Héraut Berry, *Chroniques,* 26. RSD, 3:745, says the snow began on Saint Martin's Day (November 11). On the great winter freeze of 1407/1408, see ch. 12, n. 1.

4. "Enquête," 233.

5. Ibid. Shennan, *The Parlement of Paris,* 47–48, explains *procureur,* Cousinot's indicated title.

6. "Enquête," 221–22 (Perrin Fouchier).

7. Fierro, *HDP,* s.v. "vin," "brasserie." See also Favier, *Paris au XVe siècle,* 308–10.

8. Monstrelet, *Chronique,* 1:155; RSD, 3:730 ("in tears"). Birth, death dates: Van Kerrebrouck, *Les Valois,* 118 (s.v. "Philippe de France").

9. Monstrelet, *Chronique,* 1:155. Louis's regular visits "to sup" and "cheer her up": RSD, 3:731; Vallet de Viriville, "Assassinat," 241; Schnerb, *Jean sans Peur,* 208.

10. Monstrelet, *Chronique,* 1:155–56.

11. Ibid., 1:156, says Louis had with him that night two squires and "four or six valets." RSD, 3:735, says "only five men"; Cousinot, *Geste,* 113, only three; Jacquette Griffard, "Enquête," 227, saw "five or six mounted men and three or four men on foot"; Vallet de Viriville, "Assassinat," 241–42, counts seven, including two squires and "four or five valets."

12. Monstrelet, *Chronique,* 1:156, with the two squires on "one horse." Hillairet, *Rues,* 1:551, surmises that Louis exited the palace through either the main gate in the Rue Vieille du Temple or a service entrance to the south.

13. Monstrelet, *Chronique,* 1:156–57 ("devant et derrière"). The horse in front: ibid., 1:157 ("devant lui aloit").

14. Ibid., 1:156 ("ne se hastoient").

15. "Enquête," 227 (Jacquette). For *chantoit* as "humming," see Vallet de Viriville, "Assassinat," 242 ("le duc fredonnait"); and Michelet, *History,* 2:14.

16. Geremek, *The Margins of Society,* 26.

17. "Enquête," 227 (Jacquette). The murder took place in the rue Vieille du Temple in front of the Rieux and Fouchier houses according to Bonamy, "Mémoire," 522; Collas, *Valentine de Milan,* 349–53; Hillairet, *Rues,* 1:550–51; and Lehoux, *Jean de France,* 3:106, n. 4. Sellier, *Quartier Barbette,* 58–73, locates it in an alley near the Hôtel Barbette and just off the modern Rue des Francs Bourgeois, a mistaken notion perpetuated by a historical marker placed there in 1908.

18. Jacquette saw "seven or eight" assassins surrounding Louis ("Enquête," 227) at the outset, while Drouet Prieur reported "twelve to fourteen" plus "five or six" more who appeared later (225). Jean Fovel said he saw "twenty to twenty-four" riders, not counting their comrades on foot (236). RSD, 3:735, says "seventeen"; and Monstrelet, *Chronique,* 1:155, "about eighteen." Vallet de Viriville, "Assassinat," 242–43, names a total of sixteen conspirators.

19. Jacquette saw the assassins with "swords and axes" ("Enquête," 227), and Drouet Prieur, clearly familiar with arms, specifies swords, axes, halberds, and maces (225). Witnesses along the escape route reported seeing archers, presumably with crossbows (e.g., Jean Fovel, 236), and witnesses near the crime scene saw arrows flying in the air or lying in the street.

20. Monstrelet, *Chronique,* 1:156 (saying they did so "boldly and outrageously").

21. Vallet de Viriville, "Assassinat," 242, n. 4, cites a 1399 ordinance.

22. Monstrelet, *Chronique,* 1:156.

23. Ibid., also reporting the shout "Kill him! Kill him!" (*"À mort! À mort!"*).

24. RSD, 3:735. Cousinot, *Geste des nobles,* 114; Monstrelet, *Chronique,* 1:156; and Héraut Berry, *Chroniques,* 22, all mention the severed hand as well, some saying it was the left, some the right. See also "Enquête," 217 (left hand).

25. Monstrelet, *Chronique,* 1:156–57.

26. Ibid., 1:157.

27. Of the six men, two are on the horse, one is killed (Jacob de la Merré), and one badly wounded (Robinet Huppe), leaving two unaccounted for amid several fallen torches: "Enquête," 225, 228 (one torch), 242 (two torches).

28. Ibid., 233, where Amelot Lavelle tends to a "Robinet"; Vallet de Viriville, "Assassinat," 243, citing a Robinet Huppe later compensated for injuries.

29. "Enquête," 217, 228. "Spare the duke": RSD, 3:735.

30. "Enquête," 233–34.

31. Ibid., 227.

32. Interpolated from another witness, Colin Chevalier ("Enquête," 242), who mentions blood gushing from the wrist.

33. Ibid., 227; Cochon, *Chronique normande,* 381.

34. "Enquête," 227 ("frappoient...d'estoc et de taille"). They "hammered" him: Monstrelet, *Chronique,* 1:157 ("martelèrent").

35. Cochon, *Chronique normande,* 381. A large piece of his brain: interpolated from Amelot Lavelle ("Enquête," 233).

36. "Enquête," 227.

37. Ibid., 224–25.

38. Anglo, *The Martial Arts of Renaissance Europe,* 153.

39. Monstrelet, *Chronique,* 1:157, with subsequent quotations *"Allez! Allez!"* and "Murder! Murder!"

40. "Enquête," 227–28. The returning squires, horse, and mule are interpolated from Monstrelet, *Chronique,* 1:157.

41. "Enquête," 225–26 (Drouet Prieur).

42. RSD, 3:737.

43. "Enquête," 228.

44. Ibid., 226.

45. Ibid., 238–39.

46. Ibid., 226. *"Hélas!"* has been added from the deposition of Jean Pagot, who seems to have watched the arrival of Drouet Prieur's party through a hole in his door, as described next.

47. Ibid., 234.

48. Ibid.

49. Ibid., 232–33.

50. Ibid., 239 (Simon Cagne).

51. Ibid., 222–23.

52. Ibid., 229–30.

53. Hillairet, *Rues,* 2:207, notes *oues* as a variant of *oies,* referring to the geese once roasted and sold in this street, now the Rue aux Ours (Bear Street).

54. Crossley-Holland, *Living and Dining,* 20–21, discusses indoor lighting.

55. "Enquête," 236–37, transcribes the surname as "Fouel," perhaps "Fouël," but it is more likely a variant of the widely attested "Fauvel" (*DENF,* 422, 401).

56. "Enquête," 234–35 (transcribed as "Moriset" but more likely "Moricet," attested by *DENF,* 675, s.v. "Maurice").

57. Altered from "de Bourc" (see *DENF,* 130).

58. "Enquête," 230.

59. Vaughan, *JF,* 39, quotes a 1406 list of war supplies that includes twenty thousand caltrops.

60. "Enquête," 237.

61. Ibid., 230.

Chapter Six: Post Mortem

1. "Enquête," 216.

2. The constable, a "close friend" of Louis (Nordberg, *Les ducs et la royauté,* 66), apparently learned of the murder from the men who found Louis's body and then sent his squire to the provost: Schnerb, *Jean sans Peur,* 210. The Hôtel d'Albret, located near Les Halles, was a short distance, about three hundred yards, from Guillaume's house in the Rue Béthisy (*Plan de Paris*).

3. *A Parisian Journal* (French text, Tuetey, *Journal d'un Bourgeois*), 93, n. 1.

4. "Enquête," 216–17.

5. RSD, 3:737 ("en foule"); Héraut Berry, *Chroniques,* 22.

6. "Enquête," 217.

7. Ibid.

8. Thorndike, *A History of Magic and Experimental Science,* 4:122–23.

9. "Enquête," 217.

10. Ibid. (identifying de la Merré as a "page").

11. Ibid., with next quote, "Those present told me."

12. Schnerb, *Jean sans Peur,* 211.

13. Monstrelet, *Chronique,* 1:161.

14. Ibid.

15. "Enquête," 217–18, with a list of the attendees.

16. Van Kerrebrouck, *Les Valois,* 271–89 (Anjou dynasty, Louis I and II, claim to Sicily); Guenée, *Un meurtre,* 184, on Louis II as "the highest ranking" lord.

17. Autrand, *Charles VI,* 42–46.

18. Van Kerrebrouck, *Les Valois,* 257–61 (age, titles, territories, Poitiers).

19. Vaughan, *JF,* 95.

20. Van Kerrebrouck, *Les Valois,* 260.

21. Guenée, *Un meurtre,* 141. Collections: Guiffrey, *Inventaires;* with examples in Vaughan, *Philip the Bold,* 191 (gems), 193 (books). On Berry's possible homosexuality, see Camille, "'For Our Devotion and Pleasure,'" esp. 171–74.

22. Guenée, *Un meurtre,* 142–43 ("l'idéal de son temps").

23. Guenée, *La folie,* 137–38.

24. Famiglietti, *RI,* 209, n. 23; and refs. in Guenée, *La folie,* 280, n. 65.

25. Van Kerrebrouck, *Les Valois,* 353–56; Guenée, *Un meurtre,* 141–42; Autrand, *Charles VI,* 17–19 (with reference to Poitiers).

26. Van Kerrebrouck, *Les Valois,* 364–68.

27. Vaughan, *JF,* 4, 117, 147–51. For more on John's military history, see ch. 10.

28. "Enquête," 218.

29. Ibid. specifies that *all* the gates ("toutes les portes de Paris") were closed, but Monstrelet, *Chronique,* 1:162, says all "but two," probably for essential supplies and messengers, though they were "well guarded."

30. "Enquête," 218.

31. Ibid.

32. De Baye, *Journal,* 1:206–7, with a note on the marginal sketch at the bottom of 208.

33. Froissart/Brereton, *Chronicles,* 309. See also Guenée, *Un meurtre,* 71–82.

34. "Enquête," 218.

35. Ibid.

36. Ibid.

37. Ibid.

38. Ibid.

39. Ibid., 219.

40. Batiffol, "Le Châtelet," 61: 247.

41. "Enquête," 219.

42. Ibid., 241.

43. Lehoux, *Jean de France,* 3:107.

Chapter Seven: A Mass for the Dead

1. "Enquête," 218–19.

2. Hillairet, *Rues*, 1:201; Biver and Biver, *Abbayes, monastères et couvents*, 60–61.

3. Monstrelet, *Chronique*, 1:159; "Enquête," 219. Particularly during royal funerals, churches en route to the burial site often served as way stations; see Giesey, *The Royal Funeral Ceremony*, 37.

4. Beurrier, *Histoire du monastère*, 279–87, with details.

5. Guenée, *Un meurtre*, 206. On confession, Purgatory, and the prayers of the living for the dead, see also Wieck, *Painted Prayers*, 117–18; and on last rites, 120–21.

6. Wieck, *Painted Prayers*, 117–18.

7. Plancher, *Histoire générale*, 3:201 (embalming of Philip the Bold). On embalming and other details of royal funerals, see Giesey, *The Royal Funeral Ceremony*, 19–22; and *Atlas de Paris*, 98–100.

8. "Testament," in Beurrier, *Histoire du monastère*, 297.

9. Monstrelet, *Chronique*, 1:159–60, says that these items were found the next day, although Jean Pagot, "Enquête," 234, reports seeing the severed hand right after the murder.

10. "a white shroud": Monstrelet, *Chronique*, 1:159. "A black veil": Vallet de Viriville, "Assassinat," 257. Wooden coffin: Wieck, *Painted Prayers*, 121, image 94. Images 93 and 103 illustrate the sewing of the shroud, often with "crude stitching."

11. Monstrelet, *Chronique*, 1:159.

12. Ibid. Philip of Burgundy's lead coffin (1404) weighed seven hundred pounds: Plancher, *Histoire générale*, 3:201, cited by Vaughan, *JF*, 1.

13. *Les Vigiles de Charles VII par Martial d'Auvergne* (BN MS. Fr. 5054), fol. 5, showing Louis's pall in procession.

14. Wieck, *Painted Prayers*, 122, image 95.

15. Monstrelet, *Chronique*, 1:159, with a list of royal mourners, 1:160.

16. Plancher, *Histoire générale*, 3, *preuves*, cclxxxi, col. 1; see also Bonamy, "Mémoire," 535; Vallet de Viriville, "Assassinat," 258; and Collas, *Valentine de Milan*, 359.

17. Monstrelet, *Chronique*, 1:159.

18. Ibid., 1:160.

19. From an antiphon ascribed to Pope Gregory I (d. 604) that became part of the Requiem Mass (Smith and Cheetham, *A Dictionary of Christian Antiquities*, 2:1438).

20. Wieck, *Painted Prayers*, 122–23, image 96.

21. Ibid., 122–24, with images 96 and 97.

22. RSD, 3:736. A later passage reporting Valentina Visconti's speech at court (RSD, 3:751) may allude to Christ's head (*caput*) and wounds (*vulnera*), and on September 11, 1408, the abbot of Cerisy quoted Lamentations 1:12

("Videte si est dolor sicut dolor meus"), long associated with Christ's Passion (quoted in Coville, *Jean Petit,* 238). On comparisons to Cain as well as Judas, see Guenée, *Un meurtre,* 187, 206.

23. Valentina was not at Blois but at Château-Thierry, about fifty-five miles northeast of Paris (Collas, *Valentine de Milan,* 367).

24. *A Parisian Journal,* 182 (indicating eighteen bell ringers for the funeral of Charles VI, in 1422). "A great number of knights and squires": Héraut Berry, *Chroniques,* 23; Monstrelet, *Chronique,* 1:160.

25. *Les Vigiles de Charles VII* (BN MS. Fr. 5054), fol. 5, shows a mitered bishop with crosier preceding Louis's bier.

26. Monstrelet, *Chronique,* 1:160; RSD, 3:737 (Burgundy "au convoi").

27. Monstrelet, *Chronique,* 1:160.

28. The sources mention only the starting point and destination; the route described here is conjectural but makes sense given the street layout.

29. Monstrelet, *Chronique,* 1:160.

30. Fénin, *Mémoires,* 575; Juvénal, *Histoire,* 445. See also Collas, *Valentine de Milan,* 359.

31. Monstrelet, *Chronique,* 1:160.

32. Bournon, *L'hôtel royal de Saint-Pol,* 73.

33. Beurrier, *Histoire du monastère,* 286–87; other burial details from ibid., "Testament," 298–99.

34. "Testament," in Beurrier, *Histoire du monastère,* 326, 310.

35. Beurrier, *Histoire du monastère,* 287 (identified as a "squire").

36. Ibid., 286. Vaughan, *JF,* 1–2, describes Philip the Bold's burial in clerical garb.

37. "Testament," in Beurrier, *Histoire du monastère,* 298.

38. Monstrelet, *Chronique,* 1:162. Lehoux, *Jean de France,* 3:107, n. 1, disputes this report, but practical necessity makes it likely. On provisioning Paris, see Crossley-Holland, *Living and Dining,* 67–69, which notes that in outlying regions, grain was milled and bread baked to be sold in the city.

39. RSD, 3:739, refers to "a general noise in the kingdom" about an initial suspect.

40. Sumption, *The Hundred Years War,* 1:268 (French coastal defenses), 3:173 (English surprise attack in 1340). See also Barker, *Agincourt,* 151, 160–61 (French defenses in 1415). RSD, 3:307, describes a 1405 alert involving dispatches to the borders of northern France.

41. Garcia, "Comment la nouvelle," surmises that the dispatch "was drawn up right after the reported event" (100).

42. Sumption, *The Hundred Years War,* 2:365–73, 418–19 (with map of fortresses, 367).

43. Froissart/Lettenhove, *Chronique,* 15:260.

44. Garcia, "Comment la nouvelle," 96; Sumption, *The Hundred Years War,* 3:668–69.

45. Garcia, "Comment la nouvelle," 96 (n. 4), 101 (n.16), cites Autrand, *Charles VI,* 349–50, and places Pierre de Mortain at "two [*sic*] meetings of the council."

46. Garcia, "Comment la nouvelle," 101. On Pierre's role at the French court in his brother's service, see ibid., 96.

47. Ibid., 105–7, transcribes the original, with a French translation, the basis for my own English version. The manuscript preserving the letter's contents is BN MS. Esp. 216 (Garcia, "Comment la nouvelle," 95, n. 1).

Chapter Eight: The Inquiry

1. Monstrelet, *Chronique,* 1:162.

2. *Plan de Paris* shows chains stretched across both portals; the most recent of the two (at the eastern portal) had probably been installed in 1405 on the orders of the Duke of Burgundy (RSD, 3:333).

3. Coville, *Jean Petit,* 89, one of the few modern accounts recognizing de Tignonville's detective work. See also Schnerb, *Jean sans Peur,* 213–14.

4. See Fierro, *HDP,* s.v. "cri," 816–18.

5. Dohrn–van Rossum, *History of the Hour,* 203, notes that bell ringing for deaths or funerals "spread ever more widely" in the fourteenth century. Criers: "Enquête," 241.

6. Gauvard, "Châtelet," in *DMA,* 279.

7. Batiffol, "Le Châtelet," 61: 249.

8. The standard handbook, Cappelli, *Lexicon abbreviaturarum,* lists numerous scribal abbreviations adapted from Latin into other languages.

9. Marie Fouchier's deposition, "Enquête," 219–21, stands first in the provost's investigation report.

10. Batiffol, "Le Châtelet," 61: 249.

11. Cohen, *The Crossroads of Justice,* 69–70. Gauvard, *"De grace especial,"* 129–31, notes that marks of identity, such as "name, social rank, vocation, address, age," helped guarantee the validity of the testimony and tied the inquiry to the social fabric.

12. Laurière, *Ordonnances des roys de France,* 1: 541–43 (law of 1294); Neithard Bulst, "Lois somptuaires," in *DMA,* 845–46 (with refs.).

13. Roux, *Paris in the Middle Ages,* 50 ("30 to 40 percent of men bore the baptismal name Jean").

14. "Enquête," 223–24.

15. Roux, *Paris in the Middle Ages,* 247; Greimas, *Dictionnaire de l'ancien français,* s.v. "lombart" (etym.).

16. "Enquête," 227–29.

17. Geremek, *The Margins of Society,* 253–62, discussing migration, notes that Paris had streets "bearing the names of Bretons, where natives of that region congregated" (255, n. 50). On dialects in Paris reflecting regional origin as well as class or vocation, see Lodge, *A Sociolinguistic History of Parisian*

French, 99, 105, 121–26, 135–36, 231. Robb, *The Discovery of France,* 52, notes the "hive of micro-dialects" persisting in large French cities centuries later.

18. "Enquête," 222–26.

19. Monstrelet, *Chronique,* 1: 161.

20. "Enquête," 245 (Jacques Cardon).

21. "one empty barrel" is the translation of ·i· *poinçon vuit*; and "about twelve pounds of hay" is the translation of *environ demi quarteron de foing.* On the units, see Zupko, *French Weights and Measures,* 140, 151–52; and *A Parisian Journal,* Introduction, 35, s.v. "poinson."

22. "Enquête," 241–42.

23. Geremek, *The Margins of Society,* 254.

24. "Enquête," 244–45.

25. Hillairet, *Rues,* 1: 332, citing "l'escalier conduisant aux tribunaux."

26. Vaughan, *JF,* 47.

27. Schnerb, *Jean sans Peur,* 229, likens the Clisson and Orleans attacks and even suggests the involvement of Pierre de Craon's son Antoine in the latter.

28. "Enquête," 242.

29. Ibid. Guillaume typically uses the first-person-plural pronoun (*nous*), translated throughout as "I." In this passage, the provost appears in the third person (*il*), altered to "I" in the translation.

30. Ibid., 242–43.

Chapter Nine: A Break in the Case

1. "Enquête," 243–44 (François d'Asignac).

2. Interpolated from the broker's testimony that his client wanted to see the house *"assavoir se il lui seroit bon"*—"to learn if it was good for him"—and "after having seen it, the said scholar said . . . that he would rent it."

3. Crossley-Holland, *Living and Dining,* 74–78; *Atlas de Paris,* 193 (wine transport to Paris).

4. Coville, *Jean Petit,* 89, describing the "meticulous investigation," states, "The end of the night and all the next day were filled with examinations of all sorts."

5. "Enquête," 230–32.

6. Altered from "Campignoles," following *DENF,* 163, s.v. "Campagnolle."

7. "Enquête," 238–40.

8. Ibid., 223.

9. "Nicolle du Car," in the source, suggests a woman (see *DENF,* 728, s.v. "Nicolas"), but "cirurgien" (not *-ienne*) and other grammatical details imply a man.

10. "Enquête," 241.

11. Geremek, *The Margins of Society,* 98, 143, 174, cites legal records that mention bakers' servants.

12. "Enquête," 233–34. Jean Briand: "Brian" in the source, but "Briand" is more likely (*DENF,* 141).

13. Guenée, *Un meurtre,* 10; Schnerb, *Jean sans Peur,* 209.

14. "Enquête," 229–30.

15. Ibid., 234–35.

16. Ibid., 236–37.

17. Ibid., 237–38.

18. Ibid., 246–47.

19. Ibid., 247.

20. Girard actually says a long robe of "purple" (*violet*) cloth, although most witnesses describe the red-hooded scholar's robe as "brown" (*brun*). On violet as a color sometimes used in academic garb, see Hodges, *Chaucer and Clothing*, 160, n. 3, with refs.

21. "Enquête," 247.

22. Ibid. specifies a stall "près de la Rappée." On this location, see Fierro, *Dictionnaire du Paris disparu*, 238, s.v. "Rapée (Fief de La)." The name is altered from "Lemperier," following *DENF*, 613, s.v. "Lemperière."

23. "Enquête," 248, situates her at the "[marché] aux Porées" (see *Atlas de Paris*, 197, map, item no. 17).

24. "Enquête," 248–49. The Rue au Feurre ran east of Les Halles along the north side of Les Innocents cemetery (*Atlas de Paris*, 197).

25. *Le Ménagier de Paris*, 1:xxv, xl; *Goodman of Paris*, 1, 25; Crossley-Holland, *Living and Dining*, 138–41; and Woolgar, *The Great Household*, esp. ch. 7, with examples of cooks for hire, 80, 108, 137.

26. Viollet-le-Duc, *Dictionnaire*, 2:234-41 (s.v. "boutique"). Geremek, *The Margins of Society*, 78, notes that artisans were required to practice their craft "publicly."

27. At the murder house, Jacques Cardon had confiscated a wicker basket (*pannier d'osier*, "Enquête," 245), described later as white and made of slats (*pannier d'esclices*, "Enquête," 248).

28. Ibid., 249.

29. Coville, *Jean Petit*, 89, notes Guillaume's quick grasp of "several troubling indications."

30. *Plan de Paris*, upper left quadrant.

31. "Enquête," 236–37 (Jean Fovel), with mention of the colors as a heraldic device (*devise*), suggesting livery of some sort.

32. Hindman, *Christine de Pizan's "Epistre Othéa,"* 120–21, notes John's "love of green" in particular. A contemporary image shows John at court dressed entirely in green (Pierre Salmon, *Dialogues*, Geneva, Bibliothèque publique et universitaire, MS. 165, fol. 7). Evidently following Héraut Berry, *Chroniques*, 24, both Autrand, *Charles VI*, 354, and Guenée, *Meurtre*, 9–10, mention a water carrier attached to Burgundy's palace, but the investigation report connects none of the deposed water carriers with the Hôtel of Artois. The main clue, besides the trail of caltrops, may have been the telltale livery.

33. Monstrelet, *Chronique*, 1:158, specifies that the fleeing assassins entered John's palace by a back gate (*par derrière*). A map of Paris ca. 1535 shows an east

gate in the Rue Saint-Denis and a west one in the Rue Montorgueil (or Rue Comtesse d'Artois), each situated just north (outside) of the old city wall (Rivière and Lavoye, *Tour Jean sans Peur,* 15). Since the palace predated the new wall of Charles V (1365–80) and was unlikely to have had gates *only* outside the city, it probably had a south gate as well in the Rue Mauconseil, especially since the stables were adjacent to this street, according to repair records of 1363 and 1379 (Richard, "Documents," 144, 147). Of course, if the Rue Saint-Denis gate existed in 1407, the assassins could have entered the palace grounds directly from that street moments after exiting the Rue aux Oues.

34. See notes for the end of ch. 10 on the joint Mass, etc.

Chapter Ten: Rival Dukes

1. Vaughan, *JF,* 232, 236; Schnerb, *Jean sans Peur,* 390; Van Kerrebrouck, *Les Valois,* 517–21.

2. Brantôme, *Des dames,* Discours 6, *Oeuvres complètes,* 9:472; cited by Sellier, *Quartier Barbette,* 42 (as discours 7).

3. Basin, *Histoire de Charles VII,* 1:13, the only source for this story (1:13, n. 3), but see Guenée, *Between Church and State,* 5, on Basin's devotion to the truth.

4. Brantôme (as cited above), says Louis boasted of his gallery in John's hearing, and John later entered the gallery on his own; Vallet de Viriville, "Assassinat," 249, cites a *Chronique hollandaise,* which says that Louis *showed* John the gallery, and that John recognized his wife in one of the paintings.

5. Guenée, *Un meurtre,* 145, describing John as "ugly" and pointing out numerous contrasts between the two cousins. See also Collas, *Valentine de Milan,* 320–21.

6. Collas, *Valentine de Milan,* 321.

7. Vaughan, *JF,* 28, 234–35; Famiglietti, *RI,* 55.

8. The mottos are reported variously: see Monstrelet, *Chronique,* 1:123; Vallet de Viriville, "Assassinat," 250; Van Kerrebrouck, *Les Valois,* 369, n. 12; and, for a detailed study, Hutchison, "Partisan Identity."

9. Champollion-Figeac, *Louis et Charles ducs d'Orléans,* 1:91–97. On John and wolf hunting, see Mirot, "Jean sans Peur de 1398 à 1405," 162; and Schnerb, *Jean sans Peur,* 478–81.

10. Vaughan, *Philip the Bold,* 46–47, 55–58; Famiglietti, *RI,* 24–25.

11. Pius, *I commentarii,* 1:1056–58; Pius, *The Commentaries of Pius II,* 426, cited by Vallet de Viriville, "Assassinat," 247.

12. Veenstra, *Magic and Divination,* 81–85.

13. Atiya, *The Crusade of Nicopolis.* On Philip's key role: Vaughan, *Philip the Bold,* ch. 4.

14. Vaughan, *Philip the Bold,* 66; *JF,* 3; Schnerb, *Jean sans Peur,* 63.

15. Vaughan, *Philip the Bold,* 68–69; and, for more details, Atiya, *The Crusade of Nicopolis,* ch. 4.

16. Chaucer, "The Book of the Duchess," line 1024, *Riverside Chaucer*, p. 342, includes "Walakye" in a list of hard or forbidding places to travel. Vlad III, the Impaler (1431–1476), was prince of Wallachia.

17. Vaughan, *Philip the Bold*, 69. On the destruction of Vidin (or Widden), several other cities, and also atrocities committed by the crusaders while en route, see Atiya, *The Crusade of Nicopolis*, 57–60.

18. Atiya, *The Crusade of Nicopolis*, 61–62. On mining, see also Barker, *Conquest*, 32–33.

19. Atiya, *The Crusade of Nicopolis*, 63.

20. Ibid., 63–65, gives details of the sultan's allies and route to Nicopolis.

21. Battle details from ibid., ch. 6; and Froissart/Johnes, *Chronicles*, 2:622–27.

22. Froissart/Johnes, *Chronicles*, 2:623, with "very beautiful array" from *Boucicaut*, 240, cited in Schnerb, *Jean sans Peur*, 79. On banners and pennons, see Froissart/Johnes, *Chronicles*, 2:623.

23. Atiya, *The Crusade of Nicopolis*, 87.

24. *Boucicaut*, 240; Schnerb, *Jean sans Peur*, 80.

25. *Boucicaut*, 240; Schnerb, *Jean sans Peur*, 80.

26. *Boucicaut*, 241.

27. Froissart/Johnes, *Chronicles*, 2:626; *Boucicaut*, 242–43; Schnerb, *Jean sans Peur*, 83–86.

28. *Boucicaut*, 242.

29. Ibid., 243; Froissart/Johnes, *Chronicles*, 2:626; Schnerb, *Jean sans Peur*, 85.

30. Lalande, *Jean II le Meinigre, dit Boucicaut*, 68, with refs.

31. Vaughan, *Philip the Bold*, 76–78, details various expenses contributing to the total cost; *JF*, 120 ("half a million").

32. Vaughan, *JF*, 4; Schnerb, *Jean sans Peur*, 60 (with map).

33. Guenée, *Un meurtre*, 145. John may have suffered from posttraumatic stress disorder. A French scholar writing in 1942 evoked John's horror at seeing his comrades brutally executed and his "year-long agony" awaiting execution or deliverance himself (Pocquet du Haut-Jussé, "Jean sans Peur, son but et sa méthode," 182).

34. Schnerb, *Jean sans Peur*, 103, notes a Mass for his slain comrades that John observed on the anniversary of Nicopolis for many years afterward.

35. Froissart/Johnes, *Chronicles*, 2:604, 607. Durrieu, "Jean sans Peur," 209–10, suggests that Louis was his father-in-law's informant at the French court, and, 211, that the Nicopolis disaster helped the Duke of Milan against the Florentines. On Sultan Bayezid's advance knowledge of the campaign, see Atiya, *The Crusade of Nicopolis*, 62–63.

36. Vaughan, *JF*, 230, 235.

37. Vallet de Viriville, "Assassinat," 245–46, and Kervyn de Lettenhove, *Histoire de Flandre*, 4:122–23, refer to papal letters arriving "shortly after" Philip's death and provoking John. After Philip's death (April 27, 1404), John

accompanied the bier as far as Douai, where he made his longest stop (May 5–9) before leaving for Paris (Petit, *Itinéraires,* 341–42). Thus the council may have been held at Douai, although Basin (as cited in next note) says it did not take place until after Philip's "funérailles."

38. Basin, *Histoire de Charles VII,* 1:15–19, the source for the story of the two councils and the speeches at each. Mirot, "L'État," 71, says that upon his father's death, John underwent "a complete political and moral transformation" marked by overweening ambition, hatred for his cousin, and a complete lack of scruples about how he achieved his ends.

39. Veenstra, *Magic and Divination,* 82–83, with refs. See also Vaughan, *JF,* 54, on "bogus pilgrims" used to spread propaganda.

40. Basin, *Histoire de Charles VII,* 1:17.

41. Mirot, "L'État," 71, with "subtle, wary, suspicious" from de La Marche, *Mémoires,* 316, quoted in Vaughan, *JF,* 230.

42. Vaughan, *JF,* 230.

43. Odette "brought into the court by Jean sans Peur": Van Kerrebrouck, *Les Valois,* 129.

44. Vaughan, *JF,* 230.

45. Ibid., ch. 5, detailing John's finances and noting that he "drove the Burgundian financial machine as hard as he could" (120).

46. Gascar, *Charles VI,* 135–36.

47. RSD, 3:231. On John's opposition to Louis's tax policy, see also Vaughan, *JF,* 31–32.

48. RSD, 3:231.

49. For an outline of events, see Vaughan, *JF,* 33–36; Famiglietti, *RI,* 46–51.

50. Louis de France, Duke of Guyenne, born January, 22, 1397 (Van Kerrebrouck, *Les Valois,* 117).

51. Famiglietti, *RI,* 47.

52. Marguerite: born December 8, 1393 (Van Kerrebrouck, *Les Valois,* 365). The marriage was still unconsummated in 1409: Famiglietti, *RI,* 77.

53. Famiglietti, *RI,* 46.

54. Ibid. and 230, n. 53; RSD, 3:283.

55. Guenée, *La folie,* 295 (no. 29).

56. Petit, *Itinéraires,* 350; Famiglietti, *RI,* 46.

57. RSD, 3:291–97; Monstrelet, *Chronique,* 1:108–13; Famiglietti, *RI,* 46–48; and Vaughan, *JF,* 33–36—all describe the removal of the dauphin from Paris and what followed.

58. RSD, 3:293 ("en toute hâte").

59. Van Kerrebrouck, *Les Valois,* 116–17.

60. Monstrelet, *Chronique,* 1:109.

61. RSD, 3:295.

62. Ibid. Cutting the traces: Darwin, *Louis d'Orléans,* 76, 233 (refs.).

63. RSD, 3:295, with indirect speech rendered as dialogue here and in what follows. "Sire" and "Father," typical usages, are added, following RSD's emphasis on a "respectful" and "amicable" exchange.

64. Ibid., noting Burgundy's "joy" at the dauphin's reply.

65. Ibid., citing Bavaria's threat of the queen's displeasure. Monstrelet, *Chronique,* 1:110, says Bavaria defied anyone "in the king's name" to lay a hand on the carriage.

66. RSD, 3:295 (a direct quote).

67. Ibid.; Monstrelet, *Chronique,* 1:111 (with Pouilly, the correct location, from Famiglietti, *RI,* 47 and 231, n. 59).

68. RSD, 3:297; Monstrelet, *Chronique,* 1:111.

69. RSD, 3:307.

70. Ibid.; Monstrelet, *Chronique,* 1:113.

71. RSD, 3:309.

72. Ibid.; Monstrelet, *Chronique,* 1:113; *A Parisian Journal,* 48.

73. RSD, 3:311–17, detailing the various embassies to Louis of Orleans and his scornful replies to them.

74. Ibid., 3:331.

75. Ibid., 3:333.

76. *A Parisian Journal,* 47.

77. Ibid., 48, with "Parisians were in such a panic."

78. Monstrelet, *Chronique,* 1:120.

79. Vaughan, *JF,* 139 (approx. 3,500 troops); Famiglietti, *RI,* 50 (4,560 troops).

80. Famiglietti, *RI,* 50–51, for this paragraph.

81. Monstrelet, *Chronique,* 1:124; Vaughan, *JF,* 36.

82. Petit, *Itinéraires,* 585; Famiglietti, *RI,* 54–55, with details of dinners and gifts cited in this paragraph; and Schnerb, *Jean sans Peur,* 181.

83. Vaughan, *JF,* 40–41.

84. Famiglietti, *RI,* 55.

85. Dates and ages from Van Kerrebrouck, *Les Valois,* 115, 239–40.

86. Schnerb, *Jean sans Peur,* 182.

87. Vaughan, *JF,* 38; Schnerb, *Jean sans Peur,* 182.

88. On the parallel campaigns, see Vaughan, *JF,* 38–41; and Famiglietti, *RI,* 58–60.

89. Gascar, *Charles VI,* 138. Louis cancels his expedition: Vaughan, *JF,* 38–39.

90. Vaughan, *JF,* 40, citing Monstrelet, *Chronique,* 1:135–38, but questioning whether Orleans was really to blame. Another chronicle, quoted in Monstrelet, 138–39, n. 1, says Burgundy now "knew with a certainty that the Duke of Orleans sought only to destroy and kill him."

91. Petit, *Itinéraires,* 356–57 (arriving in the capital on December 14).

92. Vaughan, *JF,* 41, tallying up the money owed (41–43).

93. Famiglietti, *RI,* 60–61 and 63 ("He probably also attributed to Louis the delay"). Nordberg, *Les ducs et la royauté,* 235, attributes the withholding of Jean's annual subsidies to Louis.

94. Schnerb, *Jean sans Peur,* 206; Nordberg, *Les ducs et la royauté,* 237, says that John's power and influence were thus "eliminated."

95. De La Marche, *Mémoires,* 317; cited by Schnerb, *Jean sans Peur,* 218. See also Vallet de Viriville, "Assassinat," 248.

96. "honor and reputation": Vallet de Viriville, "Assassinat," 252 (citing de Bauyn). John's resentment "knew no bounds": RSD, 3:448.

97. "Enquête," 243 (d'Asignac's deposition).

98. Vaughan, *JF,* 44 (dating Louis's threat to "within a month" of Anthony's possession of this territory "in December 1406").

99. Ibid., 31, 43–44; Famiglietti, *RI,* 62; Vallet de Viriville, "Assassinat," 249, n. 2 (also citing a story that Louis reversed an order sending French troops to aid John in the Liège campaign).

100. Nordberg, *Les ducs et la royauté,* 149; Famiglietti, *RI,* 62–63.

101. Vaughan, *Philip the Bold,* 73–74.

102. Vallet de Viriville, "Assassinat," 254–56, citing a *Cronica di Lucca* by a "Ser Cambio."

103. Nordberg, *Les ducs et la royauté,* 230 (with ref.). It is likely that Rapondi sent the courier.

104. Juvénal, *Histoire,* 444, 445; Schnerb, *Jean sans Peur,* 206–7.

105. From a lost chronicle by Hennotin de Clériaux (or Clairiaux), said to be one of Louis's heralds, as quoted in Favyn, *Le Théâtre d'honneur et de chevalerie,* 1:730. Vallet de Viriville (Cousinot, *Geste des nobles,* 114–15, n. 1) reproduces Favyn's excerpts from Hennotin and summarizes the same in "Assassinat," 252–53.

106. Biver and Biver, *Abbayes, monastères et couvents,* 176–91; Hillairet, *Rues,* 1:597–98 (sketch).

107. Hennotin, in Cousinot, *Geste des nobles,* 115, n. 1 (cont.). The kiss of peace (*osculum pacis*) was usual in ceremonies of reconciliation: *DMA,* 126, s.v. "baiser."

108. Hennotin, as quoted in Cousinot, *Geste des nobles,* 115, n. 1 (cont.). Van Kerrebrouck, *Les Valois,* 233 and 238 (n. 26), details the order's founding and insignia, and, 365, confirms the date of John's admission (November 20, 1407). The account of the mutual kisses that follow and Berry's "tears of joy" is also from Hennotin, as quoted in *Geste,* and Vallet de Viriville, "Assassinat," 253.

109. Plancher, *Histoire générale,* 3, *preuves,* cclxxviii, as cited in Vallet de Viriville, "Assassinat," 253.

Chapter Eleven: A Confession

1. Guenée, *Un meurtre,* 185.

2. Juvénal, *Histoire,* 445. Plancher, *Histoire,* 3:251, concurs ("personne n'en soupçonnoit le Duc Jean"). RSD, 3:737, notes John's pretense of "great sor-

row," and Cousinot, *Geste des nobles,* 115, remarks that John outdid the others in mourning.

3. For "cannon powder" (gunpowder) or *poudre à canon,* as it was often called at the time, see Smith and DeVries, *The Artillery,* 45, 237, and 246.

4. De Carbonnières, *La procédure,* 423.

5. Monstrelet, *Chronique,* 1:162. The sources vary, and I follow mainly the authoritative summary of the facts in Coville, *Jean Petit,* 90, and Guenée, *Meurtre,* 10, both of whom place the second council meeting on Friday, at the Hôtel Saint-Pol, with Guillaume himself reporting, not his lieutenant (as in *Geste,* 116).

6. Monstrelet, *Chronique,* 1:162 (paraphrasing Berry's question).

7. Ibid.

8. Héraut Berry, *Chroniques,* 24. Guenée, *Un meurtre,* 10, calls Burgundy's palace "un asile quasi inviolable."

9. Monstrelet, *Chronique,* 1:162, paraphrased from an indirect quotation, "And then King Louis [the Duke of Anjou], the Duke of Berry and the Duke of Bourbon gave him leave and permission."

10. Ibid.

11. Héraut Berry, *Chroniques,* 24; Eder, "Tignonvillana inedita," 860.

12. Héraut Berry, *Chroniques,* 24.

13. Cousinot, *Geste des nobles,* 116.

14. Monstrelet, *Chronique,* 1:162, with the "astounded" reaction, and they "began to berate him."

15. Petit, *Itinéraires,* 586; Schnerb, *Jean sans Peur,* 213.

16. Héraut Berry, *Chroniques,* 25.

17. Monstrelet, *Chronique,* 1:163.

18. Ibid.

19. *Atlas de Paris,* 106, 109; Hillairet, *Rues,* 1:381–82.

20. Monstrelet, *Chronique,* 1:163, mentions Waleran "en sa compaignie"; the bodyguards are assumed, since John had attended Louis's vigil with men-at-arms (RSD, 3:737); stairs are mentioned by Héraut Berry, *Chroniques,* 25.

21. Monstrelet, *Chronique,* 1:163, with Berry's subsequent orders to lock the doors, John's "very troubled and confused" reaction, and his exchange with Waleran.

22. Héraut Berry, *Chroniques,* 25 ("sans dire adieu").

23. Ibid.

24. Vallet de Viriville, "Assassinat," 259; RSD, 3:741.

25. Héraut Berry, *Chroniques,* 25, recounts how the three dukes then set off on their horses to see the king.

26. Guenée, *La folie,* 295, notes the interlude between spells thirty-five and thirty-six. By one account, the king was at first told only that his brother had been "beaten" (Lehoux, *Jean de France,* 3:107, n. 7; Coville, *Jean Petit,* 91–92).

27. Vallet de Viriville, "Assassinat," 260, with "jumped on a horse"; Héraut Berry, *Chroniques,* 25 ("hastily mounted a fast horse"); and Schnerb, *Jean sans Peur,* 104, 311.

28. Vallet de Viriville, "Assassinat," 260.

29. Monstrelet, *Chronique,* 1:164; *Plan de Paris* (showing John's palace about six hundred meters south of the gate).

30. *Atlas de Paris,* 51. Monstrelet, *Chronique,* 1:162, does not say which two city gates were still open but does specify (1:164) that John left the city via the Porte Saint-Denis, which must have been one of the two.

31. *Atlas de Paris,* 51 (upper sketch and text describing suburban development in the vicinity).

32. Cousinot, *Geste des nobles,* 116, and Héraut Berry, *Chroniques,* 26, reporting snow on the night of Louis's murder; see also Coville, *Jean Petit,* 94. But John's rapid progress on the roads (Schnerb, *Jean sans Peur,* 215) suggests that travel conditions were still good on Saturday, November 26.

33. Monstrelet, *Chronique,* 1:164.

34. Ibid. The sources vary on this point; see Lehoux, *Jean de France,* 3:111, n. 5.

35. Monstrelet, *Chronique,* 1:164, noting the different routes of travel to the château in Artois; Vallet de Viriville, "Assassinat," 260–61.

36. Monstrelet, *Chronique,* 1:164; Vaughan, *JF,* 47. Schnerb, *Jean sans Peur,* 215, demurs, saying John rode "without cease, not stopping anywhere except for fresh horses."

37. Héraut Berry, *Chroniques,* 25.

38. Ibid., 26.

39. Boyer, "A Day's Journey," 604.

40. Schnerb, *Jean sans Peur,* 215 (calculating the distance to Éclusier, where John crossed the Somme, as 140 kilometers).

41. Ibid.

42. Ibid., 215–16; Coville, *Jean Petit,* 94–95 (with refs.).

43. Vaughan, *JF,* 47.

44. Ibid.

45. De Baye, *Journal,* 1:208.

46. Monstrelet, *Chronique,* 1:164–65, cited by Gauvard, *"De grace especial,"* 1:166, in connection with John's flight.

47. Monstrelet, *Chronique,* 1:165.

48. Cochon, *Chronique normande,* 381. See also Monstrelet, *Chronique,* 1:166, n. 1.

Chapter Twelve: The Justification

1. Vaughan, *JF,* 69 (wine, ink, sea, rivers); RSD, 3:745–49 (frozen wells, bread, cattle, people); Monstrelet, *Chronique,* 1:165; Cousinot, *Geste des nobles,* 116–17. See also refs. in Britton, *A Meteorological Chronology,* 154–55.

2. RSD, 3:745 (slightly condensed).

3. Vaughan, *JF,* 67. See also Monstrelet, *Chronique,* 1:176, on John's return to Paris with the intent "to justify his deed and his cause."

4. Vaughan, *JF,* 68. On the Lille and Ghent conferences, see also Monstrelet, *Chronique,* 1:171. Petit, *Itinéraires,* 362, places John in Lille on December 12.

5. Vaughan, *JF,* 68.

6. Schnerb, *Jean sans Peur,* 236.

7. Jean Brandon, as summarized in ibid.

8. Vaughan, *JF,* 67, citing various Burgundian officials sent to Paris, including his chancellor (Jehan de Saulx)

9. Van Kerrebrouck, *Les Valois,* 241 and 244, n. 7.

10. Collas, *Valentine de Milan,* 367. After her Paris visit, Valentina would return to Blois (Schnerb, *Jean sans Peur,* 237).

11. RSD, 3:749–53, detailing Valentina's subsequent journey to Paris. See also Monstrelet, *Chronique,* 1:167–68. Vaughan, *JF,* 68, says Valentina saw the king on December 10 and 21.

12. RSD, 3:749, says the duchess took two sons with her, but Monstrelet, *Chronique,* 1:167, mentions only the youngest (Jean).

13. Monstrelet, *Chronique,* 1:167–68.

14. Ibid., 1:167.

15. RSD, 3:751–53, with John as Judas on 751.

16. Famiglietti, *RI,* 238–39, n. 183.

17. Monstrelet, *Chronique,* 1:168.

18. Ibid., enumerates those in attendance.

19. Ibid., 1:169.

20. Ibid.

21. Ibid., 1:169–70.

22. Vaughan, *JF,* 68–69.

23. Monstrelet, *Chronique,* 1:170–71. On *étrennes,* see Buettner, "Past Presents," 600–603.

24. RSD, 3:753.

25. Ibid.; Guenée, *La folie,* 295 (no. 36), gives the date as "after January 4."

26. Collas, *Valentine de Milan,* 376.

27. Vaughan, *JF,* 67.

28. Ibid., ch.1, details John's inheritance, and 228–29 describes the emergence of the Burgundian state as "a new power."

29. Ibid., 4.

30. Schnerb, *Jean sans Peur,* 238. On this embassy, see also Plancher, *Histoire,* 3:252–53.

31. Vaughan, *JF,* 67–68. Schnerb, *Jean sans Peur,* 238, details the negotiations leading to the Amiens meeting.

32. Famiglietti, *RI,* 66.

33. Lehoux, *Jean de France,* 3:112 and n. 4; cited by Famiglietti, *RI,* 66 and 240, n. 6. Hirschbiegel, *Étrennes,* Katalog, nos. 1430, 1478, and 1721.

34. RSD, 3:742, cited in Guenée, *Un meurtre*, 184. Bourbon's departure from the court: Monstrelet, *Chronique*, 1:173. See also Schnerb, *Jean sans Peur*, 238.

35. Vaughan, *JF*, 69.

36. Monstrelet, *Chronique*, 1:172–73; Petit, *Itinéraires*, 363 (John at Amiens, January 20–31).

37. Vaughan, *JF*, 69.

38. Cousinot, *Geste des nobles*, 117–18, notes their futile attempts at "repparacion." Famiglietti, *RI*, 67, says the two dukes gave up hope of an apology and that John had "a second justification" read out at Amiens.

39. Cousinot, *Geste des nobles*, 118. Vaughan, *JF*, 69, says John was "obdurate."

40. Famiglietti, *RI*, 67.

41. RSD, 3:747. Further details of destruction: de Baye, *Journal*, 1:212–21.

42. Héraut Berry, *Chronique*, 26, also mentioning houses and mills. RSD, 3:747, mentions livestock.

43. Monstrelet, *Chronique*, 1:165 ("Pont Neuf"); *A Parisian Journal*, 441, s.v. "Pont Saint-Michel."

44. Monstrelet, *Chronique*, 1:175–76; Cochon, *Chronique normande*, 362; and Famiglietti, *RI*, 67, all note the encounter with Anjou and Berry.

45. Monstrelet, *Chronique*, 1:176. See Littré, *Dictionnaire de la langue française*, s.v. "Noël," 4; and *A Parisian Journal*, 50 ("Noël" used to greet the king).

46. RSD, 3:752–54. Juvénal, *Histoire*, 445, says Burgundy returned to Paris with "about 1,000 men."

47. Juvénal, *Histoire*, 445.

48. Cochon, *Chronique normande*, 362, as cited in Famiglietti, *RI*, 67 and 240, n. 17.

49. Petit, *Itinéraires*, 587.

50. Monstrelet, *Chronique*, 1:177; cited in Schnerb, *Jean sans Peur*, 244.

51. Richard, "Documents." On John's tower in particular, see Plagnieux, "La Tour Jean sans Peur"; Perrault-Dabot, *L'Hôtel de Bourgogne*; and Hillairet, *Évocation*, 257–61.

52. Vaughan, *JF*, 85, with dates, cost, etc.

53. Monstrelet, *Chronique*, 1:177.

54. Schnerb, *Jean sans Peur*, 247–49, notes that Petit accompanied Philip the Bold to Avignon in 1395 to try to resolve the Schism. Guenée, *Un meurtre*, 189–90, sketches Petit's career, saying that in 1408 he was "about forty-five." RSD, 3:754, says Petit was better known for his hardiness of speech (*libera loquencia*) than for his eloquence. For more, see Coville, *Jean Petit*, chs. 1 and 2.

55. Thierry le Roy, "Rapport," 11–12. See also Coville, *Jean Petit*, 106–7, and Schnerb, *Jean sans Peur*, 244–45, 250, both noting the precision and detail of the mise-en-scène in Thierry le Roy's "Rapport."

56. Thierry le Roy, "Rapport," 12.

57. RSD, 3:755; Thierry le Roy, "Rapport," 11 ("la Grant sale...bien large"). The Grande Salle's dimensions do not survive, but another large room, the *chambre de Charlemagne,* was "fifteen fathoms long and six wide," or about ninety feet by forty-eight (Bournon, *L'hôtel royal de Saint-Pol,* 41, citing Sauval).

58. Bournon, *L'hôtel royal de Saint-Pol,* 72.

59. De Baye, *Journal,* 1:222. Cousinot, *Geste des nobles,* 119, agrees.

60. Thierry le Roy, "Rapport," 12.

61. Ibid. ("baillier par escript") also describes the sole entrance, "a window on the courtyard," entered "one by one."

62. Ibid., 12, 13.

63. Coville, *Jean Petit,* 108.

64. Thierry le Roy, "Rapport," 12–13. The distance from the east side of Burgundy's palace grounds, south along the Rue Saint-Denis, then west along the Rue de Verrerie and several other streets to the Hôtel Saint-Pol, is more than fifteen hundred meters, or about a mile, according to the *Plan de Paris.*

65. Thierry le Roy, "Rapport," 13, with "loudly" supplied by Schnerb, *Jean sans Peur,* 251.

66. Coville, "Le véritable texte," 62. See also Schnerb, *Jean sans Peur,* 251 ("prince affable").

67. Thierry le Roy, "Rapport," 13–14, with details of John's fur-trimmed scarlet robe and mail vest.

68. Ibid., 14, specifies a velour hat. The "customary black hat" is from Vaughan, *JF,* 235.

69. Thierry le Roy, "Rapport," 14, with seating details.

70. Ibid., 14–15. Cousinot, *Geste des nobles,* 119, likewise notes de Tignonville's presence on March 8.

71. De Tignonville, *The Dicts and Sayings,* 162/30.

72. Thierry le Roy, "Rapport," 15.

73. Monstrelet, *Chronique,* 1:177–244, reproducing Petit's entire oration (partly trans., Monstrelet/Johnes, 1:61–81); with briefer accounts in RSD, 3:753–65, and Thierry le Roy, "Rapport." For summaries, see Vaughan, *JF,* 70–72; and Schnerb, *Jean sans Peur,* 250–53. On the manuscript sources, see Coville, "Le véritable texte."

74. *"Radix enim omnium malorum est cupiditas"* (1 Tim. 6:10).

75. Guenée, *Meurtre,* 197, notes that Burgundy claimed to have acted "pour le tres grant bien...de tout le royaume."

76. Vaughan, *JF,* 71, quotes examples.

77. Ibid. (in summary).

78. Monstrelet, *Chronique,* 1:214–15.

79. Thierry le Roy, "Rapport," 17–19. Monstrelet, *Chronique,* 1:224–27, records much the same story.

80. List abbreviated from Vaughan, *JF,* 71–72.

81. Thierry le Roy, "Rapport," 20–21.

82. Ibid., 21, also cites Madame Berry but stresses Madame Burgundy's role. The parallel passage in Monstrelet, *Chronique,* 1:234, mentions Madame Burgundy but without special stress.

83. Monstrelet, *Chronique,* 1:242, quoted in Vaughan, *JF,* 72.

84. Thierry le Roy, "Rapport," 26; Vaughan, *JF,* 70.

85. Thierry le Roy, "Rapport," 26.

86. Ibid., 25; Schnerb, *Jean sans Peur,* 253.

87. Veenstra, *Magic and Divination,* 48–51, in a sketch of Petit's career, refers to him as such.

88. Monstrelet, *Chronique,* 1:243. RSD, 3:765, calls Petit's oration "reprehensible."

89. Vaughan, *JF,* 70.

90. Ibid., refers to copies "circulated around Europe." Coville, *Jean Petit,* ch. 5, traces the oration's written dissemination.

91. Reproduced in Vaughan, *JF,* plate 4 (black-and-white); and Guenée, *Meurtre,* plates 6–7 (color). On deluxe copies, see Coville, "Le véritable texte," 64.

92. Veenstra, *Magic and Divination,* 364, on John as "lion"; Schnerb, *Jean sans Peur,* 480, on Louis as "wolf."

93. Cochon, *Chronique normande,* 396. See Guenée, *La folie,* 295, no. 36 (with refs., n. 31).

94. Cochon, *Chronique normande,* 396; Juvénal, *Histoire,* 445 ("vendredy"); Famiglietti, *RI,* 68. RSD, 3:767, and Monstrelet, *Chronique,* 1:243–44, describe John's royal pardon. See also Vaughan, *JF,* 72.

95. Juvénal, *Histoire,* 445; RSD, 3:767; Monstrelet, *Chronique,* 1:243. For one of the letters, see Plancher, *Histoire,* 3, *preuves,* cclvi ("heart," col. 2), as cited by Famiglietti, *RI,* 68 and 240, n. 20.

96. Famiglietti, *RI,* 68.

97. Schnerb, *Jean Sans Peur,* 253–56, gives further details of the official pardon, including the royal council's consent to everything John asked for.

98. RSD, 3:767, with John's reply, "I fear no one," both as indirect quotations.

Chapter Thirteen: Amende Honorable

1. RSD, 3:767; Juvénal, *Histoire,* 446, notes the departure of Anjou and Berry; see also Famiglietti, *RI,* 68 and 240, n. 21.

2. Lehoux, *Jean de France,* 3:121–22.

3. Juvénal, *Histoire,* 445, notes that people blamed the queen; Guenée, *La folie,* 295, no. 37, with n. 32.

4. Jarry, *La vie politique de Louis de France,* 242, as cited by Guenée, *Un meurtre,* 182.

5. Lehoux, *Jean de France,* 3:122.

6. For Guillaume at the March 18 meeting, see Lehoux, *Jean de France,* 3:128, n. 5. For Burgundy "greatly displeased," see Juvénal, *Histoire,* 446.

7. Relevant documents in *CUP,* 4:146–56 (nos. 1840, 1843–44, 1847, 1849– 52); accounts in RSD, 3:722–25; Juvénal, *Histoire,* 444, 446–47; Monstrelet, *Chronique,* 1:75–76; Cousinot, *Geste des nobles,* 120–21; Héraut Berry, *Chroniques,* 32–33; and de Baye, *Journal,* 1:229–30, 231; with editorial notes in Berry and de Baye, and comments in Famiglietti, *RI,* 242, n. 23, and Gauvard, *"De grace especial,"* 228–29, n. 165.

8. De Baye, *Journal,* 1:205, specifying the presence of the dauphin and the Dukes of Anjou, Berry, and Burgundy.

9. *CUP,* 4:147 (no. 1840, "a lectionibus et sermonibus cessando"), implying that the ban went into effect soon after the executions (October 26). RSD, 3:727, notes the suspension of benefits as well but without indicating a date.

10. *CUP,* 4:148–49 (nos. 1843–44).

11. De Baye, *Journal,* 1:221. Veenstra, *Magic and Divination,* 66, connects the two incidents. Work on John's tower: Vaughan, *JF,* 85, citing dates from archival records.

12. Geremek, *The Margins of Society,* 151–52.

13. *Atlas de Paris,* 175–77, with an overview of the university and the Latin Quarter, 171–74. Favier, *Paris au XVe siècle,* 199–235, treats the university in detail, including town-and-gown disputes, 206–9.

14. Geremek, *The Margins of Society,* 147–50, supplies some demographic details.

15. Ibid., 151.

16. Jones, *Paris,* 57.

17. Cohen, *The Crossroads of Justice,* 196–97.

18. RSD, 1:98–107; Hillairet, *La rue Saint-Antoine,* 162; and Ducoudray, *Les origines du Parlement de Paris,* 707–8. RSD's account greatly favors the Church, but Ducoudray says the resulting trial "has remained mysterious."

19. Geremek, *The Margins of Society,* 149–51; Champion, *François Villon,* 1:67–69.

20. Ducoudray, *Les origines du Parlement,* 593–600; Geremek, *The Margins of Society,* 136–47.

21. Cousinot, *Geste des nobles,* 120.

22. RSD, 3:725, refers to an unprecedented "affront." Jean de Saint-Léger was the Norman who had been hanged.

23. *CUP,* 4:152–53 (no. 1850).

24. RSD, 3:725, 727, marking the change from a "popular" policy to "great displeasure" among the public.

25. Famiglietti, *RI,* 241, n. 23; Guenée, *Between Church and State,* 216, and 400, n. 507 (refs.). Juvénal, *Histoire,* 446, gives the date as May 5, probably an error.

26. Millin, *Antiquités nationales,* 3, ch. 32, 33–34, cites a plaque at Saint-Mathurin. Favier, *Paris au XVe siècle,* 415 (table B), lists de Tuillières as

lieutenant, 1404–1418, despite his excommunication as an Armagnac (i.e., Orleanist) in 1411 (*A Parisian Journal,* 59; see also French text, Tuetey, *Journal d'un Bourgeois,* 93, n. 1).

27. RSD, 3:725, with quotes from "contumacious" and "disgraceful crimes" to "all the churches in Paris."

28. Laurent Mayali, "Excommunication," in *DMA,* 506–7, notes that excommunication could entail exclusion from the sacraments and temporal punishment without damnation, but it was often abused by the Church. RSD, 3:727, refers to Guillaume's "infamiam indelebilem" ("flétrissure éternelle"), hinting at the more severe sanction.

29. Gauvard, *"De grace especial,"* 228, 232, confirming Guillaume's *amende.* On the ritual of the *amende,* see Shennan, *The Parlement of Paris,* 70–71; and Cohen, *The Crossroads of Justice,* 81, 163–65. On "unhanging," see Gauvard, "Pendre et dépendre."

30. *CUP,* 4:154–56 (no. 1852), records many details, without mention of Tignonville himself. However, Héraut Berry, *Chroniques,* 32, puts Tignonville at the scene ("ledit prevost y fust en personne"), as does Monstrelet, *Chronique,* 1:75. *Dépendre:* RSD, 3:728 ("deponerentur"); Héraut Berry ("ilz fussent despenduz").

31. Gauvard, *"De grace especial,"* 747.

32. *CUP,* 4:154 (no. 1852). Porte Saint-Denis is assumed, since this was the portal generally used for trips to Montfaucon and other ceremonial purposes. RSD, 3:729, mentions "a huge crowd of spectators."

33. See Cohen, *The Crossroads of Justice,* 169–70, on divestiture in penal rituals, especially the *amende.*

34. *CUP,* 4:154.

35. Héraut Berry, *Chroniques,* 33; RSD, 3:729.

36. *CUP,* 4:155 ("octo hore"), source of other details in this and the next paragraph, except as noted.

37. Juvénal, *Histoire,* 447.

38. *CUP,* 4:155; also mentioned by Monstrelet, *Chronique,* 1:75.

39. Héraut Berry, *Chroniques,* 32 ("ledit prevost y fust en personne").

40. *CUP,* 4:155 ("usque ad Castelletum Parisiense").

41. Ibid. ("ecclesiam Parisiensem"); RSD, 3:729; Juvénal, *Histoire,* 447, describing the procession.

42. De Baye, *Journal,* 1:231; Juvénal, *Histoire,* 447.

43. *A Parisian Journal,* 100, 253 (preaching); Favier, *Paris au XVe siècle,* 36 (bread), 228 (excommunication); *Atlas de Paris,* 116 (diagram). A map of prostitution in Favier, 81, shows several active areas near Notre-Dame (e.g., Glatigny).

44. *CUP,* 4:156, also mentioning "the many masters, doctors" and other university men on hand.

45. Ibid., 4:155.

46. Assumed from the fact that words were spoken and a proclamation read aloud on the *parvis* (Ibid., 4:156; RSD, 3:727).

47. RSD, 3:727; Héraut Berry, *Chroniques,* 32. Hillairet, *Gibets,* 41, and Favier, *Paris au XVᵉ siècle,* 207, affirm the kiss, although some scholars question whether it actually took place (e.g., Cohen, *The Crossroads of Justice,* 197).

48. Mireille Vincent-Cassy, "Baiser," in *DMA,* 126 (with refs.).

49. RSD, 3:727 ("il demandât à genoux pardon").

50. Monstrelet, *Chronique,* 1:75. Juvénal, *Histoire,* 447, implies general, sustained bell ringing.

51. RSD, 3:729.

52. Butler, *Lives of the Saints,* 4:238, notes his "great gift of casting out evil spirits"; and Caraffa, *Bibliotheca sanctorum,* 9:158–59 ("Maturino"). On the church, see Millin, *Antiquités nationales,* 3, ch. 32 (relics, p. 6); and Biver and Biver, *Abbayes, monastères et couvents,* 231–40.

53. Monstrelet, *Chronique,* 1:75.

54. Ibid., 1:76. Millin, *Antiquités nationales,* 3, ch. 32, p. 34, specifies the date.

55. Millin, *Antiquités nationales,* 3, ch. 32, pp. 33–34.

56. RSD, 3:729.

57. Monstrelet, *Chronique,* 1:75; Hillairet, *Gibets,* 37.

58. RSD, 3:727.

59. Famiglietti, *RI,* 241, n. 23.

60. De Baye, *Journal,* 1:229.

61. *CUP,* 4:156.

62. Juvénal, *Histoire,* 446–47; Lehoux, *Jean de France,* 3:122 (one of Burgundy's "creatures"). Des Essarts "less recalcitrant": de Baye, *Journal,* 1:229, n. 1.

63. *A Parisian Journal,* Introduction, 4.

64. Guenée, *Un meurtre,* 183.

Chapter Fourteen: Civil War

1. Monstrelet, *Chronique,* 1:259; Petit, *Itinéraires,* 365, showing John in Ghent for much of July. For the Liège campaign, see Vaughan, *JF,* ch. 3. On the nearly five thousand men, see Vaughan, *JF,* 141 (table: Army of 1408).

2. Famiglietti, *RI,* 70. On the battle of Othée, as it came to be known, see Monstrelet, *Chronique,* 1:362–67; and Vaughan, *JF,* 59–63, with refs.

3. Monstrelet, *Chronique,* 1:365; Vaughan, *JF,* 62.

4. Monstrelet, *Chronique,* 1:368–70; Vaughan, *JF,* 63.

5. Vaughan, *JF,* 49, citing Plancher, *Histoire générale,* 3:289.

6. Monstrelet, *Chronique,* 1:389; Vaughan, *JF,* 63.

7. Famiglietti, *RI,* 69, refers to Isabeau's actions as a "coup" against Burgundy.

8. Surmised by Collas, *Valentine de Milan,* 401.

9. De Baye, *Journal,* 1:238–39, cited in Famiglietti, *RI,* 70; Monstrelet, *Chronique,* 1:267.

10. Collas, *Valentine de Milan*, 402, indicates the Hôtel de Bohême (or Béhaigne). On this palace, see Hillairet, *Rues*, 1:389, s.v. "Coquillière (rue)."

11. De Baye, *Journal*, 1:241–42, with a summary of the proceedings in Vaughan, *JF*, 72–74.

12. Vaughan, *JF*, 73–74 (lightly edited for brevity), citing Monstrelet, *Chronique*, 1:341–48.

13. Monstrelet, *Chronique*, 1:388, with the revoked pardon, given to Valentina in writing ("lectres"), and her immediate departure.

14. Ibid., 1:388–89, also recounting how "many…began to hang their heads."

15. Vaughan, *JF*, 74.

16. Monstrelet, *Chronique*, 1:390–91. For the precise date, either November 2 or 3, and a summary of events, see Vaughan, *JF*, 74, and Famiglietti, *RI*, 70–71.

17. Mirot, "Autour de la paix de Chartres," 323, with refs., n. 3. RSD, 4:183, says the king was ill and carried secretly onto a boat.

18. *A Parisian Journal*, 49; Monstrelet, *Chronique*, 1:390–91, also mentions the chains, and messages sent from Paris to Burgundy.

19. Petit, *Itinéraires*, 368. Monstrelet, *Chronique*, 1:391–92, numbering the troops at about two thousand, "in beautiful battle array," and people "loudly shouting 'Noël!'"

20. Monstrelet, *Chronique*, 392.

21. Ibid., 393–94, with the stated cause ("anger and disappointment") and burial details. December 4 is usually specified, although Van Kerrebrouck, *Les Valois*, 234, says December 14.

22. Monstrelet, *Chronique*, 1:394.

23. Monstrelet/Johnes, *Chronicles*, 1:131 (note). Collas, *Valentine de Milan*, 423, recounts a similar deathbed speech; and, 425, notes the black clothing (citing Michelet).

24. Famiglietti, *RI*, 73, also noting the king's January announcement.

25. Vaughan, *JF*, 76, cites "interminable haggling over the exact words." Burgundy's refusal to perform an *amende honorable*: RSD, 4:185.

26. For details of the March 9 ceremony, see Monstrelet, *Chronique*, 1:395–402; RSD, 4:191–203. A Burgundian letter, quoted at length in Vaughan, *JF*, 76–78, gives many details of the mise-en-scène but leaves out the delays and mishaps that Monstrelet records.

27. Monstrelet, *Chronique*, 1:397, notes John's dismissal of five hundred men before entering the cathedral precinct.

28. Burgundian letter, quoted in Vaughan, *JF*, 77.

29. Ibid., 75.

30. Burgundian letter in ibid., 77.

31. De La Marche, *Mémoires*, 316.

32. See von Simson, *The Gothic Cathedral*, ch. 7, esp. 201–7, on the design of Chartres supporting "the weight of its great vault" and allowing it "to be luminous as no other church had been before."

33. Ibid., 160–61.

34. Monstrelet, *Chronique,* 1:397; and Burgundian letter in Vaughan, *JF,* 77, listing many of the noble attendees.

35. The Burgundian letter (Vaughan, *JF,* 77) has Louis's sons entering the palisade later, but Monstrelet, *Chronique,* 1:399, places them "behind the king," apparently from the start.

36. Monstrelet, *Chronique,* 1:398, with subsequent exchanges during the ceremony from the same source, 398–400.

37. Guenée, *La folie,* 295 (no. 40), notes that the king's next spell began "after March 9," the day of the Chartres ceremony, and lasted until "around May 23."

38. Monstrelet, *Chronique,* 1:399.

39. Ibid. ("Et lesdiz enfans riens ne respondirent").

40. Ibid., 1:399–400 (the cardinal of Bar). The book used for the oaths is a missal ("messel").

41. Ibid., 1:400.

42. Headlam, *The Story of Chartres,* 254.

43. Vaughan, *JF,* 76, refers to "this tortuous piece of diplomatic play-acting."

44. On Bernard, Berry, and the Orleanist league of Gien, see Vaughan, *JF,* 82.

45. *A Parisian Journal,* 52.

46. Ibid., 52–53.

47. RSD, 4:364, also citing Burgundy's new tax. De Baye's "walled up" turret: *Journal,* 1:335, as cited in Vaughan, *JF,* 83.

48. *A Parisian Journal,* 53.

49. Vaughan, *JF,* 83 (item no. 6), details the so-called Peace of Bicêtre.

50. Famiglietti, *RI,* 93–94, summarizes the actions taken by Charles of Orleans and Burgundy's countermoves. For John's whereabouts in 1411, see Petit, *Itinéraires,* 377–85.

51. See *DMA,* s.v. "défi."

52. For the texts, see RSD, 4:435–39, and Monstrelet, *Chronique,* 2:152–55; Vaughan, *JF,* 88–90 (English translation).

53. Guenée, *La folie,* 296, no. 45 ("after the end of July" to January 16, 1412).

54. *A Parisian Journal,* 55, specifying "the Saint-Denis side." See also Monstrelet, *Chronique,* 2:166.

55. RSD, 4:443–45. On Waleran himself, see Sumption, *The Hundred Years War,* 3:366–67.

56. RSD, 4:443–45, also cites searches and chains across the river.

57. Ibid., 4:445–47; Juvénal, *Histoire,* 466–67. See also Famiglietti, *RI,* 97. Gifts of Burgundian wine: Favier, *Paris au XVe siècle,* 149–50; Vaughan, *JF,* 98.

58. Juvénal, *Histoire,* 466–67.

59. RSD, 4:445–47 (changing "Armagnac" to the equivalent "Orleanist").

60. *A Parisian Journal,* 56. On the provost's decree, see *Journal d'un Bourgeois,* 12, n. 4. On tailors, see *HDP,* 467.

61. Vaughan, *JF,* 90.

62. RSD, 4:467, says fifty thousand, a typically outsize figure. The more accurate estimate is from Vaughan, *JF,* 139 (for "Aug.–Sept. 1411").

63. RSD, 4:467.

64. Smith and DeVries, *The Artillery,* 79, discuss the 1411 campaign in particular.

65. Vaughan, *JF,* 150–51; Contamine, *War in the Middle Ages,* 142, 148; Smith and DeVries, *The Artillery,* 19–21, 71–84.

66. Contamine, *War in the Middle Ages,* 103–4 (trebuchets used against walls), and 200–201 (gunpowder more effective against walls).

67. John's father, Philip, had bronze cannons, although iron was also in use. See Smith and DeVries, *The Artillery,* 3, 70; and 79, on Burgundian projectiles of 700 to 850 livres; and, in appendix 1, a bombard (in 1412) weighing 16,000 livres.

68. Contamine, *War in the Middle Ages,* 143–44. For the 1474 and 1475 inventories, see Smith and DeVries, *The Artillery,* appendices 2 and 3, with serpentine sizes from appendix 1.

69. Quoted in Sumption, *The Hundred Years War,* 3:224; see also Contamine, *War in the Middle Ages,* 138–39.

70. RSD, 4:469–73, recounts the siege. See also Monstrelet, *Chronique,* 2:174–77; and Vaughan, *JF,* 90.

71. Juvénal, *Histoire,* 467, also naming Bernard with his relative Charles d'Albret in a list of banished Orleanists. On Bernard's defense of Ham, see also RSD, 4:469.

72. RSD, 4:469.

73. Monstrelet, *Chronique,* 2:175–76, recounts the repairs with wood and rubble as the "cruel and sharp" assault went on.

74. RSD, 4:471.

75. Vaughan, *JF,* 90.

76. Monstrelet, *Chronique,* 2:177–78, details the widely visible "smoke and the fires" in Ham. Emissaries "dressed in black": Vaughan, *JF,* 91.

77. Vaughan, *JF,* 90, summarizes this part of the campaign.

78. *A Parisian Journal,* 55.

79. Vaughan, *JF,* 91, also notes the fall of Saint-Cloud.

80. *Atlas de Paris,* 57–59. On wartime interruptions to the city's provisioning, see Favier, *Paris au XVe siècle,* 295–97.

81. RSD, 4:513, 517.

82. *A Parisian Journal,* 57. Distance from hill to wall: *Atlas de Paris,* 217 (map).

83. *A Parisian Journal,* 57. The attempted assassination: Monstrelet, *Chronique,* 2:195–96.

84. *A Parisian Journal,* 57–58, numbers the English troops at seven to eight thousand. On the alliance, see also Famiglietti, *RI,* 101.

85. Petit, *Itinéraires,* 384, cited in Vaughan, *JF,* 92.

86. Monstrelet, *Chronique,* 2:198–99.

87. Ibid., 2:199, with quote about street lighting.

88. Figures from Lehoux, *Jean de France,* 3:243. Tipping the balance: Vaughan, *JF,* 141.

89. *A Parisian Journal,* 58, giving the date as the night of November 8.

90. Vaughan, *JF,* 93.

91. Ibid., with the ritual's origins from Brewer, *A Dictionary of Phrase and Fable,* 117. *A Parisian Journal,* 59, puts the event on "Martinmas eve" (November 10).

92. RSD, 4:551.

93. Vaughan, *JF,* 93.

94. Ibid., 158–59.

95. Famiglietti, *RI,* 102; Van Kerrebrouck, *Les Valois,* 367 (age). On the negotiations, see Vaughan, *JF,* 91–92; and Schnerb, *Jean sans Peur,* 614.

96. Famiglietti, *RI,* 100.

97. For this paragraph, see RSD, 4:627–33; Vaughan, *JF,* 94; and Monstrelet, *Chronique,* 2:236.

98. Famiglietti, *RI,* 103.

99. Ibid., 104.

100. RSD, 4:652, as trans. in Vaughan, *JF,* 95–96, with details of John's presence at the field trials earlier that year.

101. Famiglietti, *RI,* 106–7, summarizes the ensuing siege. Details in Monstrelet, *Chronique,* 2:270–83.

102. On this scourge of armies, see Barker, *Agincourt,* 180–81. The author of *Gesta Henrici Quinti,* 59, remarks that dysentery killed more soldiers than the sword.

103. Monstrelet, *Chronique,* 2:286 (trans. by Johnes, 1:223).

104. RSD, 4:705–19, detailing the treaty of Auxerre, summarized in Vaughan, *JF,* 97–98, and Famiglietti, *RI,* 107–10.

105. RSD, 4:719.

106. Ibid., 4:709.

107. Monstrelet, *Chronique,* 2:294.

108. Vaughan, *JF,* 97, citing Monstrelet ("Armagnac" changed for clarity to "Orleanist").

109. Ibid., 100 ("totally dissatisfied with the peace of Auxerre").

110. RSD, 5:7–27, and Monstrelet, *Chronique,* 2:344–50; summary in Vaughan, *JF,* 98–100, and Famiglietti, *RI,* ch. 7.

111. Famiglietti, *RI,* 115.

112. Juvénal, *Histoire,* 487–88; Famiglietti, *RI,* 129, indicating the date as August 3.

113. RSD, 5:3941; Famiglietti, *RI,* 121.

114. *A Parisian Journal,* 80.

115. RSD, 5:129; see also Monstrelet, *Chronique,* 2:399.

116. Monstrelet, *Chronique,* 2:399.

117. Petit, *Itinéraires,* 400 (for Sunday, August 20, 1413). John began to fear his own arrest: Monstrelet, *Chronique,* 2:400, also noting threats around his palace at night. Vaughan, *JF,* 101, says Burgundy now feared assassination or a public trial and execution.

118. On the publication of libels in general, see Vaughan, *JF,* 30, citing de Baye, *Journal,* 2:288. For this handbill, see refs. below.

119. Durrieu, "Jean sans Peur," 203–5, the French text; translation in Vaughan, *JF,* 230–31. Durrieu, 207, dates the letter "toward the end of Burgundy's life," while Schnerb, *Jean sans Peur,* 107, says 1411 to 1418. Libels modeled on the famous *Epistola Luciferi ad prelatos* (see Durrieu, 218–23) may have circulated when the Orleanists regained Paris in 1413. Gauvard, *"De grace especial,"* 185, implies that Burgundians were countering Orleanist libels about John as Satan's lieutenant as early as 1408.

120. Juvénal, *Histoire,* 409; quoted by Schnerb, *Jean sans Peur,* 107, with mention, 109, of a "black legend" about John.

121. Veenstra, *Magic and Divination,* 44, citing John's words as "an unfortunate excuse that could and would be used against him."

122. See Seward, *Henry V,* 131; and Veenstra, *Magic and Divination,* 135, summarizing the views of a theologian who "deplored" Burgundy's "interest in astrologers."

123. RSD, 5:149.

124. Ibid.

125. Vaughan, *JF,* 102, with ref.

126. RSD, 5:149.

127. Ibid., and 151.

128. *A Parisian Journal,* 80.

Chapter Fifteen: The Scourge of God

1. Monstrelet, *Chronique,* 1:154–55. Olivier de La Marche wrote that Louis's murder brought "many evils" to France (*Mémoires,* 317; quoted by Schnerb, *Jean sans Peur,* 218).

2. Seward, *Henry V,* 52–53; and Gies, *Joan of Arc,* 1.

3. Seward, *Henry V,* 51–52, also provides details for the gun stones delivered in October 1414.

4. Ibid., 55.

5. Ibid., 53, with details of the 1414 negotiations, including "the hand of Charles VI's daughter."

6. Ibid., 63; troop numbers and types of personnel, 54–55; fleet details and livestock, 60. Barker, *Agincourt,* 147–48, describes "sails, pennons and banners decorated with heraldic beasts and coats of arms."

7. Seward, *Henry V,* 66.

8. Ibid., with numbers of the casualties. A surviving roll lists seventeen hundred men invalided out (*Gesta Henrici Quinti,* 59, n. 5).

9. Seward, *Henry V,* 67, giving the date as September 22, with details of prior attacks.

10. Ibid., 71, with details of the attack on Fécamp.

11. Ibid., 128, 186 ("scourge" cited from a 1419 incident, with ref.). On Pierre Dubois's treatise, see Rogers, "The Age of the Hundred Years War," in Keen, *Medieval Warfare,* 136–37.

12. Seward, *Henry V,* 71, also citing the downpour, dysentery, 73; hunger, 71–72, 73; and troop numbers for each army, 70, 72.

13. On its continuing effects up to the battle, see Barker, *Agincourt,* 276.

14. Seward, *Henry V,* 74.

15. Ibid., 75–77, on the deployment of troops (with map). On the battle and its prelude, see also Keegan, *The Face of Battle,* ch. 2 (with map, 83); and Barker, *Agincourt,* ch. 15. The "best eye-witness account" (Seward, 77) is *Gesta Henrici Quinti,* ch. 13.

16. Seward, *Henry V,* 72, also notes Burgundy's brothers, Philip and Anthony ("the Duke of Brabant and the Count of Nevers").

17. Petit, *Itinéraires,* 422 (October 25, the duke spent "all day at Dijon"). By contrast, Burgundy's son, Philip, "regretted for the rest of his life that he had not fought in the campaign. Even Burgundians"—John excepted—"could not stomach an English invasion" (Seward, *Henry V,* 72–73).

18. See sources cited below in note on "le seigneur de Tignonville."

19. Seward, *Henry V,* 78, also with the "barefoot" archers and the French troops "roaring hollowly."

20. Ibid., 79–80, also noting the wooden stakes as weapons and the daggers through eye slits. Many of these details are from *Gesta Henrici Quinti,* 87–93, a vivid eyewitness account.

21. Barker, *Agincourt,* 288.

22. Seward, *Henry V,* 81, notes the small number of English casualties as well. Barker, *Agincourt,* ch. 16, provides a detailed accounting.

23. RSD, 5:574 (fourteen hundred were captured); for other figures and a sifting of the reports, see Barker, *Agincourt,* 320–21.

24. On Charles of Orleans's capture at Agincourt and subsequent captivity, see Barker, *Agincourt,* 289, 351, 356–57. On his poetry, see Claudio Galderisi, "Charles d'Orléans," in *DMA,* 262–64.

25. Seward, *Henry V,* 80; Barker, *Agincourt,* 293 (with further details). Van Kerrebrouck, *Les Valois,* 393, 401, verifies that both brothers were slain at Agincourt.

26. Monstrelet, *Chronique,* 3:115; Belleval, *Azincourt,* 259–60; Héraut Berry, *Chroniques,* 32, n. 1. Many scholars put Guillaume's death in 1414 but without citing documentary evidence.

27. See below on "the hole through which the English entered France."

28. Chaucer, "The Knight's Tale," lines 1177–80, *Riverside Chaucer*, p. 41.

29. Seward, *Henry V,* 89–90. For the hostage exchange and details of the parley, see *Gesta Henrici Quinti,* 167–75.

30. Seward, *Henry V,* 122.

31. Ibid., 105, detailing the siege and fall of Caen in ch. 9.

32. Ibid., 117, with other details of the siege of Rouen; "raided far and wide," 115; "useless mouths," 117.

33. Ibid., 132.

34. *A Parisian Journal,* 139–40; quoted in Seward, *Henry V,* 132–33.

35. *A Parisian Journal,* 142, as translated by Seward, *Henry V,* 133.

36. Seward, *Henry V,* 133.

37. RSD, 6:157–59; Favier, *Paris au XVe siècle,* 228.

38. *A Parisian Journal,* 114. On the 1418 Burgundian capture of Paris, see Vaughan, *JF,* 223–26.

39. Juvénal, *Histoire,* 541; Famiglietti, *RI,* 188–89. The death of Robert de Tuillières: *A Parisian Journal* (French text, Tuetey, *Journal d'un Bourgeois*), 93, n. 1.

40. Vaughan, *JF,* 266.

41. *A Parisian Journal,* 97–98. For dates, see Van Kerrebrouck, *Les Valois,* 117–18 (nos. 8–9), 129–30 (Charles VII).

42. Vaughan, *JF,* 273, details three meetings in the first half of July 1419.

43. Ibid., 283.

44. Ibid., ch. 10, summarizes the events, with a detailed sifting of the sources.

45. Seward, *The Hundred Years War,* 214.

46. Variously quoted in, e.g., Barker, *Agincourt,* 357; Seward, *The Hundred Years War,* 180 (the phrasing used here).

47. Seward, *Henry V,* chs. 13–14, details the Treaty of Troyes (1420) and related events.

48. Ibid., 212–13.

49. Ibid., 209 (citing sources on Henry's death). On occupied France and the regency, see Barker, *Conquest,* 46–47, detailing a December 5, 1422, agreement; and 48–49, the dauphin's competing claim.

50. Barker, *Conquest,* 62, 64–65, 115.

51. Ibid., 51–52 (oaths to Henry V); 62, 65–66 (to England), with examples of universal enforcement.

52. Ibid., 65–70, with mention of hanging, beheading, and burial alive, 66.

53. Ibid., 70–72, detailing Armagnac (Orleanist) raids, levies of *appâtis* (a type of protection racket), and their effect on the Norman peasantry.

54. Seward, *The Hundred Years War,* 201. See also Barker, *Conquest,* ch. 6.

55. *A Parisian Journal,* 204 (specifying August 1424). On the mural's size and location, see *Atlas de Paris,* 130 (diagram); and Oosterwijk, "Of Dead Kings, Dukes and Constables," 133, noting the sculpture in memory of Louis, said to have been commissioned by the Duke of Berry.

56. For the images, from a 1485 printing thought to capture the vanished mural, see Marchant, *La danse macabre* (facsimile ed.).

57. "homily in pictures": Burl, *Danse Macabre,* 52. "Death spares neither high nor low": quoted in Oosterwijk, "Of Dead Kings, Dukes and Constables," 140.

58. *A Parisian Journal,* 230–31, detailing Richard's preaching and the ensuing bonfire of the vanities.

59. Ibid., 233–35; Gies, *Joan of Arc,* 2 (voices), 21 (illiteracy), 57 (sent by God), 59–60 (armor), 81 (witchcraft). Barker, *Conquest,* details the events at Orleans, Jargeau, and Patay (ch. 8) and the coronation at Reims (ch. 9). For a briefer overview, see Seward, *The Hundred Years War,* 216–20. As civil war still divided France, not all rejoiced at Joan's victories. In September 1429, she led an army against Paris, still Burgundian, to the great outrage of the citizens (*A Parisian Journal,* 240–42).

60. Gies, *Joan of Arc,* 81, notes that the events at Orleans were "swiftly reported in Paris"; and, 109, that the coronation journey to Reims "aroused widespread excitement."

Epilogue

1. Mirot, "Raoul d'Anquetonville"; Nordberg, *Les ducs et la royauté,* 230; Famiglietti, *RI,* 238, n. 165, noting however that Raoul "must have been well over 40 years old in 1407."

2. Vallet de Viriville, "Assassinat," 247–49 (partly from Cochon, *Chronique normande,* 380–81); Schnerb, *Jean sans Peur,* 231–32.

3. This and other details are all drawn from Mirot, "Raoul d'Anquetonville," 449–52.

4. Ibid., 452.

5. Ibid., 452–53, also saying that it was he "who planned the attack." Petit, *Itinéraires,* 360, confirms that John was in Lille from August 6 to August 7.

6. Mirot, "Raoul d'Anquetonville," 457, with ref.

7. Ibid., 453.

8. Schnerb, *Jean sans Peur,* 232.

9. Ibid., 232–33.

10. Juvénal, *Histoire,* 447.

11. Monstrelet, *Chronique,* 1:351–53, 388–89, recounts what the embassy said to John, his response, and their report to the court.

12. Ibid., 1:353, describes how the two knights in the embassy "were at the engagement," although it stretches credulity to say that Guillaume, in a bid "to cultivate" Burgundy's goodwill, "joined him to fight against the Liègeois" (Famiglietti, *RI,* 241, n. 23).

13. Monstrelet, *Chronique,* 2:47; Demurger, "Guerre civile," 295. On the fate of the grand master, John of Montagu, see *A Parisian Journal,* 51; and Vaughan, *JF,* 79–80.

14. RSD, 4:341–49; Demurger, "Guerre civile," 295.

15. Tignonville, *The Dicts and Sayings,* xi, xiii–xix; Eder, "Tignonvillana inedita," 873–77.

16. Dogaer and Debae, *La librairie de Philippe le Bon,* 33 (no. 34).

17. Gauvard, *"De grace especial,"* 186 ("aucune trace de l'ordalie").

18. Cousinot, *Geste des nobles,* 121.

19. Eder, "Tignonvillana inedita," 874–75 (family tree), showing several generations of descendants.

20. Ibid., 872, and 875 (family tree), n. 5, itemizing his offices.

21. Van Kerrebrouck, *Les Valois,* 438–39.

22. Anselme, *Histoire généalogique et chronologique,* 5:196. According to a widely reported story, Jeanne refused to become Henri's mistress until she was safely married.

23. Hillairet, *Rues,* 2:636 (no. 47). See also the map in Bonamy, "Mémoire," 519, published in 1754, when the murder house still existed, occupied "by a grocer and a baker" (522). On the erroneous marker, see Collas, *Valentine de Milan,* 349–53.

24. Hillairet, *Rues,* 2:334 ("1802 to 1810"), with details of the fountain installed in 1808 and restored in 1900.

25. At the Archives départementales des Pyrénées-Atlantiques, in Pau.

A Note on the Depositions

1. "Enquête," 228.

Sources

Manuscript Sources

PARIS: ARCHIVES NATIONALES (AN)

X^{1a} 4788 (fol. 4r): Parlement, November 18, 1407 (microfilm)

PARIS: BIBLIOTHÈQUE NATIONALE (BN)

MS. fr. 5790 (fols. 36v–38v): Letter from "Lucifer" to John of Burgundy

MS. fr. 7858 (fols. 309r–320v): List of the nobles accompanying the king to Le Mans in 1392

MS. fr. 5054: *Les Vigiles de Charles VII par Martial d'Auvergne* (1484)

MS. Languedoc Doat 9 (fols. 14r–66v): The 1407 investigation report (a seventeenth-century copy)

PAU: ARCHIVES DÉPARTEMENTALES DES PYRÉNÉES-ATLANTIQUES

MS. Série E 56, famille d'Albret, année 1407: The 1407 investigation report on Louis of Orleans's assassination (original parchment scroll)

Printed Primary Sources

Basin, Thomas. *Histoire de Charles VII*. Edited and translated by Charles Samaran. 2 vols. Paris, 1933–44. Reprinted 1964–65.

Baye, Nicolas de. *Journal de Nicolas de Baye, greffier du Parlement de Paris, 1400–1417*. Edited by Alexandre Tuetey. 2 vols. Paris, 1885–1888.

Berry, le Héraut (Gilles Le Bouvier). *Les Chroniques du Roi Charles VII*. Edited by Henri Courteault and Léonce Celier. Paris, 1979.

Bonamy, Pierre Nicolas. "Mémoire sur le lieu, les circonstances et les suites de l'assassinat de Louis, duc d'Orléans, frère du roi Charles VI." *Mémoires . . . de l'Academie Royale des Inscriptions et Belles-Lettres* 21 (1754): 515–40.

Brantôme, Pierre de Bourdeilles, Abbé et Seigneur de. *Oeuvres complètes*. Edited by Ludovic Lalanne. 11 vols. Paris, 1864–82.

Chaucer, Geoffrey. *The Riverside Chaucer*. 3rd ed. Edited by Larry D. Benson. Boston, 1987.

Cochon, Pierre. *Chronique normande.* Edited by Auguste Vallet de Viriville. In *Chronique de la Pucelle,* 363–468. Paris, 1859.

Cousinot, Guillaume. *Geste des nobles.* Edited by Auguste Vallet de Viriville. In *Chronique de la Pucelle,* 105–204. Paris, 1859.

Denifle, Heinrich, and Émile Chatelain, eds. *Chartularium universitatis parisiensis.* 4 vols. Paris, 1889–1897. Reprint, 1964.

Duplès-Agier, Henri, ed. *Registre criminel du Châtelet de Paris.* 2 vols. Paris, 1861–64.

Favyn, André. *Le Théâtre d'honneur et de chevalerie.* 2 vols. Paris, 1620.

Fénin, Pierre de. *Mémoires.* Edited by Émilie Dupont. Paris, 1837. Reprint, 1965.

Froissart, Jean. *Chroniques.* Edited by J. A. Buchon. 15 vols. (= *Collection des chroniques nationales françaises,* vols. 11–25). Paris, 1824–26.

———. *Chroniques.* Edited by Joseph Kervyn de Lettenhove. 25 vols. Brussels, 1867–77.

———. *Chronicles.* Translated by Thomas Johnes. 2 vols. London, 1839.

———. *Chronicles* (Selections). Translated by Geoffrey Brereton. London, 1968.

Gesta Henrici Quinti: The Deeds of Henry the Fifth. Edited and translated by Frank Taylor and John S. Roskell. Oxford, 1975.

Juvénal des Ursins, Jean. *Histoire de Charles VI.* Edited by Joseph François Michaud et al. *Nouvelle collection des mémoires relatifs à l'histoire de France.* Vol. 2, 333–569. Paris, 1854.

La Marche, Olivier de. *Mémoires.* Ed. J.A.C. Buchon. *Choix de chroniques et mémoires sur l'histoire de France,* 295–599. Paris, 1836.

Laurière, Eusèbe de, ed. *Ordonnances des roys de France de la troisième race.* Vol. 1. Paris, 1723.

Le livre des faicts du mareschal de Boucicaut. Edited by Joseph François Michaud et al. *Nouvelle collection des mémoires relatifs à l'histoire de France.* Vol. 2, 203–332. Paris, 1854.

Le Ménagier de Paris, traité de morale et d'économie domestique, composé vers 1393 par un bourgeois parisien. 2 vols. Société des bibliophiles françois. Paris, 1846. Translated by Eileen Power as *The Goodman of Paris: A Treatise on Moral and Domestic Economy by a Citizen of Paris, c. 1393.,* 1928. Reprint, Woodbridge, Eng., 1992.

Le Roy, Thierry. "Rapport officiel…de…8 mars 1408." Edited by Louis Douët-d'Arcq. "Document inédit sur l'assassinat de Louis, duc d'Orléans (23 novembre 1407)." *Annuaire-Bulletin de la Société de l'Histoire de France* 2 (1864): pt. 2, 6–26.

Marchant, Guy. *La danse macabre de Guy Marchant.* Edited by Pierre Champion. Paris, 1925.

Metz, Guillebert de. "La description de la ville de Paris" (1434). *Paris et ses historiens aux XIVe et XVe siècles, documents et écrits originaux,* 131–236. Edited by Le Roux de Lincy and L. M. Tisserand. Paris, 1867.

Monstrelet, Enguerrand de. *Chronique*. Edited by Louis Douët-d'Arcq. 6 vols. Paris, 1857–62. Translated by Thomas Johnes as *The Chronicles*. 2 vols. London, 1853.

A Parisian Journal, 1405–1449. Translated by Janet Shirley. Oxford, 1968. Original French edition: *Journal d'un Bourgeois de Paris, 1405–1449*. Edited by Alexandre Tuetey. Paris, 1881.

Pius II, Pope (Enea Silvio Piccolomini). *I commentarii*. Edited by Luigi Totaro. Latin/Italian in 2 vols. Milan, 1984. Translated by Florence A. Gragg and Leona C. Gabel as *The Commentaries of Pius II, Books VI–IX*. Smith College Studies in History, vol. 35. Northampton, Mass., 1951.

Plancher, Urbain. *Histoire générale et particulière de Bourgogne*. 4 vols. Dijon, 1739–81. Reprint, 1968.

Queux de Saint-Hilaire, Marquis de. *Le livre des cent ballades*. Paris, 1868.

Raymond, Paul, ed. "Enquête de Prévôt de Paris sur l'Assassinat de Louis, duc d'Orléans (1407)." *Bibliothèque de l'École des Chartes* 26 (1865): 215–49.

Raynaud, Gaston, ed. *Les cent ballades, poème du XIVᵉ siècle*. Paris, 1905.

Religieux de Saint-Denis. *Chronique du Religieux de Saint-Denys (1380–1422)*. Edited by Louis Bellaguet. 6 vols. Paris, 1839–52. Reprint, 1994.

Soman, Alfred, Claude Gauvard, Mary Rouse, and Richard Rouse. "Le Châtelet de Paris au début du XVᵉ siècle d'après les fragments d'un registre d'écrous de 1412." *Bibliothèque de l'École des Chartes* 157 (1999): 565–606.

"Testament de Louis duc d'Orléans, deuxième fils de Charles cinquième," in Louis Beurrier, ed., *Histoire du monastère et convent des Pères Célestins de Paris*, 292–335. Paris, 1634.

Tignonville, Guillaume de. *The Dicts and Sayings of the Philosophers*. Translated by Stephen Scrope et al. Edited by Curt F. Bühler. Early English Text Society, Original Series, No. 211. London, 1941.

Villon, François. *The Poems of François Villon*. Translated by Galway Kinnell. Boston, 1977.

Secondary Sources

Anglo, Sydney. *The Martial Arts of Renaissance Europe*. New Haven, 2000.

Anselme de Sainte-Marie (Pierre Guibours), et al., eds. *Histoire généalogique et chronologique de la Maison royale de France*. 3rd ed. 9 vols. Paris, 1725.

Atiya, Aziz Suryal. *The Crusade of Nicopolis*. London, 1934.

Aumale, Henri d'Orléans, ed. *Chantilly, le cabinet des livres, manuscrits*. 4 vols. Paris, 1900–11.

Autrand, Françoise. *Charles VI: la folie du roi*. Paris, 1986.

Avril, François, ed. *Jean Fouquet: peintre et enlumineur du XVᵉ siècle*. Paris, 2003.

Barker, Juliet. *Agincourt: Henry V and the Battle that Made England*. New York, 2005.

———. *Conquest: The English Kingdom of France, 1417–1450*. Cambridge, Mass., 2012.

Batiffol, Louis. "Le Châtelet de Paris vers 1400." *Revue historique* 61 (1896): 225–64; 62 (1896), 225–35; 63 (1897), 42–55, 266–83.

Belleval, René de. *Azincourt*. Paris, 1865.

Bernois, Constant (Abbé). "Aveu de Guillaume du Monceau pour Thignon-ville (1482)." *Annales de la société historique et archéologique du Gatinais* 13 (1895): 74–83.

Beurrier, Louis. *Histoire du monastère et convent des Pères Célestins de Paris*. Paris, 1634.

Biver, Paul, and Marie-Louise Biver. *Abbayes, monastères et couvents de Paris*. Paris, 1970.

Bossuat, Robert, et al., eds. *Le Moyen Age*. Vol. 1 of *Dictionnaire des lettres fran-çaises*. Revised edition by Geneviève Hasenohr and Michel Zink. Paris, 1994.

Bournon, Fernand. *L'hôtel royal de Saint-Pol à Paris*. Paris, 1880.

Boyer, Marjorie Nice. "A Day's Journey in Mediaeval France." *Speculum* 26 (1951): 597–608.

Bozzolo, Carla, and Hélène Loyau, eds. *La Cour amoureuse dite de Charles VI*. 3 vols. in 2. Paris, 1982–1992.

Brachet, Auguste. *Pathologie mentale des rois de France. Louis XI et ses ascendents*. Paris, 1903.

Braudel, Fernand. *The Identity of France*. 2 vols. Translated by Siân Reynolds. New York, 1988–90.

Brewer, Rev. E. Cobham. *A Dictionary of Phrase and Fable*. New edition. London, ca. 1923.

Britton, C. E. *A Meteorological Chronology to A.D. 1450*. Meteorological Office, Geophysical Memoirs, no. 70 (no. 1, vol. 8). London, 1937.

Buettner, Brigitte. "Past Presents: New Year's Gifts at the Valois Courts, ca. 1400." *The Art Bulletin* 83 (2001): 598–625.

Burl, Aubrey. *Danse Macabre: François Villon, Poetry and Murder in Medieval France*. Stroud, Eng., 2000.

Butler, Alban. *Lives of the Saints*. Edited by Herbert Thurston and Donald Attwater. 4 vols. New York, 1956.

Camille, Michael. "'For Our Devotion and Pleasure': The Sexual Objects of Jean, Duc de Berry." *Art History* 24 (2001): 169–94.

Cappelli, Adriano. *Lexicon abbreviaturarum: dizionario di abbreviature latine ed italiane*. 6th ed. Milan, 1961.

Caraffa, Filippo, et al., eds. *Bibliotheca sanctorum*. 12 vols. Rome, 1961–69.

Carbonnières, Louis de. *La procédure devant la chambre criminelle du Parlement de Paris au XIVe siècle*. Paris, 2004.

Champion, Pierre. *François Villon: sa vie et son temps*. 2 vols. Paris, 1933.

———. *La Librairie de Charles d'Orléans*. Paris, 1910.

Champollion-Figeac, Aimé Louis. *Louis et Charles ducs d'Orléans: leur influence sur les arts, la littérature et l'esprit de leur siècle*. 3 vols. in 2. Paris, 1844.

Clanchy, Michael T. *From Memory to Written Record: England, 1066–1307.* Cambridge, Mass., 1979.

Cohen, Esther. *The Crossroads of Justice: Law and Culture in Late Medieval France.* Leiden, 1993.

Collas, Émile. *Valentine de Milan, duchesse d'Orléans.* 3rd ed. Paris, 1911.

Contamine, Philippe. *War in the Middle Ages.* Translated by Michael Jones. Oxford, 1984. Reprinted, 1986.

Coville, Alfred. *Jean Petit: La question du tyrannicide au commencement du XVe siècle.* Paris, 1932. Reprint, 1974.

———. "Le véritable texte de la justification du duc de Bourgogne par Jean Petit (8 mars 1408)." *Bibliothèque de l'École des Chartes* 72 (1911): 57–91.

Crossley-Holland, Nicole. *Living and Dining in Medieval Paris: The Household of a Fourteenth-Century Knight.* Cardiff, Wales, 1996.

Darwin, F.D.S. *Louis d'Orléans (1372–1407): A Necessary Prologue to the Tragedy of La Pucelle D'Orléans.* London, 1936.

Demay, Germain. *Inventaire des sceaux de la collection Clairambault à la Bibliothèque nationale.* 2 vols. Paris, 1885–86.

Demurger, Alain. "Guerre civile et changements du personnel administratif dans le royaume de France de 1400 à 1418: l'exemple des baillis et sénéchaux." *Francia* 6 (1978): 151–298.

Desmaze, Charles. *Le Châtelet de Paris: son organisation, ses privilèges.* Paris, 1863.

Dessalles, Léon. *Histoire du Périgord.* 3 vols. Périgueux, 1883–85.

Dictionnaire raisonné universel des arts et métiers, contenant l'histoire, la description, la police des fabriques et manufactures de France & des pays étrangers. Nouvelle édition. 5 vols. Paris, 1773.

Dogaer, Georges, and Marguerite Debae, eds. *La librairie de Philippe le Bon.* Brussels, 1967.

Dohrn–van Rossum, Gerhard. *History of the Hour: Clocks and Modern Temporal Orders.* Translated by Thomas Dunlap. Chicago, 1996.

Duby, Georges. *France in the Middle Ages, 987–1460: From Hugh Capet to Joan of Arc.* Translated by Juliet Vale. Oxford, 1991.

Ducoudray, Gustave. *Les origines du Parlement de Paris et la justice aux XIIIe et XIVe siècles.* 2 vols. Paris, 1902. Reprint, 1970.

Durrieu, Paul. "Jean sans Peur, duc de Bourgogne, Lieutenant et Procureur Général du diable ès parties d'occident." *Annuaire-Bulletin de la Société de l'Histoire de France* 24 (1887): 193–224.

Eder, Robert. "Tignonvillana inedita." *Romanische Forschungen* 33, no. 3 (1915): 851–1022.

Famiglietti, R. C. *Royal Intrigue: Crisis at the Court of Charles VI, 1392–1420.* New York, 1986.

Favier, Jean. *Paris au XVe siècle, 1380–1500.* Nouvelle histoire de Paris, vol. 4. Paris, 1974.

Fierro, Alfred. *Dictionnaire du Paris disparu: sites et monuments.* Paris, 2003.

———. *Histoire et dictionnaire de Paris*. Paris, 1996.

Garcia, Michel. "Comment la nouvelle de l'assassinat du duc d'Orléans parvint en Castille (23 novembre 1407)." In *L'Actualité et sa mise en écriture aux XVᵉ–XVIᵉ et XVIIᵉ siècles: Espagne, Italie, France et Portugal,* edited by Pierre Civil and Danielle Boillet, 95–107. Paris, 2005.

Gascar, Pierre. *Charles VI: le bal des ardents*. Paris, 1977.

Gauvard, Claude. *"De grace especial": Crime, État et Société en France à la fin du Moyen Âge*. Paris, 1991. Reprint, 2010.

———."Pendre et dépendre à la fin du Moyen Âge." *Histoire de la Justice* 4 (1991) : 5–24.

Gauvard, Claude, Alain de Libera, and Michel Zink, eds. *Dictionnaire du Moyen Âge*. Paris, 2002.

Geoscience Australia. "Astronomical Information," http://www.ga.gov.au/earth-monitoring/astronomical-information.html.

Geremek, Bronisław. *The Margins of Society in Late Medieval Paris*. Translated by Jean Birrell. Cambridge, 1987.

Gibbons, Rachel. "Isabeau of Bavaria, Queen of France (1385–1422): The Creation of an Historical Villainess." *Transactions of the Royal Historical Society,* Sixth Series, 6 (1996): 51–73.

Gies, Frances. *Joan of Arc: The Legend and the Reality*. New York, 1981.

Giesey, Ralph E. *The Royal Funeral Ceremony in Renaissance France*. Geneva, 1960.

Greimas, A. J. *Dictionnaire de l'ancien français jusqu'au milieu du XIVᵉ siècle*. Paris, 1980.

Guenée, Bernard. *Between Church and State: The Lives of Four French Prelates in the Late Middle Ages*. Translated by Arthur Goldhammer. Chicago, 1991.

———. *La folie de Charles VI: roi bien-aimé*. Paris, 2004.

———. *Un meurtre, une société: l'assassinat du duc d'Orléans, 23 novembre 1407*. Paris, 1992.

Guiffrey, J., ed. *Inventaires de Jean, duc de Berry*. 2 vols. Paris, 1894–96.

Harmand, Jacques. *Pierrefonds: la forteresse d'Orléans, les réalités*. Le Puy-en-Velay, 1983.

Headlam, Cecil. *The Story of Chartres*. London, 1902.

Hedeman, Anne D. "Pierre Salmon's Advice for a King." *Gesta* 32 (1993): 113–23.

Henneman, John B. *Olivier de Clisson and Political Society in France under Charles V and Charles VI*. Philadelphia, 1996.

Hillairet, Jacques. *Dictionnaire historique des rues de Paris*. 2 vols. 7th ed. Paris, 1979.

———. *Évocation du vieux Paris: vieux quartiers, vieilles rues, vieilles demeures historique, vestiges, annales et anecdotes*. (Vol. 1 of 3.)Revised ed. Paris, 1952.

———. *Gibets, piloris et cachots du vieux Paris*. Paris, 1956.

———. *La rue Saint-Antoine*. Paris, 1970.

SOURCES

Hindman, Sandra L. *Christine de Pizan's "Epistre Othéa": Painting and Politics at the Court of Charles VI.* Toronto, 1986.

Hirschbiegel, Jan. *Étrennes: Untersuchungen zum höfischen Geschenkverkehr im spätmittelalterlichen Frankreich der Zeit König Karls VI (1380–1422).* Munich, 2003.

Hodges, Laura F. *Chaucer and Clothing: Clerical and Academic Costume in the General Prologue to the Canterbury Tales.* Rochester, 2005.

Houston, Rab. "Literacy and Society in the West, 1500–1850." *Social History* 8 (1983): 269–93.

Hult, David, ed. *Debate of the Romance of the Rose.* Chicago, 2010.

Hutchison, Emily J. "Partisan Identity in the French Civil War, 1405–18: Reconsidering the Evidence on Livery Badges." *Journal of Medieval History* 33 (2007): 250–74.

Jarry, Eugène. *La vie politique de Louis de France, duc d'Orléans, 1372–1407.* Paris, 1889. Reprint, 1976.

Johnson, Lee. *The Paintings of Eugène Delacroix: A Critical Catalogue.* 6 vols. Oxford, 1981–93.

Jones, Colin. *Paris: Biography of a City.* 2004. Reprint, New York, 2006.

Jorga, Nicolae. *Philippe de Mézières, 1327–1405, et la croisade au XIV* siècle.* Paris, 1896.

Keegan, John. *The Face of Battle.* New York, 1976.

Keen, Maurice. *The Penguin History of Medieval Europe.* Harmondsworth, Eng., 1991.

———, ed. *Medieval Warfare: A History.* Oxford, 1999.

Kervyn de Lettenhove, Joseph. *Ducs de Bourgogne, 1383–1453.* Volume 4 of *Histoire de Flandre.* Brussels, 1849.

Laborde, Léon de. *Les ducs de bourgogne, études sur les lettres, les arts et l'industrie pendant le XV* siècle.* 3 vols. Paris, 1849–52.

Lalande, Denis. *Jean II le Meingre, dit Boucicaut (1366–1421): étude d'une biographie héroïque.* Geneva, 1988.

Le Fèvre, Antoine-Martial. *Description des curiosités des églises de Paris et des environs.* Paris, 1759.

Le Grix White, F. *Forgotten Seigneurs of the Alençonnais.* Privately printed. Penrith, ca. 1880.

Lehman, David. *The Perfect Murder: A Study in Detection.* New York, 1989.

Lehoux, Françoise. *Jean de France, duc de Berri.* 4 vols. Paris, 1966–68.

Lespinasse, Réné de. *Les métiers et corporations de la ville de Paris, XIV*–XVIII* siècle.* 3 vols. Paris, 1886–97.

Leuridan, Jacqueline, and Jacques-Albert Mallet. *Plan restitué de Paris en 1380.* Laboratoire de Cartographie Thématique, 1975. Paris (CNRS), 1999.

Littré, Émile. *Dictionnaire de la langue française.* 4 vols. (with supplement). Paris, 1873–77.

Lodge, R. Anthony. *A Sociolinguistic History of Parisian French.* Cambridge, Eng., 2004.

Lorentz, Philippe, and Dany Sandron, eds. *Atlas de Paris au Moyen Âge: espace urbain, habitat, société, religion, lieux de pouvoir.* Paris, 2006.

Mesqui, Jean, and Claude Ribéra-Pervillé. "Les châteaux de Louis d'Orléans et leurs architectes (1391–1407)." *Bulletin monumental* 138 (1980): 293–345.

Michelet, Jules. *History of France.* Translated by G. H. Smith. 2 vols. New York, 1887.

Millin, Aubin-Louis. *Antiquités nationales ou recueil de monumens.* 5 vols. Paris, 1790–99.

Mirot, Léon. "Autour de la paix de Chartres, 9 mars 1409." *Annales de Bourgogne* 3 (1931): 305–42.

———. "Jean sans Peur de 1398 à 1405 d'après les comptes de sa chambre aux deniers." *Annuaire-bulletin de la Société de l'histoire de France* 74 (1938): 129–245.

———. "L'État bourguignon-flamand au quinzième siècle." *Journal des Savants* (1942): 66–81.

———. "Raoul d'Anquetonville et le prix de l'assassinat du duc d'Orléans." *Bibliothèque de l'École des Chartes* 72 (1911): 445–58.

Morlet, Marie-Thérèse. *Dictionnaire étymologique des noms de famille.* Paris, 1991.

Nordberg, Michael. *Les ducs et la royauté: études sur la rivalité des ducs d'Orléans et de Bourgogne, 1392–1407.* Uppsala, 1964.

Oosterwijk, Sophie. "Of Dead Kings, Dukes and Constables: The Historical Context of the *Danse Macabre* in Late Medieval Paris." *Journal of the British Archaeological Association* 161 (2008): 131–62.

Perrault-Dabot, Anatole. *L'Hôtel de Bourgogne et la tour de Jean sans Peur à Paris.* Paris, 1902.

Peters, Edward. *Torture.* Expanded edition. Philadelphia, 1996.

Petit, Ernest. *Itinéraires de Philippe Le Hardi et de Jean sans Peur, ducs de Bourgogne (1363–1419).* Paris, 1888.

———. *Séjours de Charles VI: 1380–1400.* Paris, 1894.

Plagnieux, Philippe. "La Tour Jean sans Peur, une épave de la résidence parisienne des ducs de Bourgogne." *Histoire de l'art* 1/2 (1988): 11–20.

Pocquet du Haut-Jussé, Barthélémy-Amédée. "Jean sans Peur, son but et sa méthode." *Annales de Bourgogne* 14 (1942): 181–96.

Powell, James M. *Medieval Studies: An Introduction.* 2nd ed. Syracuse, 1992.

Richard, J. M. "Documents des XIIIᵉ et XIVᵉ siècles relatifs à l'hôtel de Bourgogne (ancien hôtel d'Artois) tirés du trésor des chartes d'Artois." *Bulletin de la Société de l'Histoire de Paris et de l'Île de France* 17 (1890): 137–59.

Rivière, Rémi, and Agnès Lavoye. *Tour Jean sans Peur, Hôtel de Bourgogne, 1409–1411.* Troyes, 2001.

Robb, Graham. *The Discovery of France: A Historical Geography from the Revolution to the First World War.* New York, 2007.

Robbins, Rossell Hope. *The Encyclopedia of Witchcraft and Demonology.* New York, 1959. Reprint, 1981.

Roux, Simone. *Paris in the Middle Ages.* Translated by Jo Ann McNamara. Philadelphia, 2009.

Sauval, Henri. *Histoire et recherches des antiquités de la ville de Paris.* 3 vols. Paris, 1724. Reprint, 1973.

Schnerb, Bertrand. *Jean sans Peur: le prince meurtrier.* Paris, 2005.

Sellier, Charles. *Le quartier Barbette.* Paris, 1899.

Seward, Desmond. *The Hundred Years War.* London, 1978.

———. *Henry V as Warlord.* 1987. Reprint, Harmondsworth, Eng., 2001.

Shennan, J. H. *The Parlement of Paris.* Rev. ed. Stroud, Eng., 1998.

Smith, Robert Douglas, and Kelly DeVries. *The Artillery of the Dukes of Burgundy, 1363–1477.* Woodbridge, Eng., 2005.

Smith, William, and Samuel Cheetham. *A Dictionary of Christian Antiquities.* 2 vols. Hartford, 1880.

Sumption, Jonathan. *The Hundred Years War.* 3 vols. (to date). Philadelphia, 1991–.

Thomas, Keith. *Religion and the Decline of Magic.* New York, 1971.

Thorndike, Lynn. *A History of Magic and Experimental Science.* 8 vols. New York, 1923–58.

Tuetey, Alexandre. "Une exécution à Montfaucon au XVᵉ siècle." *Bulletin de la Société de l'Histoire de Paris et de l'Île-de-France* 45 (1918): 57–60.

Vallet de Viriville, Auguste. "Assassinat du duc d'Orléans par Jean sans Peur, duc de Bourgogne." *Le Magasin de Librairie* 7 (1859): 241–82.

Van Kerrebrouck, Patrick, et al. *Les Valois.* Nouvelle Histoire Généalogique de l'Auguste Maison de France, vol. 3. Villeneuve d'Ascq, 1990.

Vaughan, Richard. *John the Fearless: The Growth of Burgundian Power.* Rev. ed. Woodbridge, Eng., 2002.

———. *Philip the Bold: The Formation of the Burgundian State.* Rev. ed. Woodbridge, Eng., 2002.

Veenstra, Jan R. *Magic and Divination at the Courts of Burgundy and France: Text and Context of Laurens Pignon's "Contre les devineurs" (1411).* Leiden, 1997.

Viollet-le-Duc, Eugène-Emmanuel. *Dictionnaire raisonné de l'architecture française du XIᵉ au XVIᵉ siècle.* 10 vols. Paris, 1858–68.

von Simson, Otto. *The Gothic Cathedral: Origins of Gothic Architecture and the Medieval Concept of Order.* 3rd ed. Princeton, 1988.

Wieck, Roger S. *Painted Prayers: The Book of Hours in Medieval and Renaissance Art.* New York, 1997.

Woolgar, C. M. *The Great Household in Late Medieval England.* New Haven, 1999.

Zupko, Ronald Edward. *French Weights and Measures before the Revolution.* Bloomington, 1978.

Illustration and Photograph Credits

―◄○►―

The parchment scroll
Conseil général des Pyrénées-Atlantiques, Service départemental des archives: E.56—1407, Titre de la famille Albret. Photo: Copyright © 2011 by Eric Jager.

Montfaucon
Drawing by Eugène Mouard, in Eugène-Emmanuel Viollet-le-Duc, *Diction-naire raisonné de l'architecture française du XIe au XVIe siècle,* vol. 5 (1861), 561, s.v. "Fourches patibulaires." Public domain.

Fifteenth-century Paris
Miracle of Dagobert, by Jean Fouquet, in *Grandes Chroniques de France* (ca. 1455–60), BnF MS. fr. 6465, fol. 56 (detail). © BnF, Dist. RMN–Grand Palais / Art Resource, NY.

The Châtelet
Place du Grand Châtelet, by Thomas Charles Naudet, Musée de la Ville de Paris, Musée Carnavalet, Paris. Scala / White Images / Art Resource, NY.

"Louis of Orleans Showing His Mistress"
"Louis d'Orléans Showing His Mistress" (ca. 1825–26), by Eugène Delacroix. Museo Thyssen-Bornemisza, Madrid / Scala / Art Resource, NY.

The Rue Vieille du Temple
Detail from "Plan of fifteenth-century Paris," in *A Parisian Journal, 1405–1449,* translated by Janet Shirley (1968), fig. 4, pp. 386–87. By permission of Oxford University Press.

The assassination
Assassinat du duc d'Orléans, by Paul Lehugeur, *Histoire de France en cent tableaux* (ca. 1890). Public domain.

The Rue Saint-Martin and the Rue Saint-Denis

Detail from "Plan of fifteenth-century Paris," in *A Parisian Journal, 1405–1449,* translated by Janet Shirley (1968), fig. 4, pp. 386–87. By permission of Oxford University Press.

Louis of Orleans

Louis d'Orléans, Cathédrale d'Amiens, Beau Pilier (sculpture, fourteenth century). Cliché: P. Y. Corbel–DRAC de Picardie.

A funeral procession

Vespers for the Dead, by Jean Fouquet, *Les heures d'Étienne Chevalier* (ca. 1445), Musée Condé, Chantilly, MS. fr. 71, fol. 27. Erich Lessing / Art Resource, NY.

Jacques Cardon's inventory

Conseil général des Pyrénées-Atlantiques, Service départemental des archives: E.56 — 1407, Titre de la famille Albret. Photo: Copyright © 2011 by Peg Eby-Jager.

John of Burgundy

Portrait of Jan zonder Vrees, Hertog van Bourgandië, Anonymous (ca. 1450), Koninklijk Museum voor Schone Kunsten, Antwerp. © Lukas Art in Flanders VZW.

Duke John's tower

Tour Jean sans Peur, pencil drawing by Hippolyte Destailleur (1822–1893). © BnF, Dist. RMN–Grand Palais / Art Resource, NY.

Siege of a fortified town

Siege of Mortagne (1378), in Jean de Wavrin, *Chronique d'Angleterre,* British Library MS. Royal 14 E. IV, fol. 23 (c. 1470). HIP / Art Resource, NY.

Danse Macabre

The Priest and the Laborer, facsimile of an illustration in *La Danse Macabre Nouvelle,* by Guyot Marchant (ca. 1500). Kharbine-Tapabor / The Art Archive at Art Resource, NY.

The Rue Vieille du Temple today

Photo: Copyright © 2011 by Eric Jager.

Index

About the Author

———◁◦▷———

ERIC JAGER is an award-winning professor of English at UCLA. He holds a PhD from the University of Michigan and is the author of *The Last Duel, The Book of the Heart,* and *The Tempter's Voice,* as well as numerous articles for acclaimed academic journals. He lives in Los Angeles.

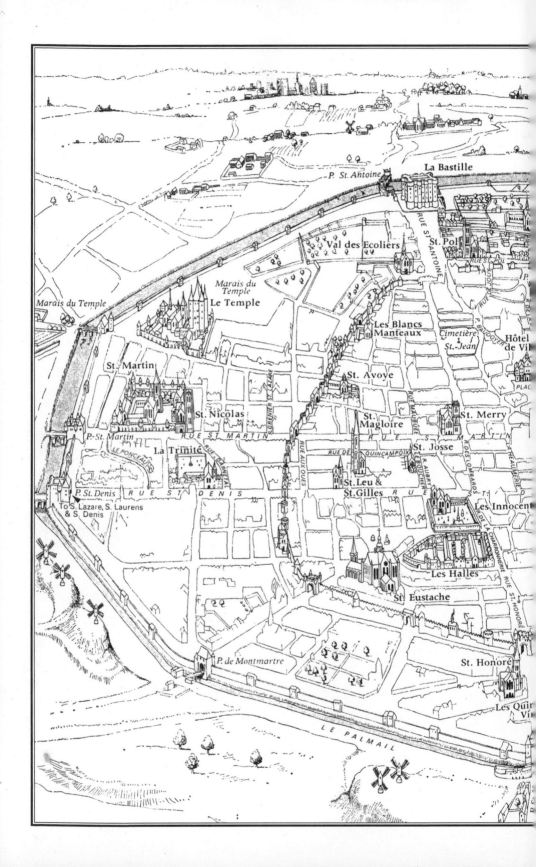